lonely planet

EAST COAST AUSTRALIA

Sarah Reid, Cristian Bonetto,
Caoimhe Hanrahan-Lawrence, Trent Holden,
Phillip Tang, Jessica Lockhart

Meet our writers

ALBERTO LOYO/SHUTTERSTOCK

Sarah Reid

@sarahreidtravels

Byron Bay–based travel journalist and positive-impact travel advocate Sarah is a big fan of exploring Australia – even her own backyard (p92) – with Indigenous guides.

Cristian Bonetto

@rexcat75

Melbourne-born Cristian is as passionate about his home town as he is about his espressos. Indeed, his favourite experience is wandering through Melbourne's laneways (p137) from Flinders Street to the State Library, coffee in hand, wintry skies above.

Caoimhe Hanrahan-Lawrence

Caoimhe is a Wiradjuri writer from rural New South Wales, currently living in Sydney on Wangal-Eora land. They can't pass up a regional museum (with the Eden Killer Whale Museum, p115, a case in point) and have a penchant for overnight bus trips.

Trent Holden

@hombreholden

A Geelong-based writer, Trent has a fondness for megacities – the more chaotic the better. On the flip side, he's equally happy among remote wilderness areas and national parks, with Victoria's rugged coastline (p162) a favourite hiking destination.

Brisbane & Southeast Queensland 178
Noosa 2hrs
Brisbane
Toowoomba
Gold Coast
Tweed Heads
Sydney 8hrs
Byron Bay
Ballina
Moree
Glen Innes
Grafton
Yamba
Bourke
Byron Bay & North Coast New South Wales 76
Coffs Harbour
Nambucca Heads
Tamworth
Kempsey
Broken Hill
NEW SOUTH WALES
Port Macquarie
Dubbo
Hunter Valley
Taree
Forster-Tuncurry
Wollemi National Park
Newcastle 74
Mildura
Blue Mountains National Park
Hay
Murray River
Sydney 40
Jervis Bay 3hrs
Wagga Wagga
Wollongong
Goulburn
CANBERRA
Nowra
SOUTH PACIFIC OCEAN
Echuca
Albury
ACT
Batemans Bay
South Coast New South Wales 100
Melbourne 130
Bega
VICTORIA
Eden
Great Ocean Road 1¼hrs
TASMAN SEA
Bairnsdale
Portland
Geelong
Mallacoota
Lakes Entrance
Warrnambool
Sale
Croajingalong National Park
Wilsons Promontory National Park
The Gippsland Coast 164
Bass Strait
Great Ocean Road 158
0 500 km
0 250 miles

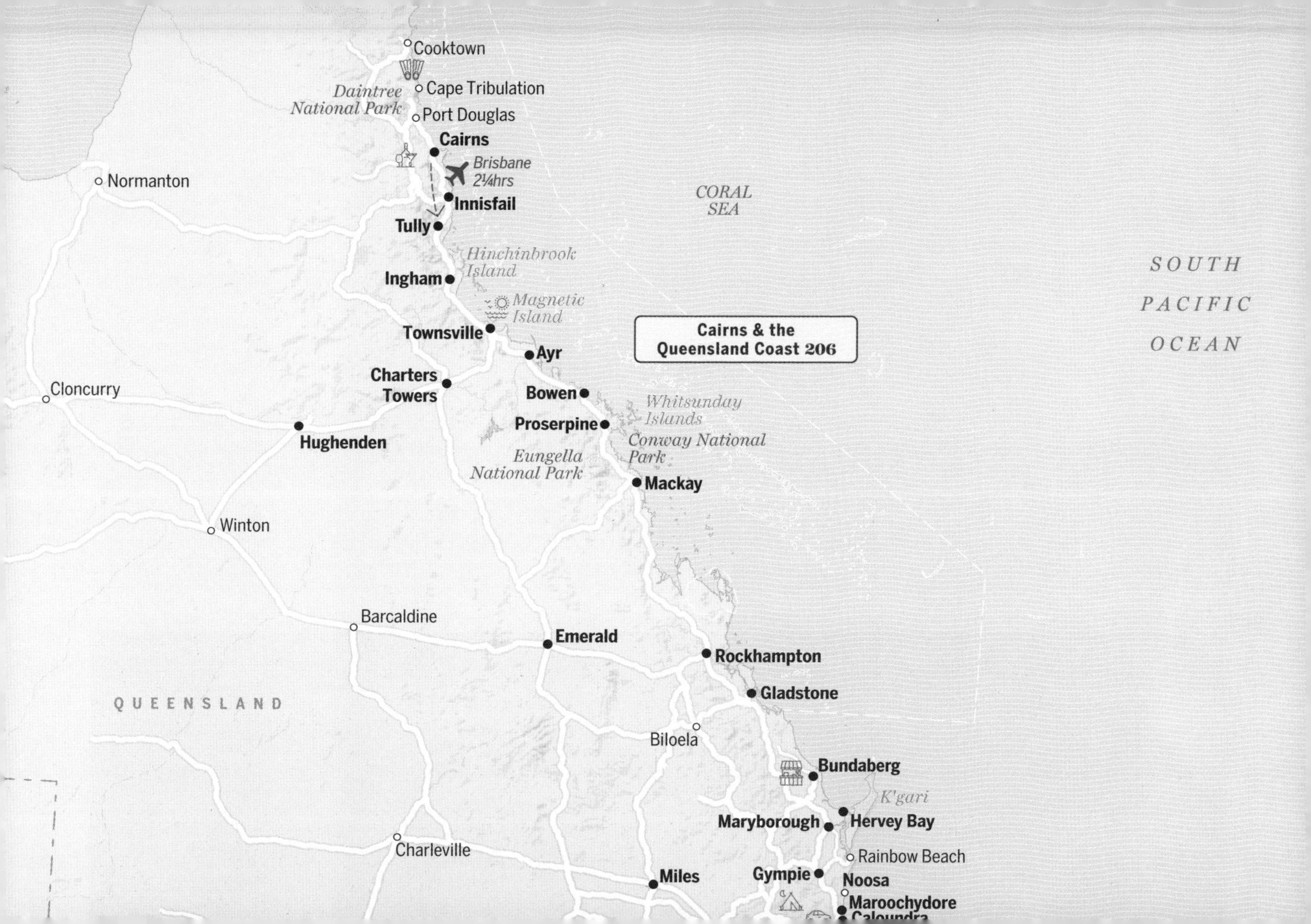

Cooktown
Cape Tribulation
Daintree National Park
Port Douglas
Cairns
Brisbane 2¼hrs
Normanton
Innisfail
CORAL SEA
Tully
Hinchinbrook Island
SOUTH PACIFIC OCEAN
Ingham
Magnetic Island
Townsville
Cairns & the Queensland Coast 206
Ayr
Charters Towers
Cloncurry
Bowen
Whitsunday Islands
Proserpine
Hughenden
Conway National Park
Eungella National Park
Mackay
Winton
Barcaldine
Emerald
Rockhampton
Gladstone
QUEENSLAND
Biloela
Bundaberg
K'gari
Maryborough
Hervey Bay
Charleville
Rainbow Beach
Miles
Gympie
Noosa
Maroochydore

Immerse yourself in ancient rainforests. Discover the sustainability secrets of the world's oldest living cultures. Feast on fresh seasonal seafood paired with sophisticated local wines. Marvel at the biodiversity of blockbuster marine ecosystems. Sip award-winning coffee while exploring urban street art. Spot native wildlife on a hike to a lush waterfall. Learn the stories behind architectural icons. Camp on an island. Enjoy a remote beach all to yourself – and perhaps see a kangaroo or two.

This is East Coast Australia.

TURN THE PAGE AND START PLANNING YOUR NEXT BEST TRIP →

Twelve Apostles (p160), Victoria

Phillip Tang

@mrtangtangtang

Phillip grew up in Sydney before calling London and Mexico City home, but the raucous caucus of rainbow lorikeets (p64) in jacaranda trees always summons him back. Besides, Sydney is like the Greatest Culinary Hits of Asia (p50).

Jessica Lockhart

@WynneLockhart

An award-winning Canadian journalist, Jessica researched this book while living in Mapleton, Queensland. Her favourite weekend getaway is North Stradbroke Island/Minjerribah (p192), where mobs of kangaroos casually graze on suburban lawns.

PREVIOUS SPREAD: CALAM PHOTOGRAPHY/SHUTTERSTOCK

Contents

RENEEFAIRHURST/SHUTTERSTOCK

Scuba diving, Northern Great Barrier Reef (p233)

Acknowledgement of Country

Lonely Planet would like to acknowledge all First Nations people throughout this country, who have nurtured and maintained the land since time immemorial. This guide was written on, and is written about, the lands of many diverse nations.

We recognise the unique and ongoing connection that Aboriginal and Torres Strait Islander peoples have to land and waters and thank them for their efforts to preserve them. We pay our respects to Elders past and present and extend this respect to any Aboriginal or Torres Strait Islander people who may be reading this guide.

We also recognise the ongoing efforts of Aboriginal and Torres Strait Islander peoples for reconciliation, justice, and social, cultural and economic self-determination. Sovereignty was never ceded. Australia always was, and always will be, Aboriginal and Torres Strait Islander land.

Cultural Sensitivity Warning

Aboriginal and Torres Strait Islander readers are advised that this guide may contain names and images of people who have since passed away.

FIRST NATIONS STATS

Australia's East Coast is home to more than 40 Indigenous nations.

The largest populations of Indigenous Australians live in New South Wales and Queensland (62.3%).

Some 9.5% of Indigenous Australians speak a traditional language at home.

INDIGENOUS CULTURE

Aboriginal and Torres Strait Islander peoples maintain a strong and continuing connection to their Country (traditional lands) stretching all the way along Australia's East Coast, making it one of the best places in Australia to connect with the world's oldest living cultures through arts, food and an excellent range of Indigenous-led tourism experiences.

Left Kuku Yalanji man applying ochre markings
Right Kuku Yalanji guide, Mossman River, Daintree National Park (p214)
Below Bush tucker (native pepperberry)

→ WHOSE COUNTRY?

Learning about whose Country you're visiting adds a rich layer to your experience. Each Aboriginal and Torres Strait Islander group has its own culture, customs, lore and dialect.

▶ Discover more about Australia's First Nations people on p126.

MATT MUNRO/LONELY PLANET

URBAN CULTURE

Superb Indigenous galleries, museums and cultural centres can be found in East Coast cities, along with urban bush-tucker walks and innovative and authentic Indigenous-focused experiences.

TOP RIGHT: MATT MUNRO/LONELY PLANET
RIGHT: BLUE GUM/SHUTTERSTOCK

INDIGENOUS DINING

Indigenous chefs are making their mark on Australia's culinary scene. Bundjalung chef Mark Olive translates indigenous flavours for sophisticated modern palates at his Sydney Opera House restaurant, Midden (p124).

Best Indigenous Culture Experiences

▶ **Explore Queensland's Daintree Rainforest with a Kuku Yalanji guide.** (p224)

▶ **Go on a cultural stand-up paddleboarding adventure on the Coffs Coast.** (p82)

▶ **Take an Aboriginal tour of Sydney Harbour on a Tribal Warrior boat cruise.** (p56)

▶ **Immerse yourself in the Aboriginal culture of the NSW South Coast on a Yuin retreat.** (p124)

▶ **Discover the Aboriginal art, culture and stories of Naarm (Melbourne).** (p146)

FUN FACTS

The Great Barrier Reef is home to more than 600 coral species.

There are more than 35 ocean pools in Sydney, carved out of the rock face.

Humpback whales travel up to 10,000km on their annual migration from Antarctica to the East Coast.

AQUATIC **ESCAPADES**

With more than 100 beaches in Sydney alone, Australia's East Coast was made for fun in, on and around the water. From snorkelling on the Great Barrier Reef to surfing the legendary point breaks of NSW to chasing waterfalls in coastal forests and watching whales frolic along the coast, the region is ripe for aquatic pleasures. Get ready to dive in!

Left Surfing, Duranbah (p98), New South Wales
Right Humpback whale, Hervey Bay
Below Lifeguard on duty

→ WHALE WATCHING

Each year between May and November, thousands of humpback whales migrate along the East Coast from their Southern Ocean feeding grounds to mate and calve in warmer waters.

UWE BERGWITZ/SHUTTERSTOCK

GREAT BARRIER BEAUTY

The world's largest living organism may be under threat, but Queensland's marine icon is still an incredible sight. Take a day trip or stay overnight on an island or a floating pontoon.

▸ Visit the reef from Townsville (p220) or Cairns (p223).

RIGHT: LEV KROPOTOV/SHUTTERSTOCK, LEFT: VISIAL COLLECTIVE/SHUTTERSTOCK

↑ LIFE'S A BEACH

There are hundreds – if not thousands – of sandy havens to discover along Australia's East Coast. Stick to lifeguard-patrolled beaches wherever possible, and always check for croc and stinger warning signs.

▸ See p60 for the lowdown on Sydney's beaches.

Best Aquatic Experiences

▸ **Dive into the glorious Great Barrier Reef.** (p232)

▸ **Paddle in waterfalls and idyllic freshwater waterholes in Queensland and beyond.** (p212)

▸ **Surf Byron Bay's famous waves – or learn to.** (p92)

▸ **Scuba dive with placid grey nurse sharks off the north coast of NSW.** (p86)

▸ **Take a boat trip to the mysterious Skull Rock at Gippsland's Wilsons Promontory.** (p173)

EPIC HIKES & WALKS

You can hike between ancient rainforest trees, along wild coastal trails and deep in the Aussie bush on Australia's East Coast, with hundreds of trails to choose from, including accessible options. Even short walks require a degree of preparation; check national park websites for tips.

Cape Tribulation

Accessible Daintree wanders

Three of the four short but beautiful boardwalks in the heart of Queensland's Daintree Rainforest are wheelchair accessible. Weaving through a lush mangrove habitat, the Madja Boardwalk (1.2km circuit/45 minutes) is a particularly mesmerising meander. Look for fish, crabs, and maybe even a saltie below.

90min drive from Cairns

▶ p212

NORTHERN TERRITORY

WESTERN AUSTRALIA

SOUTH AUSTRALIA

Kalgoorlie-Boulder

Port Augusta

Great Australian Bight

Esperance

Adelaide

Warrnambool

Great Ocean Walk

Leave the road behind

Bus from Melbourne to Apollo Bay and explore Victoria's Great Ocean Road slowly on this block-buster route (110km one way/six to eight days), ending at the iconic Twelve Apostles (pictured). Camp on the trail or stay nearby, or sample sections of the trail on invigorating day hikes.

3hr drive from Melbourne ▶ p162

FROM LEFT: RONGJUN GUAN/SHUTTERSTOCK, POSNOV/GETTY IMAGES, PHOTOS BRIANSCANTLEBURY/SHUTTERSTOCK

K'gari (formerly Fraser Island)

Wild walks galore

There are more than 40 marked trails on the world's largest sand island. Pack a picnic and follow the Lake Wabby Walk (8.2km return/three to four hours; pictured above) through the rainforest to the track's namesake, where you can enjoy a dip before scrambling up a sand blow to a great lookout.

20min drive from Hervey Bay plus a 30min ferry ▶ p236

Gondwana Rainforests

Hike to waterfalls

Stretching from Southeast Queensland down to Newcastle, the UNESCO-listed Gondwana Rainforests are criss-crossed with walking trails. For waterfalls, try the Crystal Showers Walk (3.2km return/90 minutes; pictured above) in Dorrigo National Park, and enjoy the gorgeous Waterfall Way drive to reach the trailhead.

1hr drive from Coffs Harbour ▶ p88

Blue Mountains

Aboriginal rock art

Near Glenbrook, the Red Hands Cave Walking Track (8km loop/two hours) offers a rich taste of Blue Mountains hiking. The trail winds through bushland to one of the most impressive Aboriginal stencil galleries in the Sydney Basin.

1hr drive from Sydney ▶ p70

Wilsons Promontory

Southern Prom highlight

Among the most memorable of the Gippsland national park's walks is the 19.1km trek (one way) to mainland Australia's most southerly lighthouse, built in 1859, where you can spend up to two nights before retracing your steps.

3hr drive from Melbourne ▶ p172

NOSH BY NUMBERS

Twenty-five percent of Australia's fresh produce is grown in Bundaberg, Queensland.

Seventy million oysters are produced annually in NSW.

There are more than 2000 cafes and coffee shops in Melbourne.

COASTAL **CUISINE**

From the farm-fresh produce of Bundaberg to the plump oysters of the NSW coast and the fine wines of the Mornington Peninsula, Australia's East Coast is an epicurean delight. Discover lauded regional restaurants redefining modern Australian fine dining, kick back in cool cafes offering much more than avo on toast, feast on fresh seafood straight off the trawlers, and explore the vibrant multicultural culinary scenes of Sydney and Melbourne.

Left Cafe breakfast, Melbourne (p130)
Right Dish with bush-tucker ingredients (p196)
Below Freshly shucked oysters

→ BUSH TUCKER

Look out for East Coast staples including lemon myrtle, warrigal greens and saltbush on restaurant menus, or join an Indigenous tour to learn about traditional uses for native plants.

▶ For more bush-tucker staples see p196.

JACKSON STOCK PHOTOGRAPHY/SHUTTERSTOCK

TIPPING TIPS

It's customary to leave some small change in the tip jar for a cafe meal. Tip 10% to 15% for good service at restaurants.

RIGHT: JONATHON STOKES/LONELY PLANET
LEFT: LISA HOLMEN PHOTOGRAPHY/SHUTTERSTOCK

↑ ZERO-FOOD-MILE TREATS

From buckets of berries to trays of oysters, many East Coast producers sell fresh food directly from their farms; look out for signs and roadside stalls.

Best Coastal Culinary Experiences

- **Stock up at the farm gates of the Bundaberg food bowl.** (p226)
- **Eat your way around the coastal fine diners of the NSW Northern Rivers.** (p96)
- **Enjoy a Mod Oz lunch one day and yum cha brunch the next in cosmopolitan Sydney.** (p50)
- **Slurp fresh oysters on the South Coast of NSW.** (p113)
- **Fill your picnic hamper at historic South Melbourne Market.** (p148)

↘ KOALA COUNTRY

Koalas are native to the eucalypt forests of eastern Australia, making it the only place you can observe the iconic marsupials wild in their native environment – a heart-melting experience.

Koalas are easier to spot at dawn and dusk, when they're at their most active.

WORLDSWILDLIFEWONDERS/SHUTTERSTOCK

WILDLIFE **WONDERS**

With two of the world's most biodiverse rainforest systems – the Daintree Rainforest and the Gondwana Rainforests of Australia – among its impressive clutch of globally important habitats, Australia's East Coast brims with native wildlife-watching opportunities. From cassowaries to koalas, many of the region's incredible creatures are found nowhere else on Earth.

Best Wildlife Experiences

- **Look for cassowaries in Queensland's Wet Tropics World Heritage Area.** (p215)
- **Listen for ancient birds in the Gondwana Rainforests.** (p88)
- **Swim with seals on the NSW South Coast.** (p111)
- **Spot wombats, kangaroos, emus and more on a Wilsons Prom wander.** (p172)

ISLAND TIME

Dotted along the East Coast are hundreds of islands with a remarkable diversity of attractions, from dazzling coral reefs to Indigenous culture, and luxury glamping to colonial history. Better yet, many of these islands are easily visited on day trips from the coast, while others tempt you to stay a while.

TOP: JACKSON STOCK PHOTOGRAPHY/SHUTTERSTOCK, BOTTOM: CO LEONG/SHUTTERSTOCK

↑ CASTAWAY CAMPING

It's possible to camp on dozens of East Coast islands, particularly in Queensland. Fitzroy Island is an easy option from Cairns; in the Whitsundays, Scamper (whitsundaycamping.com.au) can rent gear and ferry you to your island of choice.

Best Island Experiences

- **Snorkel just steps from your Great Barrier Reef island eco-hotel.** (p232)
- **Get off-grid on a 4WD K'gari trip.** (p237)
- **Swim, camp and whale-watch on Straddie.** (p192)
- **Uncover the convict history of Cockatoo Island.** (p55)
- **Spot koalas on Gippsland's Raymond Island.** (p171)

★ ISLAND DREAMING

From Queensland's K'gari to NSW's Baranguba Montague Island, many East Coast isles play important roles in Indigenous culture. Learn more on tours.

Above left Whitsunday Islands (p236)
Left K'gari (p238)

CRAFT DRINKS & WINE

A great glass of local wine is never far away on the East Coast, home to 10 wine regions within easy reach of the sea between Southeast Queensland and Victoria's Great Ocean Road. Craft breweries are even more abundant, along with an ever-expanding network of distilleries, most with cellar doors. Cheers!

★ GOING SOFT?

Booze-free craft bevvies are booming Down Under. Australia's first 'non-alc' bar, Brunswick Aces, opened in Melbourne in 2020; now non-alc brands such as Heaps Normal are becoming the new normal.

TOP: BEX WALTON/FLICKR/CC BY 2.0. BOTTOM: ANDREW ROBINS PHOTOGRAPHY/SHUTTERSTOCK

Best Wine & Craft Drinks Experiences

- **Pick your favourite craft brewery on the Sunshine Coast.** (p190)
- **Enjoy cocktails with harbour views in Sydney.** (p52)
- **Get buzzed in Melbourne's coffee and small-bar scenes.** (p143)
- **Tour the cellar doors of Gippsland and the Mornington Peninsula.** (p168; p152)

★ NATURAL WINE

The natural – also known as minimal-intervention – wine movement, which allows the local terroir to shine, is also big in Australia. Imbibe the trend on the Mornington Peninsula and beyond.

Above left Aunty Peg's (p143), Melbourne
Left Mornington Peninsula vineyard (p152)

SYDNEY HARBOUR BRIDGE CLIMBS

There are four main options for climbing Sydney's architectural icon. For a different perspective on the harbour city, opt for the Burrawa Climb, with an Indigenous storyteller as your guide.

ANASTASIA MYASNIKOVA/SHUTTERSTOCK

ARCHITECTURE & THE ARTS

Whether you prefer to see art hanging in galleries or plastered across laneways, there's plenty of both to be discovered in the cities of the East Coast, with a smattering of excellent regional galleries beyond. Architecture fans will also find much to appreciate, from Sydney's convict-built relics to the opulent buildings of Melbourne that sprang up during the city's post-gold-rush period.

Best Art & Architecture Experiences

- **Take a backstage tour of the Sydney Opera House.** (p47)
- **Discover the architectural wonders of Melbourne's Collins St.** (p139)
- **Tour the recreated studio of a famed Tweed artist.** (p98)
- **Purchase meaningful souvenirs at the Cairns Indigenous Art Fair.** (p225)

Christmas Day, Boxing Day, New Year's Day and 26 January are public holidays. Shops may be closed.

← Sydney New Year's Eve Fireworks

At 9pm and midnight, Sydney Harbour is lit up with several tonnes of dazzling fireworks.

▶ sydneynewyearseve.com

Woodford Folk Festival

The 200-hectare property of Woodfordia is transformed for the last six days of the year, hosting music, theatre, comedy and more.

▶ woodfordfolkfestival.com

→ Australian Open

Tennis fans descend on Melbourne in January for the first tennis Grand Slam event of the year.

▶ ausopen.com

DECEMBER

Australian summers are often very humid.

JANUARY

East Coast Australia in SUMMER

The heat attracts spiders and snakes. Take care when bushwalking, and check your shoes before putting them on to avoid a surprise.

FROM LEFT: MARTI BUG CATCHER/SHUTTERSTOCK, FILEDIMAGE/SHUTTERSTOCK, HOLLI/SHUTTERSTOCK, AIYOSHI597/SHUTTERSTOCK, BACKGROUND: AUTAU/SHUTTERSTOCK

↘ Sydney Mardi Gras

Sydney celebrates the strength and diversity of the LGBTIQ+ community in late February or early March with public events and the famed parade.

▶ mardigras.org.au

↑ Lunar New Year

Australia's large Chinese community celebrates the Lunar New Year with events up and down the East Coast.

FEBRUARY

Rain is not uncommon in summer, especially in the tropics.

This is bushfire season, and some regional areas will be affected by fires.

Demand for accommodation peaks during December and January. View tours and overnight adventures in advance at lonelyplanet.com.

Packing Notes

Wear light, breathable fabrics and SPF50+ sunscreen, and keep a water bottle handy.

← Noosa Festival of Surfing

In mid-March, celebrate surf culture and watch competitions, including the world's largest surfing-dog competition.

▶ noosafestivalofsurfing.com

↙ Melbourne International Comedy Festival

Australian and international comedians converge on Melbourne for this celebrated comedy festival from late March.

▶ comedyfestival.com.au

MARCH

Queensland and northern NSW remain wet and humid.

APRIL

East Coast Australia in AUTUMN

↙ Sydney Royal Easter Show

Australia's largest annual event, the Easter Show offers amusement rides, a fair and agricultural events.

▶ eastershow.com.au

↗ Anzac Day

On 25 April Australians commemorate the service of Australian and New Zealand troops. It is a public holiday.

It begins to cool down, though days are usually sunny.

MAY

The southern regions are colder than the rest of the country.

Easter

Good Friday and Easter Monday are public holidays. This four-day weekend is a popular time to travel and visit family.

Packing Notes

Swap the umbrella for a raincoat, and layer up for variable weather.

East Coast Australia in WINTER

Winter is tourism low season, so you will likely avoid large crowds and score some bargains on travel and accommodation.

↗ Vivid Sydney

Sydney is at its most colourful during Vivid, with landmarks transforming through light projections from late May to mid-June.

▶ vividsydney.com

↘ Laura Quinkan Dance Festival

More than 25 Indigenous troupes from Cape York gather in June to compete in contemporary and traditional dance.

▶ lauraquinkanfestival.com.au

NAIDOC Week

Across the country, the first full week in July is dedicated to honouring Australia's Indigenous peoples.

▶ naidoc.org.au

JUNE

Winter is usually dry, though some areas experience rainfall.

JULY

FROM LEFT: POOKROOK/SHUTTERSTOCK, CHAMELEONSEYE/SHUTTERSTOCK, AREYOUBEN/SHUTTERSTOCK, JACKSON STOCK PHOTOGRAPHY/SHUTTERSTOCK, BACKGROUND: IAMMOTOS /SHUTTERSTOCK

← Humpback Highway

The East Coast whale-watching season is in full swing. Take a boat tour or watch the spectacle from the shore.

↑ Hamilton Island Race Week

This week-long yacht race in late August skirts the Great Barrier Reef.

▶ hamiltonislandraceweek.com.au

Pop Up North Queensland

Biennial PUNQ showcases contemporary visual, immersive and performance art for nearly three weeks in August.

▶ umbrella.org.au/punq

AUGUST

Days are cooler, but sunburn is still a risk; continue to use sunscreen.

Temperatures drop at night, with morning frosts in the south.

Packing Notes

A jumper and coat are warm enough during the day. Pack warm pyjamas.

Visitor crowds remain smaller during September and October, though school holidays fall between late September and early October.

Brisbane Festival

September is dedicated to this showcase of Brisbane's diverse artistic culture.

▶ brisbanefestival.com.au

Quandamooka Festival

The Quandamooka peoples from North Stradbroke Island/Minjerribah share their rich culture over two days in September.

SEPTEMBER

The days are sunny, making sun safety a must.

OCTOBER

East Coast Australia in SPRING

FROM LEFT: POC/SHUTTERSTOCK, NEALE COUSLAND/SHUTTERSTOCK, FILEDIMAGE/SHUTTERSTOCK
BACKGROUND: BEN JEAYES/SHUTTERSTOCK

↘ AFL Grand Final

Cheer for your favourite team during the final match of the Australian Rules football season in late September.

Melbourne

▶ afl.org.au

Brisbane International Film Festival

This four-day celebration of the films that have shaped us falls in late November.

▶ biff.com.au

Sculpture by the Sea

From late October Sydney's Bondi Beach hosts this free exhibition featuring sculptures along its 2km coastal walk.

▶ sculpturebythesea.com

↓ Melbourne Cup

The race that stops the nation: events occur Australia-wide to commemorate the famous horse race in early November.

▶ vrc.com.au

NOVEMBER

Evenings are cool in the south; perfect for outdoor dining.

The humidity begins to rise in the north.

Though the days are comfortably warm, the seas remain cool. Prepare for a slight shock if you go for a dip in the south.

Packing Notes

Have a broad-brimmed hat for daytime, and a light jacket for after dark.

SYDNEY & SOUTH COAST NSW

Trip Builder

TAKE YOUR PICK OF MUST-SEES AND HIDDEN GEMS

From its iconic architecture to its glittering harbour, it's easy to be entranced by Sydney. When you've filled up on glitz and gourmet, head out to the Blue Mountains for a memorable hike, or pack the car for a scenic South Coast road trip.

Trip Notes

Hub towns Sydney, Wollongong

How long Allow around two weeks

Getting around Use buses, trains, ferries and the light-rail network to get around Sydney, then hire a car for a South Coast road trip. It's two hours by train from Sydney to Katoomba, in the heart of the Blue Mountains.

Tips Access to national parks can be restricted by bushfires, erosion and other issues. Check the latest alerts at nationalparks.nsw.gov.au before you go.

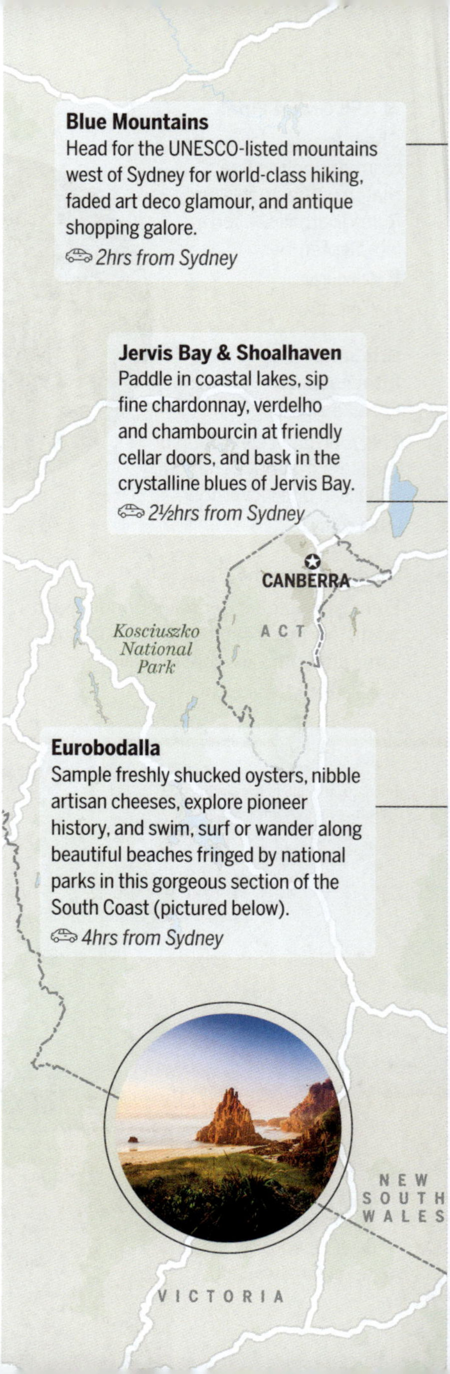

Blue Mountains
Head for the UNESCO-listed mountains west of Sydney for world-class hiking, faded art deco glamour, and antique shopping galore.
2hrs from Sydney

Jervis Bay & Shoalhaven
Paddle in coastal lakes, sip fine chardonnay, verdelho and chambourcin at friendly cellar doors, and bask in the crystalline blues of Jervis Bay.
2½hrs from Sydney

Eurobodalla
Sample freshly shucked oysters, nibble artisan cheeses, explore pioneer history, and swim, surf or wander along beautiful beaches fringed by national parks in this gorgeous section of the South Coast (pictured below).
4hrs from Sydney

FROM LEFT: MICHAEL XIAOS/SHUTTERSTOCK, MARI_MAY/SHUTTERSTOCK, PHILLIP WITTKE/SHUTTERSTOCK

Sydney

Step back into history, then down into the underground after-dark scene of the NSW capital, where you can also eat your way around the world without leaving the city.

1½hrs from Melbourne

Royal National Park

Discover the many draws of this iconic national park, from the Aboriginal rock carvings near Bundeena to its wild walks, surprising rock formations and blissful beaches.

1hr from Sydney

Illawarra

Go searching for urban glow-worms, discover an unexpected slice of serenity near Wollongong and feel the power of the ocean at an explosive natural attraction at Kiama (pictured right), all just a short hop from the state capital.

1½hrs from Sydney

Sapphire Coast

Go diving and hiking, fossick for gold, and learn about the region's intriguing whale story at the southern end of the South Coast, where the deep blue sea glitters like a precious gem.

5hrs from Sydney

NORTHERN NSW
Trip Builder

TAKE YOUR PICK OF MUST-SEES AND HIDDEN GEMS

Beautiful beaches and atmospheric towns dot the entire North Coast of NSW, with its northern tip particularly well known for acclaimed restaurants, cool cafes and watering holes, hip boutique hotels and wellness options galore.

Trip Notes

Hub towns Byron Bay, Kingscliff

How long Allow at least a week

Getting around Hiring a car, ideally at Ballina Byron Gateway Airport or Gold Coast Airport, is the best way to explore beyond central Byron Bay, though there are some wildlife- and culinary-based tour options.

Tip Book accommodation and popular restaurants well ahead, particularly during school holidays and festival periods.

Tweed Hinterland
Driving this farming region's winding country roads is an experience in itself. You'll find farm gates, restaurants, cafes, a top distillery and a renowned Murwillumbah gallery.
20mins from Gold Coast Airport

Nightcap National Park
Part of the Gondwana Rainforests of Australia, this dramatic national park has brand-new visitor facilities, including a new lookout perched above 100m-high Minyon Falls.
45mins from Byron Bay

NEW SOUTH WALES

Clarence Coast
Surf uncrowded waves, pitch a tent by the beach, and feast on fresh prawns straight off the trawlers before heading back up the coast, or down to Sydney.
1¼hrs from Byron Bay

FROM LEFT: JACKSCOTT/SHUTTERSTOCK, TRAPPY76/SHUTTERSTOCK, RUGLIG/SHUTTERSTOCK

Tweed Coast

Kingscliff is the Tweed's holiday accommodation HQ, with great beaches and eats to be found here, as well as in Casuarina, Cabarita and Pottsville to the south.

25mins from Gold Coast Airport

Brunswick Heads

The once-sleepy fishing village now has a food scene to be reckoned with. Three holiday parks nestle alongside the idyllic Brunswick River, and there's a great historic pub shaded by poinciana trees.

15mins from Byron Bay

Byron Bay

Watch the sun rise from Australia's most easterly point before working your way around the popular holiday town's famous beaches and hot-ticket eateries.

30mins from Ballina Byron Gateway Airport

Lennox Head & East Ballina

Enjoy leisurely coastal walks and linger in cafes and pubs overlooking the Pacific Ocean in this low-key corner of the Northern Rivers.

25mins from Ballina Byron Gateway Airport

Byron Bay Hinterland

Dotted with Federation buildings, many of them housing cafes, restaurants and boutiques, the hinterland villages of Bangalow, Newrybar, Federal and Mullumbimby have become destinations in their own right.

15mins from Byron Bay

MELBOURNE & COASTAL VICTORIA
Trip Builder

TAKE YOUR PICK OF MUST-SEES AND HIDDEN GEMS

Enjoy the artistic and culinary delights of Melbourne, then venture beyond the big smoke to discover awesome outdoor adventures, laid-back beach towns and, yes, more great food and craft drinks along Victoria's southeastern coastline.

Trip Notes

Hub town Melbourne

How long Allow 10 to 14 days

Getting around Melbourne has an efficient public transport network, with connections to the Mornington Peninsula, Gippsland and the Great Ocean Road, though it's more convenient to have a car to explore beyond the city.

Tip While it's generally warm enough for a heart-starting ocean dip in southern NSW in winter, Victoria's beaches are best enjoyed by swimmers during the summer months.

FROM LEFT: PAUL HARDING 00/SHUTTERSTOCK, LKONYA/ SHUTTERSTOCK, YOHANES PAULUS BISMA/SHUTTERSTOCK

Melbourne
Appreciate architecture, seek out street art, feast at some of Australia's best restaurants and explore the vibrant neighbourhoods of the nation's capital of cool.
1½hrs from Sydney

Great Ocean Road
Soak up sublime coastal views and eat your way through the beach towns of Victoria's most famous driving route, or savour the scenery on the six-day Great Ocean Walk.
1½hrs from Melbourne

Lakes Entrance

Sign up for a heli-SUP tour or go kayaking with the kids at this popular coastal Gippsland family holiday destination.

4hrs from Melbourne

Mallacoota

Relax on a houseboat (no licence required) or simply soak up the easy-going vibe of this remote East Gippsland beach town.

6½hrs from Melbourne

Great Southern Rail Trail

Get on your bike and tackle this 72km Gippsland cycleway, or veer off the trail to tour the region's cool-climate wineries, distillery doors and breweries.

1½hrs from Melbourne

Wilsons Promontory

Lace your boots for spectacular national park trails and laze on bone-white beaches lapped by turquoise water while keeping an eye out for native wildlife.

4hrs from Melbourne

Mornington Peninsula

Indulge in the gourmet pleasures of this scenic wine region dotted with cellar doors, great restaurants and cafes. Top off the day with a scenic coastal stroll.

1hr from Melbourne

SOUTHEAST QUEENSLAND Trip Builder

TAKE YOUR PICK OF MUST-SEES AND HIDDEN GEMS

Queensland is known as the Sunshine State, but its southeastern corner bags the most sunny days – ideal for bouncing between golden beaches and cool craft breweries, and exploring the lush hinterland regions beyond.

Trip Notes

Hub towns Brisbane, Gold Coast, Noosa

How long Allow at least a week

Getting around It's easy to navigate central Brisbane and the Gold Coast via public transport, but a car is more convenient for exploring the Sunshine Coast and Gold Coast hinterland regions.

Tip It costs just $7.25 per person per night to camp in Queensland national parks – handy if you're travelling in a camper. You'll usually need to bring your own drinking water.

Sunshine Coast Hinterland
Leave the beach behind for a day or two to camp out in national parks, fill your picnic basket at charming country town markets, tick off a hike or two and maybe even spot an elusive platypus.
1½hrs from Brisbane

Scenic Rim
Visit a camel farm with a difference, tour wineries and a quirky brewery, and admire exquisite mountain scenery and more in this emerging tourism destination.
1hr from Brisbane

Noosa

Stroll the seriously scenic Coastal Walk in this postcard-perfect Sunshine Coast holiday hub until you find your perfect beach. Then spend an afternoon exploring the Sunshine Coast's burgeoning craft-beer scene.

2hrs from Brisbane

Brisbane

Top off a day exploring the Queensland capital's excellent museums and galleries with a swim at Southbank or a cool drink by the Brisbane River.

1½hrs from Sydney

North Stradbroke Island/ Minjerribah

Escape to easily accessible Straddie for a day (or more) of whale watching, exploring Aboriginal connections, and beach fun.

, 1½hrs from Brisbane

Gold Coast

Experience the Glitter Strip's transformation from greasy-spoon territory to a seaside city with culinary clout – and some killer cocktail bars.

1hr from Brisbane

Gold Coast Hinterland

Go for a hike in search of waterfalls and glow-worms in the lush, ancient rainforests rising up behind the Gold Coast.

45mins from Surfers Paradise

TROPICAL NORTH QUEENSLAND
Trip Builder

TAKE YOUR PICK OF MUST-SEES AND HIDDEN GEMS

Cairns is an unmissable stop on any East Coast traveller's itinerary, but the fun doesn't end at this buzzy gateway to the Great Barrier Reef and the Daintree Rainforest, with oodles of attractions dotted all the way along this lush stretch of coastline.

Trip Notes

Hub towns Cairns, Port Douglas, Townsville

How long Allow nine to 14 days

Getting around Hire a car at Cairns Airport, or book a tour; most tours include hotel transfers.

Tips The humidity is lower during the June to October dry season, and stinger suits aren't required for marine activities, making this time ideal for outdoor exploration. Visit at the beginning or end of the season to avoid the bulk of the crowds.

CLOCKWISE FROM LEFT: BRETT ANDERSEN/SHUTTERSTOCK, ALEXPURPLE/SHUTTERSTOCK, MAXIMILIANE WAGNER/SHUTTERSTOCK

Cooktown
Embark on a road trip to historic Cooktown via the storied 4WD-only Bloomfield Track, or via the longer, sealed inland route, which takes roughly the same amount of time.
4½hrs from Cairns

Port Douglas
Relax poolside at one of the holiday town's many resorts, enjoy long walks (and maybe a swim) at fabulous Four Mile Beach and make the most of the easy access to the Daintree Rainforest's Mossman Gorge.
1hr from Cairns

Atherton Tablelands
Chase waterfalls, swim in crater lakes, spot quirky wildlife and explore an incredible outdoor museum in the refreshingly cool hills above Cairns.
1½hrs from Cairns

Cape Tribulation
Immerse yourself in the heart of the otherworldly Daintree Rainforest on a day (or longer) trip to 'Cape Trib', where the rainforest meets the Great Barrier Reef.
2½hrs from Cairns

Great Barrier Reef
Sign up for an outer-reef day trip for the best snorkelling and diving in the iconic marine park, or enjoy the reef for longer on an overnight experience.
1½hrs from Cairns or Port Douglas

Cairns
Sultry Cairns has been upgraded with flash hotels and a hip small-bar scene, making the multicultural seaside city a fantastic base for reef and rainforest excursions.
2¼hrs from Brisbane

Cassowary Coast
Discover hidden beaches, kick back at relaxed pubs, and look out for the formidable feathered namesake of this laid-back coastal region between Cairns and Townsville.
1½hrs from Cairns

Townsville
Go koala-spotting on Magnetic Island, and sign up for a day trip to snorkel or dive the Museum of Underwater Art (MOUA) at John Brewer Reef.
4½hrs from Cairns

7 Things to Know About EAST COAST AUSTRALIA

INSIDER TIPS TO HIT THE GROUND RUNNING

1 Most Australians Live Here

Australia's population mostly lives in the eastern states, and almost half the country lives in Brisbane, Sydney or Melbourne. However, given the size of this part of the continent, there's still plenty of room to breathe. The East Coast is full of friendly, tight-knit small towns and natural expanses where you can be alone with the gum trees.

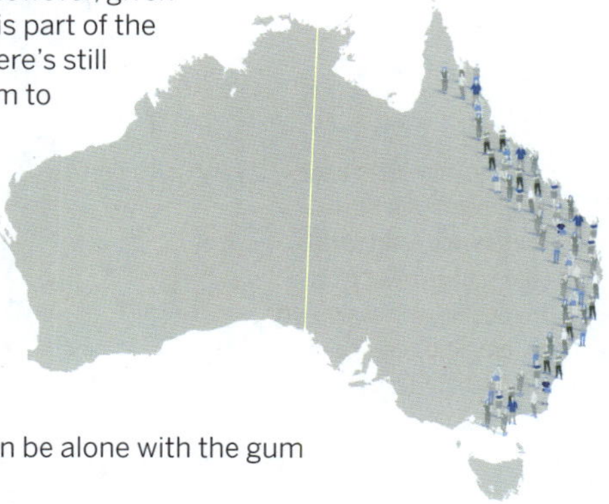

2 It's Bigger Than You Think!

No, really. It takes around 10 hours to drive from Sydney to Melbourne, and three hours to fly from Melbourne to Cairns. Make sure to check your travel time beforehand. Don't worry, Australians fall into this trap as well: many a local has embarked on a half-hour drive only to arrive an hour later than planned.

▶ For information on Getting Around see p244

3 Local Accents Vary

While regional accents in Australia are less defined than in some other countries, Aussies can usually distinguish between someone from Melbourne and someone from Sydney – and will almost definitely be able to identify someone from Far North Queensland!

4 Coffee Is Serious Business

Australians – especially Sydneysiders and Melburnians – love their coffee. If an Aussie recommends a cafe, they probably know what they're talking about.

FROM LEFT: SUDARSAN THOBIAS/SHUTTERSTOCK, ASTUDIO/SHUTTERSTOCK, KIRASOLLY/SHUTTERSTOCK, NORA HACHIO/SHUTTERSTOCK, OXY_GEN/SHUTTERSTOCK

5 The Animals Are Rather Special

And they (mostly) won't hurt you. Most of the world's marsupials are found in Australia, and the East Coast is full of creatures you won't find anywhere else on Earth. To name just a few, weedy sea dragons, wobbegong sharks and bandy-bandy snakes are all unique to this slice of the globe.

6 Colloquialisms Are Celebrated

You may think you know English, but sometimes speaking 'Australian' is something entirely different. Australians are known to shorten words, add vowels or change meanings. Here's a quick guide to the many 'o's in Aussie slang:

Ambo An ambulance driver

Arvo An afternoon

Avo Are you getting the hang of it? This is an avocado.

Bottle-o A bottle shop. This term is so common that many pubs will label their attached bottle shop a bottle-o.

Defo Definitely!

Garbo No, not the 1930s actress (far from it). This is a shortened form of 'garbage collector'.

Journo A journalist

Muso A musician

Relo A relative or family member

Servo A petrol station (formerly called a 'service station') or sometimes a convenience store

Smoko A quick break from work. Though the word comes from 'smoke break', a smoko no longer requires a cigarette.

7 Sun Safety Is No Joke

Even when it's overcast, sun-conscious Aussies will tell you to slip, slop, slap: slip on a long-sleeved shirt, slop on some sunscreen and slap on a hat. The sun is harsher here than in most other countries, and sunburn is an all-too-easy way to ruin your holiday.

▶ For more Safe Travel measures see p246

Read, Listen, Watch & Follow

READ

Too Much Lip (Melissa Lucashenko; 2018) An Aboriginal woman rides a stolen motorcycle to visit her dying grandfather.

Picnic at Hanging Rock (Joan Lindsay; 1967) Haunting classic about mysterious schoolgirl disappearances.

Dark Emu (Bruce Pascoe; 2014) Challenges assumptions about Aboriginal culture before colonisation.

Cloudstreet (Tim Winton; 1991) A classic Aussie novel by a master storyteller about two Perth families.

LISTEN

Barkaa
The current matriarch of Australian rap, the Malyangapa and Barkindji woman (pictured right) won an Aria award for her 2024 EP *Big Tidda*.

Paul Kelly
Hear his early work in *Under the Sun* (1987), enjoy the more experimental *Life Is Fine* (2017) and delight in his greatest hits in *Songs from the South* (1997).

Pete Murray
The folk rock singer-songwriter's 2025 album *Longing* is perfect for East Coast road trips.

Warm Red Earth Podcast Hidden and often surprising aspects of Australian history.

BRENDON THORNE/STRINGER/GETTY IMAGES

Like A Version A long-running weekly feature on radio station Triple J, where artists cover new and classic tracks.

WATCH

Boy Swallows Universe (2024) Drama series following a young boy growing up in the suburbs of 1980s Brisbane.

Bluey (2018–) Brisbane inspired the setting for this beloved animated series about a six-year-old blue heeler puppy.

Playing Beatie Bow (1986) Based on Ruth Park's award-winning novel, this film transports viewers to 1873 Sydney.

The Castle (1997) Typifies Australian humour and is full of quotable moments. Set in suburban Melbourne.

Muriel's Wedding (1994; pictured right) ABBA-loving Muriel (Toni Collette) tries to escape her small-town life.

COLLECTION CHRISTOPHEL/ALAMY STOCK PHOTO

FOLLOW

@astrokirsten
Wiradjuri astronomer Kirsten Banks on the Australian night sky.

@gabscanu
Incredible photos of Australia.

@celestebarber
The queen of keeping-it-real comedy.

@adrianwidjy
Eating spots in Sydney.

@chrishemsworth
Just as charming off-screen.

SYDNEY

BEACHES | FOOD | HISTORY

RESEARCHED BY PHILLIP TANG AND SARAH REID

ELIAS BITAR/SHUTTERSTOCK

SYDNEY
Trip Builder

Listen in on local brunch gossip at a garden cafe, then hike, surf or do sweet, sandy nothing at any of the city's 100-plus beaches. Delight in fusion flavours in Australia's premier multicultural city, then sip drinks with a view across the endlessly captivating harbour.

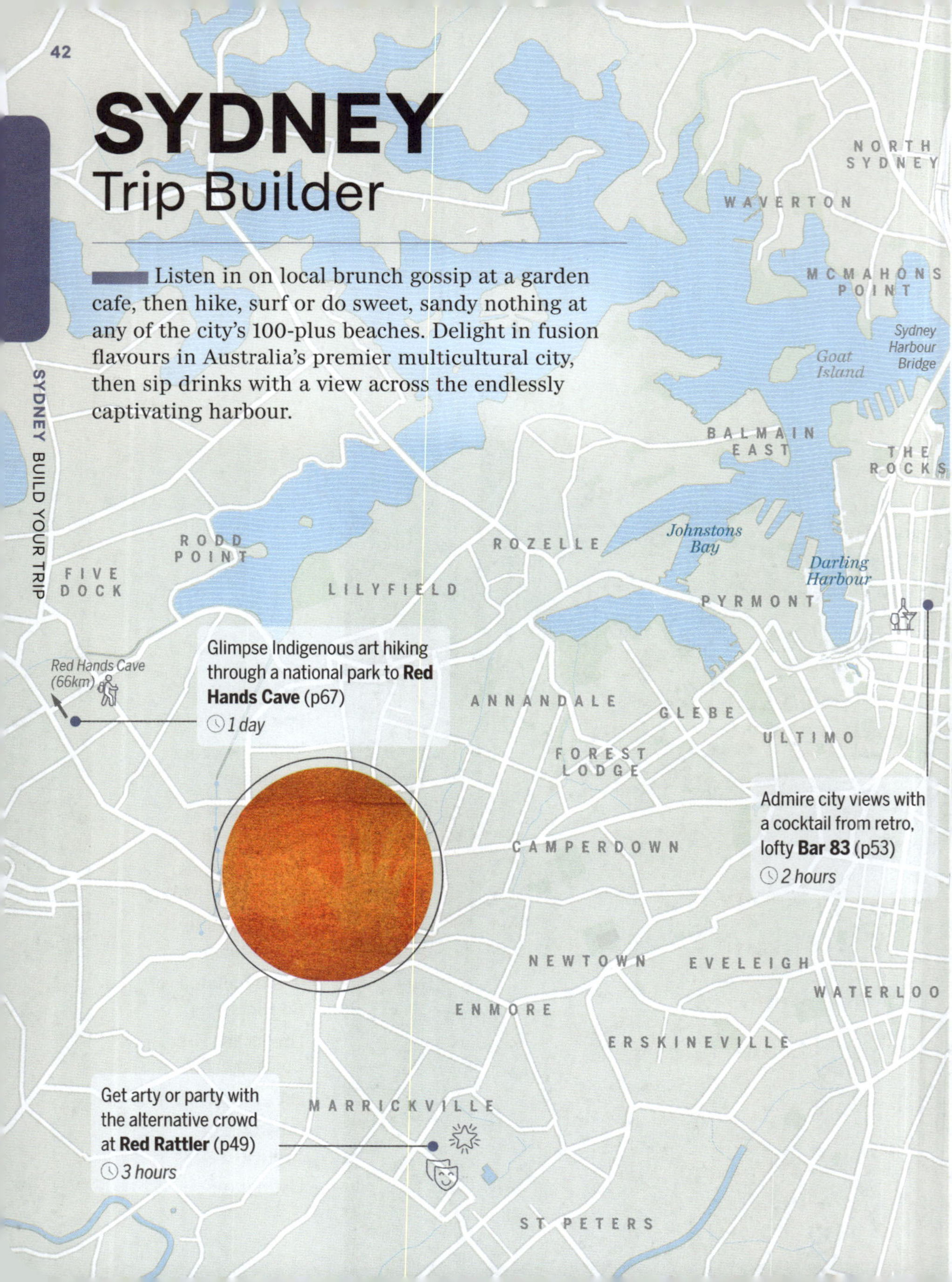

Glimpse Indigenous art hiking through a national park to **Red Hands Cave** (p67)
1 day

Admire city views with a cocktail from retro, lofty **Bar 83** (p53)
2 hours

Get arty or party with the alternative crowd at **Red Rattler** (p49)
3 hours

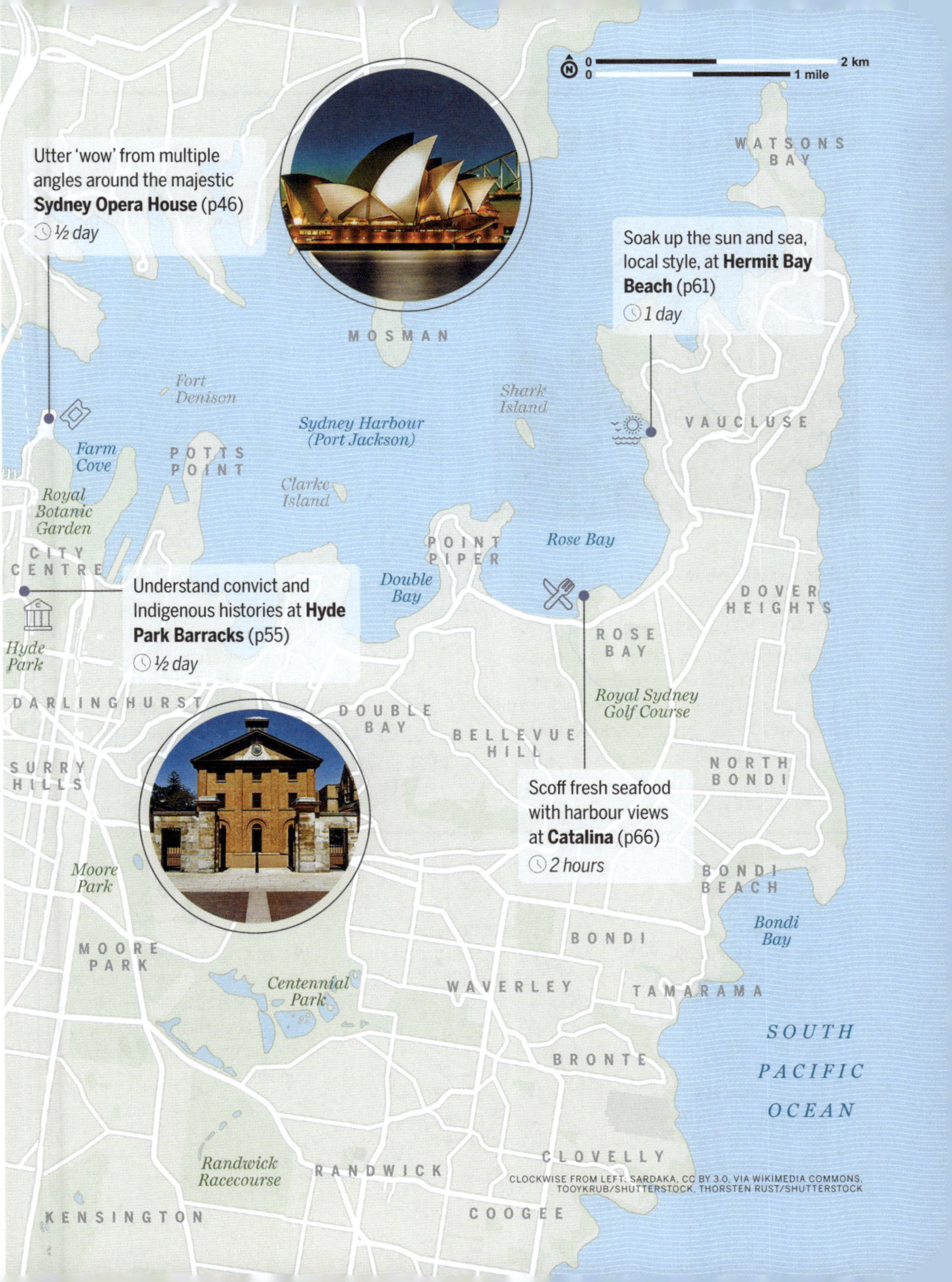

CLOCKWISE FROM LEFT: SARDAKA, CC BY 3.0, VIA WIKIMEDIA COMMONS, TOOYKRUB/SHUTTERSTOCK, THORSTEN RUST/SHUTTERSTOCK

Practicalities

EIGENBLAU/SHUTTERSTOCK

ARRIVING

Sydney Airport Taxis to the city cost a flat fee of $60. Trains from beneath the terminal cost around $22 each for the short journey into the city.

Central Station Country and interstate trains arrive at Central Station, at the southern end of the city centre. Local trains are downstairs, or head to Railway Sq for buses. Long-distance coaches stop in front of Central Station.

HOW MUCH FOR A

Serve of fish and chips $17

Private surfing lesson $100

Glass of wine $14

GETTING AROUND

Opal Purchase an Opal Card or use the app for all public transport. It's slightly more expensive to tap and pay with a credit/debit card.

Train, bus & light rail Train lines (including new metro lines) radiate from Central Station. Buses are especially useful for reaching the beaches and parts of the Inner West. Light rail (tram) is useful for city-hopping in the central business district, and trips to Pyrmont, Glebe, Surry Hills, Moore Park and Randwick.

Ferries Head all around the harbour and up the river to Parramatta. Most people take a ferry to get to Manly in the north because you get the harbour views as a bonus.

WHEN TO GO

DEC–FEB
Peak season coincides with summer school holidays and hot weather

MAR–JUN
Warm but with occasional downpours

JUL & AUG
Chilly nights but usually sunny days

SEP–NOV
Spring is usually dry and warm

EATING & DRINKING

The city truly celebrates Australia's place on the Pacific Rim, pairing the freshest local ingredients – excellent seafood is a particular highlight – with the flavours of Asia, the Mediterranean and beyond. One tradition that has gone global is the easy-going Sydney cafe. The blueprint for this is Bills in Darlinghurst, with its large communal table. Here, late chef Bill Granger popularised, maybe even invented, smashed avocado on toast (pictured bottom right). Cafes are still good for a solid, often adventurous meal. The Inner West is brimful with them.

Best cocktail wizardry
Eau-de-Vie (p67)

Best contemporary dining
Margaret (p66)

CONNECT & FIND YOUR WAY

Wi-fi Free at most accommodation, cafes and shopping centres. A prepaid SIM card for your (unlocked) phone costs around $2; a month of data and unlimited national calls and texts costs $13 to $40 or more.

Navigation Some roads are kilometres long, forking off and changing names; for example, Oxford St starts as Liverpool St and becomes Bondi Rd.

WHERE TO STAY

Book ahead around weekends and big events. Prices, even in the budget class, are high.

Neighbourhood	Atmosphere
City centre	Convenient transport and numerous Asian restaurants, but noisy, with high prices.
Circular Quay & the Rocks	Big-ticket sights, vibrant nightlife and top hotels and restaurants. Made for tourists, with matching high prices.
Newtown & the Inner West	Far from beaches, but bohemian with great cafes and interesting shops. Priced for locals.
Surry Hills & Darlinghurst	Sydney's hippest eating and drinking precinct and the heart of the gay scene. Hilly with few sights.
Bondi & the Eastern Beaches	Sand, surf and sunbathers. A slow bus ride to the city.
Manly	Beautiful beaches and a privileged community feel, but not much to do in bad weather.

CHEAP FERRIES

Transport on Saturday and Sunday is price capped, so weekends are good for ferry-hopping or out-of-town trips. Problem is, everyone else thinks so too.

MONEY

ATMs are plentiful, and some charge fewer foreign-transaction fees if you withdraw from a bank that is part of the international ATM network of your bank back home.

01 Sydney Harbour SCENES

WALKING | VIEWS | FAMILY

Inspired by yacht sails and surrounded by water, the glorious Sydney Opera House is an iconic symbol of Australia. The building's majestic curves dominate Sydney Harbour and look impressive from every angle. Visitors may be many, but you can still find special points of view for private gazing at different times of the day.

RICHIE CHAN/SHUTTERSTOCK

How to

Getting here There are plenty of trains, buses, ferries and light-rail stops at nearby Circular Quay.

When to go There are fewer visitors on weekdays and after 7pm weekends. Sunsets are always magical.

Cost There is no entrance or entry fee to explore the exterior of the Sydney Opera House or to view the light show.

Circumnavigate the Opera House Not many people know that you can stroll right around the base of the Opera House.

BENNY MARTY/SHUTTERSTOCK

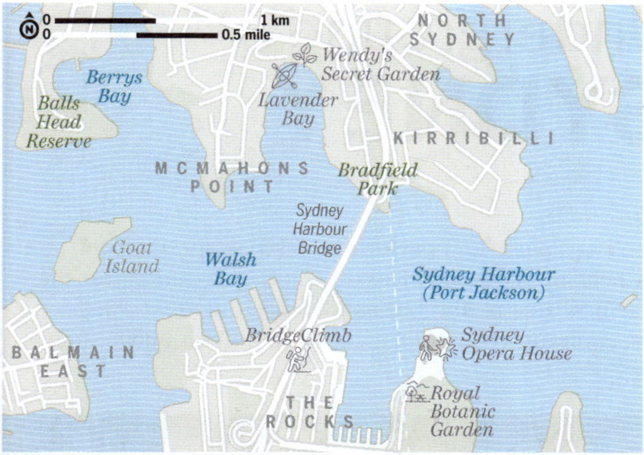

Wendy Whiteley's Secret Garden Australian artist Brett Whiteley and his then-wife Wendy built a home at lovely Lavender Bay in 1970. After Brett's death, Wendy worked to establish a garden on the difficult, sloping site, and today the expansive space (free and open to visitors) is filled with Australian plants and offers harbour views and a glimpse of the Opera House.

Get the blood pumping Don a headset, a safety cord and a grey jumpsuit for **BridgeClimb**: a guided three-hour ascent of Sydney Harbour Bridge that'll get you a white-knuckle view of the Opera House as the wind whips up. Options aside from the classic ascent include the Burrawa Climb, guided by an Indigenous storyteller who shares some of Sydney's lesser-known history on the way up. For a quieter perspective, kayak at dawn as the sun kisses the surrounding waters. Departing from places like Lavender Bay boat ramp, most tours include a guide, all gear and a briefing for novices.

Picnic break Enjoy an alfresco meal under Moreton Bay fig trees on the crowd-free Tarpeian Lawn at the edge of the **Royal Botanic Garden**, adjacent to the Opera House.

Light show *Badu Gili* is a light show of Aboriginal art projected onto the Opera House at sunset. It's been such a hit that it's become a daily event.

Top left Sydney Opera House
Bottom left BridgeClimb, Sydney Harbour Bridge

Inside the Opera House

If you fall in love with the Sydney Opera House, or want to, you can take a tour inside for lesser-seen delights.

Peek at the six fine performance spaces that stage around 40 shows a week – and it's not all opera. Modern concerts, theatre and stand-up comedy happen here too, so book ahead for events. The Concert Hall features panoramic screens showcasing past performances, and is especially impressive for architecture lovers with its radiant art deco shell design. Some tours take you backstage to see actors rehearsing, or even into a green room for breakfast.

02 Underground SYDNEY

ART | NIGHTLIFE | LGBTIQ+

Sydney's underground art, party and performance scene sprang from restrictive drinking laws. Check out edgy galleries during the day, and after the sun sets invite yourself to fringe theatre and places to dance the night away. Rockers, writers, dreamers, community-minded artists and allies all have their own enclaves.

AAP/ALAMY

How to

Getting here Parties happen around Redfern and the Inner West and are advertised on social-media pages, sometimes with secret locations only revealed on the night.

When to go Art and performance spaces are hot year-round, but book ahead for events around the Gay and Lesbian Mardi Gras.

Cost Party nights and performances are usually ticketed, while bars and pubs cost sweet nothing.

What to wear Check social-media snaps to see what's hot.

AAP/ALAMY

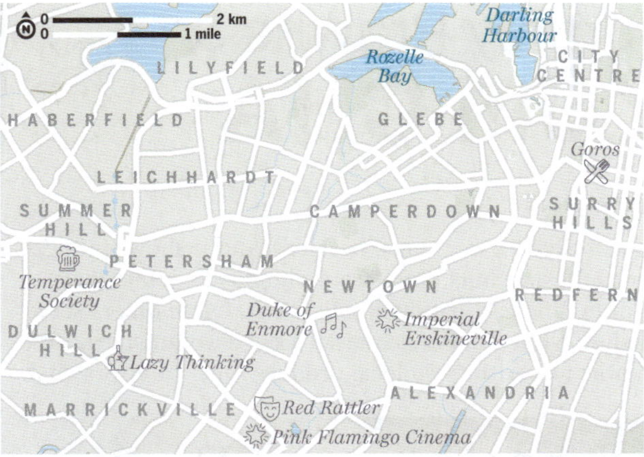

Bars, pubs and theatre Heritage-listed in 2025 for its deep historical and cultural significance, the **Imperial Erskineville** (of *Priscilla, Queen of the Desert* fame) is the most iconic place in Sydney to catch a drag show. Alternative performers are also under the spotlight at the **Red Rattler** community-run theatre in Marrickville. In Surry Hills, **Goros** is an *anime*-themed restaurant-bar with karaoke, arcade games and a young crowd. The **Temperance Society** bar is a tiny, unexpected slice of artistic life in stuffy Summer Hill, attracting writers and creatives to its dark Victorian interior to sup locally sourced beer and wine. Live music and poetry have sometimes been spiced up with presentations on topics such as 'Women in electronic-music history'.

Party nights Regular parties with a carnival of fantastical, gender-bending performances go off at **Honcho Disko**. **Heaps Gay** events are magnets for a mixed crowd (the space isn't just gay and lesbian, despite the name), who come for live bands, DJs and death-dropping hype girls. If that still feels too commercial, look up **Bad Dog** (baddog.net.au), which thinks leather is conservative and prefers to stretch the boundaries of what a queer party should be.

Look out for Burning Man–inspired festivals **Burning Seed** and **Dragon Dreaming** in country New South Wales.

Top left Imperial Erskineville
Bottom left Lazy Thinking

Underground Sounds

Lazy Thinking is an Inner West record bar with underground gigs every night of the week. Entry is by donation, which supports local artists. Expect an arty, indie vibe. The **Duke of Enmore** is an alternative rock 'n' roll hub in the Inner West with gigs on most evenings, including punk, goth and metal, plus trivia and karaoke. Film buffs should check out **Pink Flamingo Cinema**, an underground cinema hosted in a Marrickville warehouse that screens carefully curated obscure and cult films.

■ **Tips by Jovana Subotic,** *an underground electronic music nerd, reformer Pilates and yoga teacher, and witch @mysticvisions*

03 Yummy Prawns & YUM CHA

EATING | MULTICULTURAL | DRINKING

Nearly half of Sydney's residents were born overseas, and it shows in the city's wealth of dining options. Restaurants range from pho noodle joints that evoke a trip to Vietnam to dumpling-cart banquet halls. Persian fine diners serve pomegranate-bejewelled dishes, while Thai-kitsch bistros sell coconut snacks to go. Everything tastes authentic, just with fresh local produce (and fatter prawns).

PHAIAPIROM/SHUTTERSTOCK

How to

When to go Book ahead for weekends, and even from midweek in the warmer months.

How to get here All the areas in the CBD are easily walkable from places like Circular Quay. Other areas are best reached by public transport or Uber.

BYO If you're having more than a couple of drinks, it can be better value to bring your own beer or bottle of wine. Restaurants will state if they're BYO; corkage is usually around $15 per bottle of wine.

BERNADETTE TSAN/SHUTTERSTOCK

CHEDIMA/SHUTTERSTOCK

Far left top Yum cha selection
Far left bottom Dessert, Mango Coco
Left Vietnamese pho

In the CBD, groups of friends congregate at Korean restaurants like **Basax** for sticky fried chicken. Casual Thai restaurants line Campbell St, off George St in Haymarket. Sydney's Thai community gossips over desserts at bistros like **Mango Coco** between grocery shopping.

The 'food courts' of Dixon and Sussex Streets in Chinatown are actually bustling indoor hawker stands like you might find in Indonesia, Thailand, Singapore and Vietnam. Yum cha is a weekend brunch ritual for the Cantonese community. You can turn up hungry at the red-and-gold banquet halls of Haymarket and nab a bamboo steamer of prawn dumplings right off the trolleys within minutes.

The Lebanese community first called Surry Hills and Redfern home in the 1880s, and that legacy lingers in Persian, Turkish and Middle Eastern restaurants.

The Inner West neighbourhood of Marrickville has a stretch of good Vietnamese restaurants from the train station to Marrickville Rd. It's the real deal, just with updated interiors for the hip crowd.

Newtown is Sydney's plant-based capital, with a dozen vegan Japanese, Vietnamese, Thai, gelato, 'butchery', 'cheese' and dumpling joints on King St. The epicentre is **Gigi Pizzeria**.

A 25-minute express train from Central Station whizzes you to the other CBD, Parramatta, where cottages in the adjacent Harris Park have become restaurants and dessert diners serving dishes from every region of India.

Best Hidden Asian Diners

Cabramatta's **Battambang Restaurant** is a long-time fave with Khmer locals seeking home-style dishes. Try the dry Phnom Penh noodles and a serving of crispy deep-fried intestines.

Grab some sticky rice and take yourself to flavour town with juicy barbecued ox tongue, spiced pork sausages and papaya salad at **Lao Village** in Fairfield. Where have you been all my life?

Hidden between a roadside petrol station and a car wash, little **2 Foodies** in Mt Pritchard has pho broth so deep, rich and hearty you'd be lucky to eat one this good even if you grew up in a Vietnamese household.

Tips by Kevin La, *food blogger and content creator from southwest Sydney @sydneyfoodboy*

04 Bar Crawl with A VIEW

DRINKING | VIEWS | HARBOUR

Toast the smashing views of Sydney's harbour, beach and twinkling lights. Drink at giddy heights gazing across the Opera House, or ditch the crowds and kick back in a park with the trees framing the water.

PHOTOHOLGIC/SHUTTERSTOCK

Best Cocktail Bars

PS40, CBD Try the hot and cold Africola.

Bar Demo, Newtown Fantastic cocktails and low-intervention wines.

Cantina OK, CBD Ridiculous agave selection.

Ramblin Rascal, CBD Vibey and divey. Order a Boilermaker and kick back.

Huelo Bar, Newtown Hidden behind a general store, with $3 happy-hour oysters.

Tips by Chau Tran, *bartender at Burrow Bar* *@burrow_bar, @chaueth*

Trip Notes

Getting here and around Featured bars are within walking distance of city train stations. For Bondi, take bus 333.

When to go Summer for long, scorching days; crisp, sunny winter for fewer crowds and no summer downpours.

Non-alc night out Sydney's non-alcoholic scene is thriving, with local distilleries producing gin, beer and other tipples with all the botanicals and none of the hangovers.

Drinking dens Raining? Cosy up in a moody cocktail bar (p67).

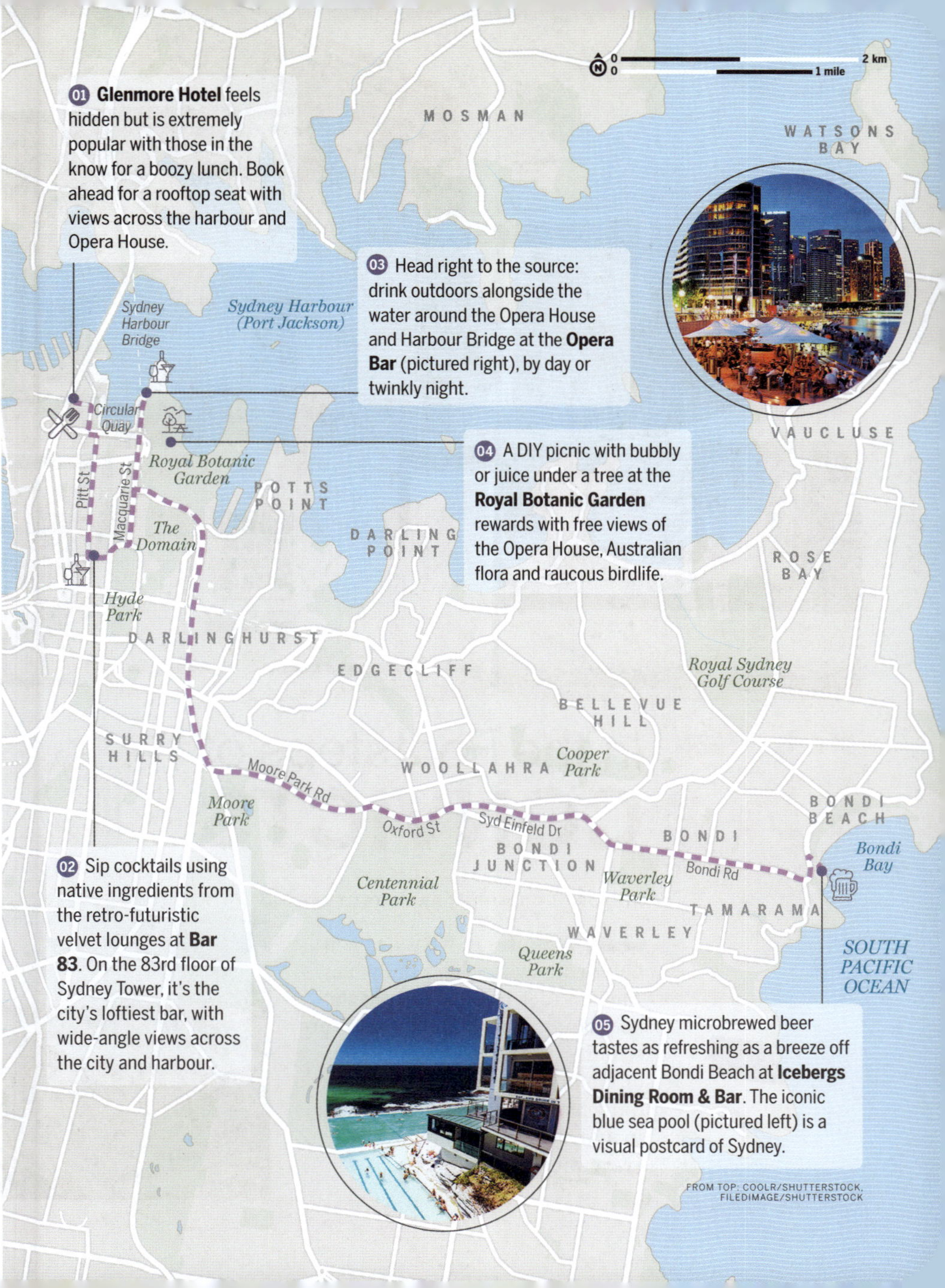

01 **Glenmore Hotel** feels hidden but is extremely popular with those in the know for a boozy lunch. Book ahead for a rooftop seat with views across the harbour and Opera House.

03 Head right to the source: drink outdoors alongside the water around the Opera House and Harbour Bridge at the **Opera Bar** (pictured right), by day or twinkly night.

04 A DIY picnic with bubbly or juice under a tree at the **Royal Botanic Garden** rewards with free views of the Opera House, Australian flora and raucous birdlife.

02 Sip cocktails using native ingredients from the retro-futuristic velvet lounges at **Bar 83**. On the 83rd floor of Sydney Tower, it's the city's loftiest bar, with wide-angle views across the city and harbour.

05 Sydney microbrewed beer tastes as refreshing as a breeze off adjacent Bondi Beach at **Icebergs Dining Room & Bar**. The iconic blue sea pool (pictured left) is a visual postcard of Sydney.

FROM TOP: COOLR/SHUTTERSTOCK, FILEDIMAGE/SHUTTERSTOCK

05 In the Footsteps of CONVICTS

HISTORY | CULTURE | ARCHITECTURE

Glimpses of what has gone before are everywhere in Sydney. Ancient rock carvings adorn the headlands, convict-hewn roads are still in service, and large chunks of the harbour look much as they did when the First Fleet muscled in and changed absolutely everything else.

CLAUDINE VAN MASSENHOVE/SHUTTERSTOCK

How to

Getting here and around Hyde Park Barracks is outside St James Station, or from Circular Quay it's an interesting 15-minute walk down Macquarie St with its historic buildings.

When to go The city centre can get hectic with office lunchers during the week, making weekends the quieter option.

Museums of History Learn more about this collection of 11 museums and historic houses in Sydney at mhnsw.au.

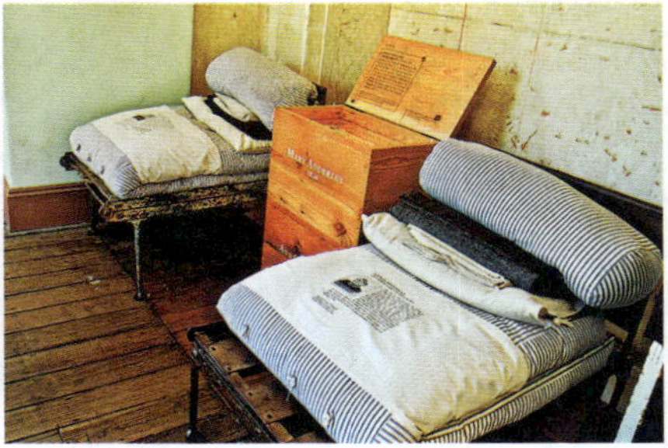

GIRLWANDER1982/SHUTTERSTOCK

Convict Sites

Start with the place convicts called home: **Hyde Park Barracks**. Not only were convicts housed here, but convict stonecutters, bricklayers and carpenters built the handsome building that is today a modern museum. A 2020 refurbishment added interactive installations, theatrical events and displays that turn dry history into an exploration of human struggle.

Cockatoo Island was a harsh place of punishment, with the cat-o'-nine-tails and underground solitary cells. As at Hyde Park Barracks, the system here was based on work, and inmates were controlled by a system of bells. Tours of Cockatoo Island (cockatooisland.gov.au) give insights into its history, or you can get a ferry here from Circular Quay and explore.

DANIEL DE PETRO/SHUTTERSTOCK

Indigenous Plants

While First Fleeters came close to starvation in the early years, local Aboriginal tribes had millennia of knowledge of living off the land. See examples of edible plants harvested by the Gadigal, Dharug and Dharawal peoples in the Cadi Jam Ora (First Encounters) beds of the **Royal Botanic Garden**.

Left Cockatoo Island
Above left Hyde Park Barracks
Above right Hyde Park Barracks interior

Aboriginal Sydney

Sydney is the land of the Eora nation. It is an important place for all Aboriginal people and they wish to tell their own stories of their survival. Learn some on an eye-opening 90-minute walking tour of the Rocks with **Dreamtime Southern X**.

Hear Dreaming stories and learn about cultural sites as you sail across Sydney Harbour on a **Tribal Warrior** cultural cruise. Tour profits are reinvested in Indigenous family programs.

The **Australian Museum** (australian.museum/learn/first-nations) has a rich Aboriginal and Torres Strait Islander collection, with Indigenous-guided Waranara Tours available.

And you can even climb the Sydney Harbour Bridge with an Indigenous guide on the Burrawa Climb (p47).

The Rocks

Known as Tallawoladah to its original inhabitants, the Gadigal people, Sydney's oldest neighbourhood was the hub of convict- and

Rat Time Capsule

When renovators lifted the floorboards of the convict wards at Hyde Park Barracks in 1979, they discovered a time capsule: convict-era rats had stolen boarders' clothing and other everyday items to fashion their nests. The dry environment under the floor had preserved 120,000 pieces. It's no wonder the nests were so extensive: convicts complained of packs of rats nipping at their faces throughout the night.

Today, the barracks display 4000 items from this treasure trove of coins, leather, rosary beads, hammock rope, aprons, bonnets, cotton spools, dresses and brooches. There are even a few rat skeletons!

ALEX CIMBAL/SHUTTERSTOCK

Left Hammocks, Hyde Park Barracks (p55)
Below Outdoor market, The Rocks

wharf-trading life in the early 19th century. Today, the Rocks is a place of glitzy shops and bars in the shadow of the Harbour Bridge. Colonial marks are still here, though, and they come alive with a tour, but you can easily wander around yourself, time-jumping with lunch in a modern-day cafe or shopping at the outdoor market. Architecture highlights are the sandstone splendour of **Sydney Observatory**, the brick warehouses of **Campbell's Stores**, and **Sergeant Major's Row** of terrace houses.

Archaeological digs have discovered the remains of households, and there are a number of museum sites to visit here, the main one being the **Big Dig Archaeology Education Centre**. Tucked away down a laneway, **The Rocks Discovery Museum** digs deep into the area's history on an artefact-rich tour. Sensitive attention is given to the Gadigal people, and there are interesting tales of early colonial characters.

First Contact

James Cook's monument-marked landing place is on the southern side of the park in Kurnell, 45 minutes south of the CBD. The **Kurnell Visitor Centre** conveys the impact of European arrival on the local Aboriginal people, and has information on the surrounding wetlands and Cook's life and expeditions.

FRANK MARTINS/SHUTTERSTOCK

Further out west, several interesting historic houses date from the very earliest days of colonial settlement. Parramatta was founded with First Fleet convict labour when Sydney Cove proved to be lousy for growing veggies.

■ **By Paula Jane Byrne**
Historian Paula Jane Byrne is an adjunct fellow in humanities at Western Sydney University and author of Criminal Law and Colonial Subject. *ResearchGate @Paula-Jane-Byrne*

Life for the First Convicts

SURVIVAL OF THE FITTEST IN SYDNEY TOWN

For the early convicts arriving at present-day Circular Quay, Sydney was a place of control and punishment. The system allowed little ways that convicts could shape their own lives, but it was also fickle, and they could be lashed, imprisoned or retransported to another part of the NSW coast.

Left Arrival of the First Fleet at Sydney Cove
Middle Parramatta Female Factory
Right Convict gang, Sydney

PICTORIAL PRESS LTD/ALAMY

Beginnings

The eastern side of Sydney Cove – Warrane in the language of Traditional Owners, the Gadigal – is the site of the first permanent European settlement in Australia. It was established on Gadigal Country in 1788.

The original shoreline is marked by bronze discs in the pavement. Looking up the hill into the city, imagine two even rows of brick huts, allocated to convicts in 1792.

On the western side of Circular Quay, the Rocks was the commercial area of convict life. Houses were carved up, and lofts, garden space and sheds were rented out in the early 1800s. Convicts exchanged rations, rum and even stolen goods as rent. They raised income from working after hours: after finishing their government work, they were able to hire themselves out as labourers, in a kind of gig economy.

The rum brought into the houses gave landlords ideas, and numerous informal public houses opened up. If you owned one glass or even a cooking pot you were in business.

Tragic Second Fleet

Train your gaze on the centre of Circular Quay and imagine the first wharf here, where convicts landed on arrival. In 1789 the Second Fleet arrived in Warrane and 486 convicts were brought on shore. Many were starving and ill with scurvy, and soon died. Standing here, imagine the shock and horror that day. Some convicts fainted, while others crept upon their knees or were carried on the backs of others.

The convicts had been transported by a merchant slaving company with no interest in keeping their human cargo alive. They would not make any money by selling them, so what was the point in feeding them?

HISTORIC COLLECTION/ALAMY

HISTORY AND ART COLLECTION/ALAMY

Female & Male Convicts

Each ship was its own little culture that depended on the personality of the captain.

For women this could mean the difference between repeated rape or cohabitation with a sailor or officer, or doing business on board washing clothes or trading in articles bought at ports. When female convicts landed after 1813 they were taken up the Parramatta River by boat to the Parramatta Female Factory (parramattafemalefactoryfriends.com.au). You can take the same route by ferry to Parramatta and see the factory.

> In 1789 the Second Fleet arrived in Warrane and 486 convicts were brought on shore. Many were starving and ill with scurvy, and soon died.

Male convicts had set work hours, and to be found in the street outside these hours was an offence. Work was in the building industry and the stores, where rations were distributed and produce taken in. When male convicts arrived, they were told to find lodgings for themselves in the squalid Rocks. It was (and is) a maze that resembled an Irish village, with higgledy-piggledy streets and no street numbers so people could not be easily found by the constables.

The English government owned the labour of the convicts, not the convicts themselves. Convicts were sentenced to work for seven or 14 years, or for life. Alternatively, the governor could pardon them, and then they lived as if free. The last convict ship arrived in NSW in 1850 after much opposition to (not sympathy for) the convicts. Anti-convict sentiment formed part of the movement for democracy.

Convict Labour

Walk through Sydney and imagine the hewn stone, the mortar, the limewash and the cut wood. This labour was extracted from male convicts by fear of the lash. Many convict-made buildings and other constructions are still visible today.

St James' Church 179 King St

Supreme Court building Elizabeth St

Man-O' War steps Near the Botanic Gardens

Parliament House Macquarie St

Mint Museum Macquarie St

Parts of the Sydney Conservatorium of Music Near the Botanic Gardens

National Trust Centre Observatory Hill

Cadmans Cottage The Rocks

Hyde Park Barracks Macquarie St

Argyle Cut The Rocks

06 Let's BEACH

BEACHES | NATURE | SURFING

Nowhere else does the city kiss the sea so spectacularly. Sydneysiders are blessed with over 100 beaches, each with its own personality. Hidden strands favour sunbathing with a book, and some stretches of dramatic water are known only to surfers.

ALEKSANDAR TODOROVIC/SHUTTERSTOCK

How to

Getting here and around The eastern beaches can be reached from the city centre by bus. For the north, take a ferry from Circular Quay to Manly.

When to go Sunny weekdays can be quieter, especially in the mornings. Cloudy days see fewer crowds and more locals and surfers.

Surf safety Sydney's lifeguards and volunteer surf lifesavers watch over certain stretches of major beaches, marked with red-and-yellow flags, where it's safest to swim.

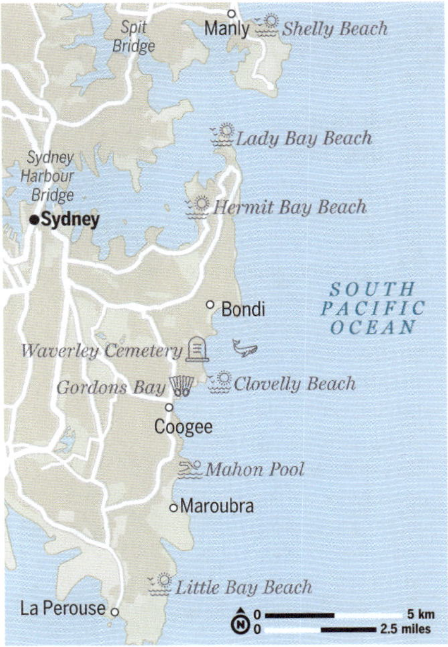

Social Swimming

Clovelly Beach is all concrete, so you can laze back and have a drink or jump straight off the platform into the water. Afterwards, there's a good bowlo (lawn bowls club) uphill for a drink and a game with friends. Plus **Clovelly Bowling & Recreation Club** has the best views over the coast of any bowlo in the world.

Quiet Swimming

Mahon Pool near Maroubra is calm and less busy than most beaches, but with dramatic surf at its edges. At **Little Bay Beach**, south of Malabar, you can't even see any buildings, just the beautiful flat water and outcrops for snorkelling. It's very quiet, with mostly local swimmers. Quiet **Hermit Bay Beach**, at the end of Nielsen Park's walking trails, faces the distant Harbour Bridge. It's ideal for reading

AIYOSHI597/SHUTTERSTOCK

Top left Clovelly Beach
Bottom left Mahon Pool

a book on the soft wheatgrass under shady trees. You don't even need to touch the sand; you can launch off a little rock wall into the water. **Shelly Beach** in Manly is protected from wild weather. There are no southerly winds, so you can take in the serenity.

Ocean Pools

If you have young kids or shark paranoia – or the surf just doesn't excite you – you can chill out at one of Sydney's approximately 35 artificial ocean pools, located up and down the coast and inside the harbour. Most are free. Some, like **Mahon Pool** and **Bronte Bogey Hole**, are what are known as bogey holes: natural-looking rock pools where you can safely splash about and snorkel, even while the surf surges in. Calm **McIver's Ladies Baths** (also known as Coogee Women's Baths) is open only to women and children; **Fairlight Beach Rock Pool** is similarly quiet and family-friendly. Others, like **Maccallum**

Surfing for Beginners

The most important thing at the beginning is just to get out there. Your paddling won't get stronger unless you're in the water all the time. Sydney beaches can be crowded, but don't let that deter you. Focus on getting your own waves.

Stay away from Bondi – it's so busy. Manly is relaxed and best for starting out. It can be quite protected, unlike Bondi and Maroubra, whose aggressive waves can dump you. South Cronulla is a long, more isolated beach with loads of space to find your own stretch.

■ **Lucy Small,**
surfer and activist
@saltwaterpilgrim

DARIA NIPOT/SHUTTERSTOCK

Nude Beach

Lady Bay Beach is Australia's oldest nudist beach. It's not just for ladies – gay men, straight couples and international visitors have sought solace in the calm, blue waters in their birthday suits for decades. Shrug off your clothing and the distant city, sheltered by Lady Bay's two rocky natural piers.

ANDY333/SHUTTERSTOCK

Pool and the famous **Bondi Icebergs**, resemble swimming pools. The ocean pools normally close one day a week so the seaweed can be cleaned out.

Walking & Snorkelling

The most famous beachside walk is the spectacular **Bondi to Coogee**, but there are plenty of trails (walkingcoastalsydney.com.au), with some of the most surprising ones around the harbour. The **Harbour Bridge to Spit Bridge** walk and the **Spit Bridge to Manly** walk are excellent stretches. Or do the 80km **Bondi to Manly** stretch over a few days (bonditomanly.com). One of the best snorkelling spots is **Gordons Bay**, where a free underwater nature trail has been set up, as is **Shelly Beach**, next to Manly.

Whale Watching

Each year, more than 50,000 humpback and southern right whales pass along Sydney's coast between May and November as they migrate between Antarctica and the warmer waters of the Pacific. It's easy to spot their spouts from the cliffs – grab a perch at **Waverley Cemetery** and keep an eye out for breaches and spouts.

WONGYMARK1/SHUTTERSTOCK

Left Surfing, Cronulla Beach
Top right Lady Bay Beach
Above right Humpback whale, Manly Beach

CREATURES
of Sydney

01

02

03

04

05

06

01 Ibis

Sydney's 'bin chicken' fossicks for food scraps in park bins and is drawn to tourists snacking at Circular Quay.

02 Silver gull

Loves screeching 'kwarwh' and fighting other seagulls for chips at the beach.

03 Laughing kookaburra

The bird emblem of NSW. If you don't hear them in Centennial Park, any other national park is a safe bet.

04 Australian magpie

Swoops from trees at joggers, cyclists and jumpy tourists in September (and around) to protect its chicks.

05 Sulphur-crested cockatoo

So rowdy, so Sydney, this parrot rules from Mrs Macquarie's Point to the outer suburbs.

06 Rainbow lorikeet

This parrot flocks for colourful – and noisy – sunset orchestras across Sydney.

07 Flying fox

Look up for another Hyde Park and Centennial Park nightly visitor as this bat, silhouetted against the sky, seeks eucalyptus pollen.

07

08

09

10

11

12

13

08 Huntsman spider

After summer downpours, this fist-sized visitor dries off on bedroom walls looking deadly – but it's not.

09 Sydney funnel-web spider

The world's second-most-venomous spider adores Sydney gardens after rain. Relax: no deaths have occurred since an antivenin was devised in 1981.

10 Eastern water dragon

Even lizards love Sydney's water and sun, especially in Lane Cove National Park and the bush around Parsley Bay.

11 Lace monitor (goanna)

Look out for this giant, gentle lizard sunbathing along the Manly Scenic Walkway.

12 Brushtail possum

Catch the possum's retro-reflective eyes at night as it scurries around Hyde Park.

13 Brush-turkey

Wanders leafy North Shore suburbs scratching up million-dollar gardens.

Listings

BEST OF THE REST

Sociable Eating

Farmhouse $$

Has a sociable common table where you can dig into simple and scrumptious oysters and cod in now cosmopolitan Kings Cross.

Chat Thai $

Reasonably priced, loaded with flavour and constantly buzzing. A go-to for meeting up with friends and family, with a Thai dish to please everyone.

Ms G's $$

Loud, brash and delicious Chinese fusion. The mixed bar and communal-warehouse vibe means you'll quickly feel part of the local eating scene.

Seafood & Views

Catalina $$$

The seafood is so fresh that you could go fishing out the window at this Rose Bay classic. The inventive, varied set menu makes any special occasion sparkle.

Pilu at Freshwater $$$

Brilliant Sardinian seafood know-how and Italian wines, backing a northern beach.

Ripples Chowder Bay $$$

Elevated terrace with scenic harbour perspectives and punchy salmon and prawn dishes. The port and occasional naval ship in dock will suit those with industrial tastes.

Sydney Fish Market $$

Enjoy a fresh seafood feast overlooking Blackwattle Bay or buy fresh fish to cook at home at Sydney's $836-million new fish market.

Felons Seafood $$

Chow down on plump oysters, ceviche tostadas, elevated fish and chips and more at this 300-seater on Manly Wharf, surrounded by the big blue.

Aussie Fusion

Ester $$$

Well-sourced Australian seafood prepared with global influences in Chippendale. Don't miss the blood-sausage sandwich or the excellent vegan set menu.

LuMi Dining $$$

Totally delicious blends of Italian and Japanese influences. Tasting menus are a tour de force. In the city.

Margaret $$$

Top chef Neil Perry's Double Bay restaurant is known for its steak, but the raw entrées and wood-fire-grilled fish are also excellent.

Bathers' Pavilion $$$

At Balmoral Beach, the modern French-Aussie seasonal menu focuses on produce from small local providers, with plenty of seafood.

MAYURA POJANAPORN/SHUTTERSTOCK

Chat Thai

Neptune's Grotto $$$

A moody underground restaurant near Circular Quay offering spins on traditional Italian.

Nature & First Nations

Guringai Aboriginal Tours

This Aboriginal-owned and -operated tour company offers excellent insights into the cultural heritage of beautiful Ku-ring-gai Chase National Park on its three-hour Basin Track Tour.

Red Hands Cave

Heading deeper into Ku-ring-gai Chase National Park, the Resolute picnic area has faint Aboriginal handprints in ochre at Red Hands Cave. Then, the Resolute Track heads past an Aboriginal engraving site.

Bondi Rock Engravings

Aboriginal rock engravings at Ben Buckler Point in North Bondi feature a whale and a turtle, with two shields and an eel close by. See more engravings at the nearby golf course.

Whale Watching Sydney

Learn about the importance of whales in Aboriginal cultures on a whale-watching trip between mid-May and November on a three-hour tour.

Drinking Dens

Eau-de-Vie $$$

Hidden away, but worth tracking down for its cocktail wizardry when you've had enough of the endless sunshine.

Lazybones Lounge $$

Head out of the city centre and discover the gloriously mellow vibes and live music at this low-lit Marrickville star that will take you as you are.

MIN JING/SHUTTERSTOCK

Art Gallery of NSW

Uncle Ming's Bar $$

A dark Chinese cave of cinema fantasies lives in this small bar secreted in a basement by a shirt shop. It's an atmospheric spot for leisurely exploration of the cocktail or dumpling menu.

Shady Pines Saloon $$

From the laneway entrance (look for the white door) you'd never guess there was a subterranean honky-tonk bar in urban-boho Darlinghurst.

Free Fun

Art Gallery of NSW

One of the main players of museum life in Sydney, with loads to see in its free sections, including regular concerts, screenings and children's activities. Free guided tours are offered on various themes.

Chau Chak Wing Museum

This museum at the University of Sydney exhibits Indigenous cultural objects and Australian, European and Asian art. The Mummy Room keeps kids amused with a 2500-year-old Egyptian mummified cat.

White Rabbit

Cutting-edge, contemporary Chinese art (works produced since 2000) that is edgy, funny, sexy and idiosyncratic. In many ways this is Sydney's best contemporary-art gallery.

Green Spaces & Beaches

Wandering the city's parks, gardens and national parks (though there's a vehicle fee) is gratis, and rolling out your towel on the sand is an Australian birthright.

Sydney Harbour

You can walk over that other great icon, the Sydney Harbour Bridge, and wander through Luna Park (there's a charge for rides).

Historical Buildings

Many of Sydney's most beautiful old buildings are free to enter, including the Customs House, the Mint, St Mary's Cathedral, the State Library and the GPO. For political entertainment, visit Parliament House on sitting days.

Architectural Gems

Window-shoppers should peruse the exquisite Queen Victoria Building and the Strand Arcade. For more modern architectural thrills, check out Central Park and the nearby Dr Chau Chak Wing Building.

Cinema Under the Stars

Sunset Cinema

Its two outdoor cinema locations at North Sydney Oval and Bondi Beach's Dolphin Court are among several popular summer-night choices. Take a picnic, but no booze: they're licensed.

Moonlight Cinema

Take a picnic and join the bats under the stars in magnificent Centennial Park. A mix of new-release blockbuster, kid-friendly, art-house and classic films is screened at sunset from December to March.

Westpac Openair

Risk being distracted by the incredible city views where the screen juts up over the water at Mrs Macquarie's Point from early January to mid-February.

MAURIZIO CALLARI/SHUTTERSTOCK

Queen Victoria Building

Coffee, Cake & Ice Cream

Bourke Street Bakery $

A Surry Hills institution, with additional outlets also in Barangaroo, North Sydney, Marrickville and beyond.

Reuben Hills $$

The star is the fantastic single-origin coffee, roasted on the premises in Surry Hills, but the refreshing homemade *horchata* (rice milk), stellar fried chicken, tacos and *baleadas* (Honduran tortillas) are no slouches either.

Grounds of the City $$

You won't notice the crowds of the QVB inside this Parisian-style cafe. An oasis of vintage decor and excellent coffee, this is a recharging pit stop on any city-centre adventure.

Cow & the Moon $

This fabulous Enmore ice-creamery has won national and international awards for its inventive gelato flavours.

Black Star Pastry $

Gourmet pies and delicious sweets, including its social-media star, watermelon cake. Stores in the CBD, Newtown and beyond.

Koi Dessert Bar $$

Coffee is also served, but MasterChef Australia star Reynold Poernomo's fabulous desserts are the star at this Chippendale sweet-tooth haven.

Pablo & Rusty's Sydney CBD $

With the city centre's best coffee, this place means you don't even need to go to Melbourne.

TRAVEL_ADVENTURE/SHUTTERSTOCK

Koi Dessert Bar

Australiana & Aboriginal Art

RM Williams

Everything you need for the fair-dinkum jackaroo look.

Strand Hatters

Complete your *Crocodile Dundee* ensemble with an Akubra hat.

Aboriginal & Pacific Art

Represents community-based Aboriginal and Pacific Islander art from a gallery in Waterloo.

Australian Wine Centre

Stock up on the top Aussie drops.

Gannon House Gallery

Inspiring selection of Aboriginal art in the Rocks, purchased directly from artists.

Ken Done Gallery

Browse bright and joyful art featuring Australian landscapes and icons, and don't miss the gift shop.

Opal Minded

Opal aficionados love this jewellery shop.

07 Blue Mountains MAGIC

VINTAGE | CULTURE | VIEWS

A favourite rest stop for high society in the 1800s, the Blue Mountains region has luxury and style in spades. Explore arts, culture and architecture, eat lunch in a cosy cafe or drink an artisanal cocktail in an atmospheric bar. After you've recharged your batteries indoors, venture out into the area's glorious natural bounty.

MAXIMILIANE WAGNER/SHUTTERSTOCK

How to

Getting here Trains on the Blue Mountains line leave regularly from Sydney's Central Station. The gateway town of Glenbrook is about an hour by car along the Great Western Hwy from Sydney.

When to go March and April, with light crowds, is a great time to hike. Avoid hot, busy December through February.

Call ahead Some shops and restaurants are closed on Monday, and local businesses close early on the weekend.

SLOW WALKER/SHUTTERSTOCK

Indoor Pursuits

Champagne Charlie's cocktail bar in Katoomba's historic Carrington Hotel (1883) transports you to a bygone era of glitz, glamour and free-flowing sparkling wine. Take a seat under the stained-glass dome and choose from a menu of traditional and modern cocktails, an extensive range of wines, and beer from the Carrington's own Katoomba Brewing Company.

Drawing its inspiration from Shanghai teahouses, the Hydro Majestic Hotel's **Salon du Thé** encompasses the building's former Billiards Room and Cats Alley ladies' lounge. Have an afternoon pot of tea after walking in the gardens, or try a refreshin, tea-inspired cocktails before dining at the hotel's Wintergarden restaurant.

WENDELL TEODORO/GETTY IMAGES

Salacious Australian Art

The historic house of renowned Australian artist and author Norman Lindsay now showcases his numerous paintings, sculptures, etchings, and illustrations from his children's novel *The Magic Pudding*. Expect lush gardens, unique art and a view into Lindsay's sometimes scandalous life.

Left Hydro Majestic Hotel
Above left View of the Three Sisters
Above right Carrington Hotel

Vintage Shopping

Hunt for treasure in this popular antiquing destination. Run by veteran art and antiques dealer Steven Archer, the **Katoomba Antique Centre** also contains a small camera museum. Vinyl enthusiasts shouldn't miss the nearby **Velvet Fog Record Bar**, with a wide range of rare albums. **MacArthur's Arcade** has everything from china to furniture to vintage clothing. Downstairs is **Mr Pickwick's Fine Old Books**, home to 60,000 vintage and secondhand volumes, and across the road in the old post office is the **Katoomba Vintage Emporium**.

Vintage-clothing enthusiasts will love **Leura Vintage**, with its wonderful array of fabulous frocks. **Hazelbrook Cottage Antique Centre** offers a rustic collection of furniture and period Australiana.

Hiking the Blue Mountains

Prince Henry Cliff Walk
Connecting Katoomba and Leura, this moderate hike passes the famed Three Sisters, with views of Ruined Castle and three waterfalls. The track follows the base of the cliffs that make up Katoomba and Leura, allowing you to view the Jamison Valley from the ground floor.

Grand Cliff Top Walk
Designed to be walked over two days, this newer 19km trail hugs the spectacular cliffs between Wentworth Falls and Katoomba, with surreal views of valleys, sandstone peaks and waterfalls on the way.

For significant hikes, fill out a trip intention form, and borrow a personal locator beacon from a tourist information centre or police station.

B-E/SHUTTERSTOCK

Far left Prince Henry Cliff Walk
Left Katoomba Antiques Centre
Below Red Hands Cave

Outdoor Delights

Hiking in Blackheath is almost up there with the Grand Canyon walk, but there are many easier and less-crowded walks that don't skimp on beautiful views of the Grose Valley. The **Fairfax heritage walk** is a level 1.8km track that is entirely wheelchair accessible. Visit in spring to see the waratahs and vibrant wildflowers in full bloom.

The whimsical name, relatively short distance and swimming hole at the end make the **Jellybean track** a favourite with families during the sunny months. An 8km loop track takes you to **Red Hands Cave**. View axe-carving grooves and the vibrant hand-stencil gallery created by the local Dharug people. The stencils in the Red Hands Cave are between 500 and 1600 years old and are some of the best hand-stencil art in Sydney and its surrounds.

Pies & Sweet Treats

Every Australian town has a pie shop that you absolutely must try, and Blackheath is no different. The **Bakehouse on Wentworth** is a local and tourist favourite, with unforgettable pies. This is a great place to fuel up before heading off on a hike.

A staple in many children's trips to the Blue Mountains, the **Candy Store Leura** has walls lined with boiled lollies and chocolates ranging from Australian classics to modern and imported sweets.

SARDAKA, CC BY-SA 4.0, VIA WIKIMEDIA COMMONS

08 Fine Newcastle **FARE**

CHIC CAFES | HIP BARS | EAT STREETS

Once a gritty industrial city, today's Newcastle – affectionately known as 'Newy' – has transformed into one of Australia's most happening dining destinations. With an ever-increasing array of cool cafes, top-notch restaurants and buzzy bars, and the Hunter Valley wine region right on its doorstep, it's the kind of place where you'll want to arrive hungry – and thirsty.

ALEX JACK PHOTOGRAPHY

How to

Getting around Cruise between eateries on an e-bike for just $2 per 10 minutes or $10 per day courtesy of Newcastle's Bykko scheme.

When to go April is Newcastle Food Month, with oodles of culinary events, masterclasses, 'plate date' deals and more.

While you're here Fully reopened in 2026, the reimagined Newcastle Art Gallery holds one of Australia's most significant collections, with works by Australian masters and more. The gallery's Hilliers cafe adds to the town's food offerings.

FORT WHISKEY PTY LTD

Left Momo
Bottom left Coal & Cedar

Cool Cafes

This relaxed seaside city was made for cafe culture. For ocean views with your smoked-salmon bagel, head to **Mereweather Surfhouse**, or tuck into scrambled eggs with macadamia pesto at **Estabar**, opposite Newcastle's main beach. In the city centre, **Momo** serves an innovative all-vegan menu (though cow's milk is available for coffees), while **Mockingbird** in Hamilton is the place to go when you're in the mood to pair your morning coffee with something more adventurous than avo toast – red velvet pancakes with Persian candy floss, perhaps?

Top Tables

Newcastle's fine-dining scene is on the up, with produce-driven **Flotilla**, Italian-influenced **Humbug** and French-inspired **Bistro Penny** all bagging a coveted 'hat' in the SMH Good Food Guide 2026 Awards. Relaxed Humbug serves terrific pastas – perfect for a special night out that won't break the bank.

Eat Streets

Newcastle has birthed several 'eat streets' packed with restaurants and bars. Among the best known is **Darby Street** in Cooks Hill, just south of the city centre, where you'll find more than 20 restaurants, bars and cafes along a 400m stretch between Queen and Bull Sts. In Hamilton, west of the city centre, **Beaumont Street** offers antique shopping by day and a thriving bar and restaurant scene by night. Right in the city, **King Street** and **Hunter Street** are also packed with drinking and dining options.

Bar Hopping

Coal & Cedar Cocktails are mixed with flair at this hard-to-find New York–style speakeasy.

Koutetsu The quirky vibe of this West End bar hints at its former life as a pawn shop.

Grain Store With a rotating selection of 21 craft beers on tap, the warehouse-turned-bar is a top spot for a pint and a burger.

Customs House Hotel Drink in the history of this watering hole, which has a great beer garden.

King Street This three-level live music venue with several bars was enlarged and renovated in 2023.

BYRON BAY & NORTH COAST NEW SOUTH WALES

BEAUTIFUL BEACHES | RAINFOREST HIKING | COASTAL DINING

RESEARCHED BY SARAH REID

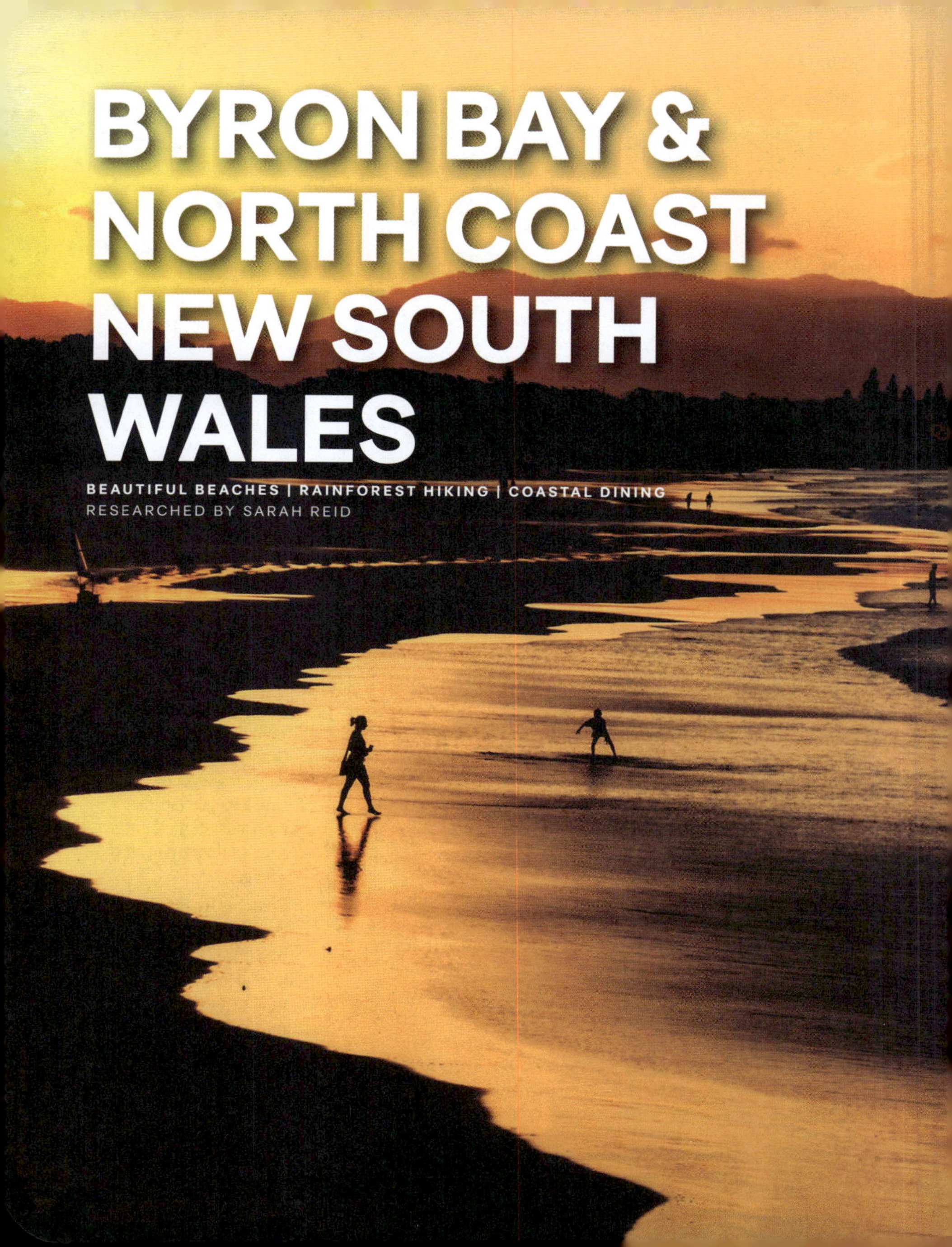

BYRON BAY & NORTH COAST NSW
Trip Builder

Lush farmlands and pockets of World Heritage–listed rainforest fringe lazy beach towns all the way along the NSW North Coast, many of them now just as well known for their culinary offerings as for their surf breaks and laid-back vibe.

NICK FOX/SHUTTERSTOCK

Practicalities

ARRIVING

Gold Coast Airport Convenient entry point to the Tweed region.

Ballina Byron Gateway Airport Shuttles and taxis run to Byron Bay.

Coffs Harbour Airport Receives domestic flights from major cities.

CONNECT

Wi-fi is typically free at hotels but not always available at cafes; purchase a local SIM card to stay connected.

MONEY

You'll pay Sydney prices for food and lodgings in the Byron Bay region. Expect a 10 to 15% dining surcharge on Sundays and public holidays.

WHERE TO STAY

Location	Atmosphere
Tweed Coast & Hinterland	Small boutique hotels and B&Bs.
Byron Bay	Boutique hotels, hostels, holiday apartments and campgrounds aplenty. Book ahead.
Mid-North Coast	Family-friendly resorts and campgrounds.
Barrington Coast	Ideal base for a budget family beach holiday.
Port Stephens	Smart boutique resorts, B&Bs and camping.

GETTING AROUND

Hire car & camper Renting a car is the best way to explore. Bookings are required for camping in all NSW national parks; wild camping is prohibited by some councils.

Taxi & rideshare Both widely available, but best booked ahead.

Train & bus A train service runs from Sydney to Casino. Greyhound buses run from Sydney to Brisbane via Byron Bay.

TOP: NEWEARTH.MAMA/SHUTTERSTOCK
BOTTOM: MAODOLTEE/SHUTTERSTOCK

EATING & DRINKING

The northern end of the North Coast has an exciting culinary scene, with wholesome cafe fare and relaxed coastal fine dining showcasing local seafood and, increasingly, native ingredients. The trend is rapidly filtering southward, adding new options to towns along the coast.

Best coastal fine diner
Pipit, Pottsville (p97)

Must-try craft beer
Stone & Wood Pacific Ale (p99; pictured bottom left)

DEC–FEB
Ideal beach weather; book accommodation well ahead

MAR–MAY
Warm days with fewer crowds, except for busy Easter

JUN–AUG
Cooler temps perfect for hiking; still warm enough for a swim

SEP–NOV
Spring flowers, warm days and fewer crowds

09 A Perfect Port Stephens WEEKEND

GREAT BEACHES | SCENIC WALKS | ICONIC WILDLIFE

Just two hours north of Sydney, Port Stephens offers the ultimate nature hit with its beaches, coastal walks, wildlife encounters and massive sand dunes surrounding an immense natural harbour. It always feels like the weekend here, where seafood rules local menus.

RUGLIG/SHUTTERSTOCK

Dolphins & Whales

Port Stephens is famous for its bottlenose dolphins. Humpback whales join the party in winter, making it a great time to book a cetacean-watching cruise. You can also opt to 'join the pod' with Dolphin Swim Australia, which holds a permit from NSW Parks to operate responsible wild dolphin swims.

Trip Notes

Getting around There's a good local bus network, including services to Newcastle.

When to go October to April for wild dolphin swims; late May to early November for whale watching.

Seafood Try Little Nel, Little Beach Boathouse, Rick Stein at Bannisters, and Sandpipers, or grab a tray of fresh oysters at Holberts Oyster Supplies.

Local tipples A winery, distillery and brewery can all be found at B.Farm, overlooking the vines.

01 Get your bearings – and enjoy incredible views – atop Tomaree Head (161m), reached via the invigorating **Tomaree Head Summit Walk** (2.2km return). A side trail leads to WWII gun emplacements.

02 Cool off with a dip at **Zenith Beach**, below Tomaree Head, arguably the most dramatic of the 26 beautiful beaches to choose from in Port Stephens.

03 Contribute to the rehabilitation and conservation of an Aussie icon by visiting the recently opened **Port Stephens Koala Sanctuary**. There's also glamping accommodation.

04 Stake out a top spot to watch the sunset – ideally over a drink at waterside bar-restaurant the Deck – at **Soldiers Point**, located on a peninsula jutting into the Karuah River.

05 Experience the famous shifting seaside dunes of **Worimi Conservation Lands** on a quad-bike tour with Aboriginal-owned Sand Dune Adventures.

FROM TOP: IAN WOOLCOCK/SHUTTERSTOCK, 365 FOCUS PHOTOGRAPHY/SHUTTERSTOCK

10 Coffs Coast CULTURE

SACRED SITES | ADVENTURE | BUSH TUCKER

Known for its Big Banana and string of beautiful beaches, the Coffs Coast also has a rich Aboriginal culture. This is Gumbaynggirr Country, home to one of the largest coastal Aboriginal nations in NSW. Gumbaynggirr people have maintained a profound connection to the natural landscape, and this connection can be explored through experiences ranging from dance to a paddling tour.

How to

Cost A 2½-hour SUP tour with Wajaana Yaam Adventure Tours costs $95/40 for adults/kids.

Bush foods Look out for the Aboriginal-owned Bakirindi Bush Foods stall at the Harbourside Markets held on the Coffs Harbour Jetty Foreshore every Sunday (8am to 2pm).

Solitary Islands Coastal Walk The 60km trail passes several cultural sites, including Look At Me Now Headland at Emerald Beach, which plays an integral part in the Creation story of Gumbaynggirr Country.

Cultural paddle Hosted on three culturally significant creek systems in the Solitary Islands Marine Park, stand-up paddleboarding excursions with **Wajaana Yaam Adventure Tours** pair fun on the water with fascinating insights into the Gumbaynggirr connection to this idyllic ecosystem. Along the way, your guide will share Dreaming stories, reveal the traditional uses of local plants and collect bush tucker to sample.

Aboriginal art and dance At Corindi Beach, the **Yarrawarra Aboriginal Cultural Centre** is home to the Wadjar Regional Indigenous Gallery and the Jalumbo Keeping Place. Here you can see paintings, ceramics, prints, photos and sculpture by regional Aboriginal artists, and view artefacts representing more than 4000 years of Aboriginal life in the area.

You can also learn about Gumbaynggirr culture through stories, song and dance during the **Giingan**

WAJAANA YAAM ADVENTURE TOURS

Arrawarra Fish Traps

On the northern side of the Arrawarra Headland, a series of stone fish traps appear at low tide. Dated to be around 5000 years old, the Arrawarra fish traps form an important part of a wider cultural landscape in Gumbaynggirr Country that Gumbaynggirr people have a continuing connection to. Highlighting the ingenuity of local Aboriginal people since time immemorial, the traps are a complex structure and the practices for using them are also complex, involving Gumbaynggirr language, song and an innate connection with ocean, dolphins and seasonal changes.

Clark Webb, *Gumbaynggirr man, CEO of the Bularri Muurlay Nyanggan Aboriginal Corporation and owner-operator of Wajaana Yaam Adventure Tours @wajaanayaam*

Gumbaynggirr Cultural Experience led by the Bularri Muurlay Nyanggan Aboriginal Corporation. Watch the Wajaarr Ngaarlu dancers perform and take part in a smoking ceremony before enjoying Aunty Jenny's damper. Then you'll join an interpretative walk along the Gumgali Track to scenic Korora Lookout.

Indigenous food Try a warrigal greens (native spinach) quiche with salad and bush tomato relish at the Yarrawarra Aboriginal Cultural Centre's **Songlines Bush Cafe**, or head to the **Nyanggan Gapi Cafe** at Niigi Niigi (Sealy Lookout) in the Orara East State Forest to try Indigenous flavours in a wattleseed brownie or a lemon-myrtle muffin.

Above Stand-up paddleboarding with Wajaana Yaam Adventure Tours

LOCAL PRODUCE
from the Source

01

02

03

04

01 Crab, Tweed Heads

Three crab species are harvested from the Tweed River; go on a crab-catching adventure with Tweed Eco Cruises.

02 Seafood, Yamba

Also known for its prawns, Yamba is a popular place to hook snapper, flathead (pictured), whiting and more – or purchase it fresh or cooked from Yamba's Fisho.

03 Macadamias, Byron Bay Hinterland

The birthplace of Australia's commercial macadamia-farming industry remains a great place to sample this rich, buttery native nut.

04 Bananas, Coffs Harbour

Did you even go on an East Coast road trip if you didn't get a selfie at the Big Banana?

05 Strawberries, Port Macquarie

Pick your own hydroponic strawberries year-round at Ricardoes, just off the Pacific Hwy north of the Hastings River.

06 Honey, Taree

Fragrant, gooey honey is a staple at Taree's

05

06

08

07

09

11

10

excellent Thursday Produce Market.

07 Oysters, Central Coast

Slurp down Sydney rock and Pacific oysters at the Hawkesbury River Oyster Shed, just off the highway at Mooney Mooney.

08 Prawns, Ballina

The home of the Big Prawn is famous for its local shellfish, known for their large size and sweet taste.

09 Avocados, Port Stephens

Pick up fresh, creamy avocados at the Bobs Farm Avocados stall on Nelson Bay Rd from June to November.

10 Artisan cheese, Macleay Valley Coast

This fertile farming region also produces delicious buffalo cheeses; try them at Eungai Creek Buffalo's cafe in Tamban.

11 Wine, Hunter Valley

Less than an hour inland from Newcastle, the Hunter Valley is Australia's oldest wine-growing region, with more than 150 cellar doors.

01 ZCW/SHUTTERSTOCK, **02** PICTURE PARTNERS/SHUTTERSTOCK, **03** POPOVAPHOTO/GETTY IMAGES, **04** CRBELLETTE/SHUTTERSTOCK, **05** NICK PASCHALIS/SHUTTERSTOCK, **06** KOVALEVA_KA/SHUTTERSTOCK, **07** YUDA CHEN/SHUTTERSTOCK, **08** SPAYDER PAUK_79/SHUTTERSTOCK, **09** PIXBANK CZ/SHUTTERSTOCK, **10** NEW AFRICA/SHUTTERSTOCK, **11** MARCO CASAVECCHIA/SHUTTERSTOCK

11 Dive into the North COAST

SHARK DIVING | SNORKELLING | MARINE WONDERS

The Great Barrier Reef isn't the only great place to go scuba diving in Australia. North Coast NSW is one of the best places in the world to dive with critically endangered grey nurse sharks, a large, placid species that gathers in several spots along the coast at different periods throughout the year.

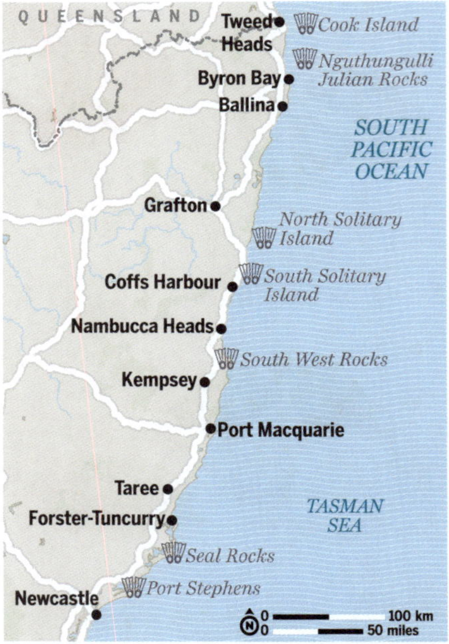

How to

When to go The water temperature can dip below 20°C on the North Coast in winter, but there's no bad time of year to go diving (just bad weather). All operators rent wetsuits.

Qualification Some shark dive spots are suitable for open-water divers, while others require advanced open-water certification. Check with your operator.

Snorkelling There's great snorkelling at many dive sites; some operators allow snorkellers to join trips at a reduced cost.

Shark Diving

Nguthungulli Julian Rocks Temperate and tropical waters meet at this rocky outcrop off Byron Bay, attracting more than 1000 marine species, including over 530 species of fish. Grey nurse sharks (which grow up to 3.6m long) aggregate here from June to November, but as soon as they leave another major attraction arrives: beautifully patterned (and similarly docile) leopard sharks, which stick around until May, along with huge manta rays. Bottom-dwelling wobbegong sharks can be seen year-round.

South West Rocks Running 125m right through Fish Rock, which lies 2km off South West Rocks on the Mid-North Coast, **Fish Rock Cave** offers year-round grey nurse sightings, along with a plethora of other marine life, from moray eels to friendly blue groupers. In the summer months,

grey nurse sharks rest in the azure cave entrance, presenting an incredible photographic opportunity. While Nitrox certification isn't essential, it's recommended for this dive.

Forster and Seal Rocks On the Barrington Coast, Forster and nearby Seal Rocks are home to more than a dozen dive sites. Many of these are also visited by grey nurse sharks year-round. Top picks include the Pinnacle, a deeper dive off Forster (where the dive operators are located), and Big Rock at Seal Rocks, which is surrounded by several gutters patrolled by graceful grey nurse sharks.

Other Fantastic North Coast Dives

Cook Island Green turtles are the main attraction at this relatively shallow dive site just off Tweed Heads.

North Solitary Island Colourful anemones carpet the sea floor in this section of the Solitary Islands Marine Park.

South Solitary Island This shallow dive site off Coffs Harbour is great for learning, and there's plenty of temperate marine life, similar to Byron Bay's.

Port Stephens A popular dive site off Port Stephens is the Looking Glass at Broughton Island, a narrow trench where grey nurse sharks aggregate.

David Robinson, *shark ecologist, founder of the Cape Byron Leopard Shark Project and owner of Sundive Byron Bay* *@sundivebyronbay*

Above left School of fish, Nguthungulli Julian Rocks

12 Gondwana Hikes GALORE

RAINFOREST | HIKING | WATERFALLS

Comprising more than 30 national parks and reserves between southeast Queensland and Newcastle, the UNESCO-listed Gondwana Rainforests of Australia holds the world's most extensive areas of subtropical rainforest. Get your Gondwana fix on these great hikes near the coast in the NSW section.

OZBEACHES/SHUTTERSTOCK

How to

Getting around You'll need your own car to access most Gondwana parks.

When to go Hiking is excellent year-round, though the risk of dehydration and heat stroke increases in summer.

Safety Always tell someone where you're going and when you plan to return, and pack adequate water and gear.

Parks pass Visiting several NSW national parks with parking fees? It may be cheaper to purchase an annual multi-parks pass ($65; nationalparks.nsw.gov.au).

MICHELLE HOLIHAN/SHUTTERSTOCK

Minyon Falls Loop, Nightcap National Park

Distance 13km

Duration Three to four hours

Just 45 minutes west of Byron Bay, this hike takes you from the top of Minyon Falls to the base of the magnificent waterfall, some 100m below. Tracing the **Nightcap** escarpment, the track begins in wet sclerophyll forest before descending into a cooler subtropical wonderland as the rainforest canopy closes in towards the bottom of the valley. Enjoy a dip in the natural waterfall pool before hiking up the other side of the escarpment for front-on views of the falls from the **Minyon Grass Picnic Area** before walking back to the trailhead along the road (1km).

JACKSCOTT/SHUTTERSTOCK

Bushfires

More than 50% of the Gondwana Rainforests burned during Australia's 2019–20 bushfires, and the habitats of rare and threatened flora and fauna suffered catastrophic damage. Nearly all affected tourism infrastructure has since reopened, though, and the rainforest continues to recover with the assistance of governments, Aboriginal groups, scientists and local communities.

Top left Minyon Falls
Left Nightcap National Park
Above Kookaburra, Nightcap National Park

Iluka Rainforest Walking Track, Iluka Nature Reserve

Distance 5.2km return

Duration One to three hours

In Iluka Nature Reserve, near Yamba, the Iluka Rainforest Walking Track offers an easy stroll through lush coastal forest to **Iluka Bluff** in neighbouring Bundjalung National Park. Look out for the brightly coloured noisy pitta, and listen for the sharp crack of the whipbird. The Bluff is a great spot for a picnic lunch and a swim (or snorkel) before heading back the same way, with great whale watching from late May to early November.

Crystal Shower Walk, Dorrigo National Park

Distance 4.4km return

Duration 90 minutes

Mist-shrouded rainforest towers above you on this short but stunning walk in Dorrigo National Park, an hour's drive west of Coffs Harbour

Quirky Gondwana Wildlife

Alberts lyrebird Look for this shy bird scratching for soil-dwelling invertebrates. In winter and early spring you might hear the male's unique call mimicking sounds he's heard over the years, or see him do his magnificent tail fan dance.

Red-legged pademelon If you're still and quiet, you can see these small macropods feeding on fruit and leaves in the early morning and late afternoon.

Land mullet The largest member of the skink family is often mistaken for a snake.

Lamington crayfish Usually a bright turquoise, this large freshwater crayfish is typically seen in rainforest creeks above 300m.

■ **Wendy Bithell,**
ecotour guide and founder of Vision Walks Eco-Tours @visionwalks

IMOGEN WARREN/SHUTTERSTOCK

CHARLIE BLACKER/SHUTTERSTOCK

Far left Red-legged pademelon
Left New England National Park
Below Lamington crayfish

via the Waterfall Way scenic drive. The trail takes you behind the fairy-tale **Crystal Shower Falls**, and a suspension bridge carries you across the valley in front of the falls for Insta-worthy views. Return the same way or extend the walk by looping back via Tristania Falls on the Wonga Walk, which adds 2.2km to the journey. Don't miss the **Skywalk Lookout** next to the Rainforest Centre on your way out, nor the charming hinterland town of **Bellingen** on the drive back to the coast.

Cascades Track, New England National Park

Distance 5.7km loop

Duration Three hours

An hour southwest of Dorrigo National Park, New England National Park hugs the Great Escarpment, some 1500m above sea level. A highlight is the Cascades Track, which takes you past vivid green moss-covered boulders, flourishing ferns and gushing cascades. Look out for unusual fungi and the velvet worm, a living fossil that looks like a velvety caterpillar. This rough track has short, steep hills that could be challenging for small children.

ANDYWAK/SHUTTERSTOCK

13 First Light in BYRON BAY

SALUTE THE SUN | CULTURAL WALKS | COOL CAFES

Australia's most easterly town, Byron Bay is the first place on the mainland to see the dawn. Best from the cliffs of Walgun Cape Byron, which is topped by a 1901 lighthouse, this soul-stirring experience is just one of many reasons to rise early with the locals, when this NSW North Coast holiday town is at its most serene.

NAOMI CREEK/SHUTTERSTOCK

How to

When to go June to October for whale watching, or the March–May and September–November shoulder seasons for warm beach weather with fewer crowds.

Wildlife Wallabies can often be seen grazing on the cape in the early mornings.

Free yoga Hotels including Elements of Byron and Crystalbrook Byron offer complimentary morning yoga.

Surf lesson For one-on-one tuition, try Rusty Miller Surf, run by the local surfing icon and his daughter Taylor.

WILL DAY/SHUTTERSTOCK

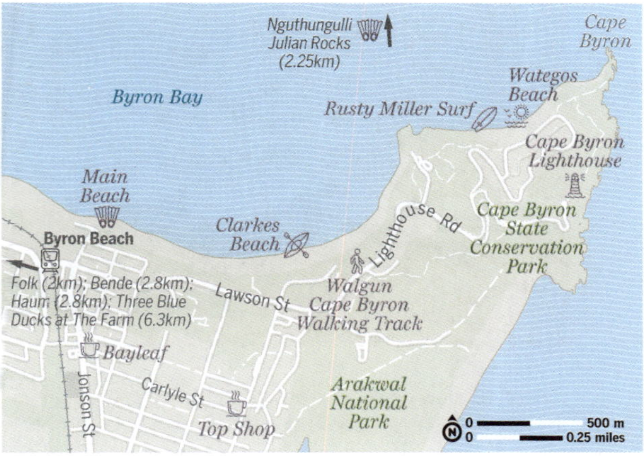

Seize the Morning

On land Many locals begin their day with an invigorating walk on the **Cape Byron Walking Track**, which makes a 3.7km loop around the rainforest-clad headland. If you begin early enough, you can enjoy the sunrise en route. Whales swim close to the cape and dolphins can be spotted year-round along with turtles, sharks and rays when the ocean is calm and clear.

The walking track also forms part of the **Byron Bay History Trail**; look for the QR codes revealing insights into the early days of British settlement. To learn more about the deep cultural significance of Byron to Arakwal Bundjalung people, book a walking tour with Traditional Custodian Delta Kay of **Explore Byron Bay**.

In the water Beat the crowds by paddling out for a surf at sunrise, when you can also score a parking spot without too much effort. With the wind often picking up later in the day, aim for an early-morning scuba dive at **Nguthungulli Julian Rocks Nature Reserve**. There are two shipwrecks you can snorkel independently right off **Main Beach**; calm sea days are also ideal for an early-morning kayaking tour (two operators are based at Clarkes Beach).

At the studio Whether you're into yoga, Pilates, barre, saunas or ice baths, Byron has your morning wellness routine covered. Local favourites include **Haum** for holistic classes, and **Bende** for yoga, Pilates and barre classes.

Far left top Sunrise, Main Beach
Far left bottom Surfer, Byron Bay

Brunch O'Clock

Bayleaf The Byron institution pairs smooth coffee with wholesome brunch dishes including the ever-popular scrambled special (eggs on sourdough with dill, chilli, marinated feta, salad greens and salsa verde).

Folk Near the northern entrance to town, this relaxed garden cafe presents its plant-based dishes beautifully.

Top Shop The former 1950s milk bar opens onto a grassy knoll, perfect for relaxing with a latte and an açai bowl or pastry.

Three Blue Ducks at The Farm Ideal for families: kids can meet the farm animals or hit the playground while parents linger over a decadent brunch showcasing home-grown produce.

The Byron Bay Experience

PARADISE REDEFINED

Between its eye-watering property prices and trending eateries, today's Byron Bay is a bit different from the sleepy coastal idyll 'discovered' by surfers in the 1950s, with hippies hot on their sandy heels. Scratch Byron's highly Instagrammable surface, however, and you'll discover a destination that still has plenty of substance.

Left Surfers, Byron Bay
Right Cafe, Byron Bay
Middle Cape Byron Lighthouse

NAOMI CREEK/SHUTTERSTOCK

'Cheer up, slow down, chill out', goes the welcome sign at the northern entrance to Byron Bay. The middle part of this mantra is easy enough to master, as you'll likely find yourself in a queue of traffic by the time you see it.

Such are the trade-offs of the ever-increasing popularity of this iconic Northern Rivers beach town, which now receives more than 2.2 million visitors per year – that's around 183 tourists for each of its 10,900-odd residents. But dramatic headlines describing Byron as a 'paradise lost' only tell one side of the story.

An important meeting place for Bundjalung nation clans for more than 22,000 years, this genetically blessed corner of NSW – known as Gabanbaa to the local Arakwal people – changed forever when European settlers arrived in the late 1800s. First cedar-getters and farmers set about felling a 75,000-hectare swathe of tropical lowland rainforest stretching from Byron to Lismore known as the Big Scrub; only 1% of this still stands today. Then sand-mining operations turned Byron's exquisite coastline into a barren wasteland. More extractive industries followed, with the Byron Bay township of the 1950s and '60s described in local historical records as 'reeking from the stench' of local piggery, abattoir and whaling factories.

It wasn't until these industries had all wound down by the early 1980s that Byron (originally named Cavvanba, an Anglicised version of Gabanbaa) began to transform back into a version of the paradise maintained by the Arakwal, who secured a historic Indigenous Land Use Agreement in 2001 that led to the formation of Arakwal National Park. Industrial workers transitioned to jobs in the service

AMPUEROLEONARDO/GETTY IMAGES

LUIS CRISTOFORI/SHUTTERSTOCK

industry, including tourism, and proposed developments with the potential to compromise the regeneration of Byron's natural environment, or the lifestyles of its new wave of alternative, eco-conscious locals, were passionately resisted.

Byron Today

That today's Byron is still a low-rise beach town in a gorgeous natural setting with a strong community spirit, despite the increasing pressures of housing (un)affordability, climate change and urban development, is really quite extraordinary. And while locals may complain about how busy, expensive and pretentious their home has become, many will concede that Byron's popularity has its benefits, with the town now boasting one of Australia's finest regional dining scenes, a packed calendar of cultural events and a booming sustainable-fashion industry. Dotted with lauded restaurants and independent boutiques of their own, hinterland villages such as Bangalow and Federal, as well as nearby beach towns including Brunswick Heads and Lennox Head, have also become destinations in their own right.

> This iconic Northern Rivers beach town now receives more than 2.2 million visitors per year.

Sure, reality-TV stars might now outnumber barefoot surfers at the Beach Hotel. And the days of scoring Byron's famous waves to yourself are long gone. But it's impossible to deny that Byron is still a special place.

How to 'Do' Byron

While it may seem more environmentally and socially responsible to stay away from destinations struggling with overtourism, planning an eco-conscious visit that supports the local community is often a more sustainable choice.

In Byron, this means avoiding unhosted holiday rentals outside the town centre, which are a major contributor to Byron's housing crisis, and supporting locally owned businesses committed to sustainable operations, so your money benefits the community as well as the environment. It means treading gently on the fragile ecosystem, and respecting local culture and laws. These small gestures protect Byron's natural beauty and individual character.

14 Eat the TWEED

GOURMET PRODUCE | CRAFT DRINKS | COUNTRY DRIVES

At NSW's northeastern tip, the Tweed region's rich volcanic soils brim with fresh produce, which travels just metres to the plates of the region's ever-increasing array of restaurants. Home to one of the Tweed's top tables (Paper Daisy), the Hamptons-meets-NSW-coast Halcyon House hotel makes a fine base to explore the exciting local food and drinks scene between beach swims.

ARTUR BEGEL/SHUTTERSTOCK

How to

Getting around Navigating the Tweed's winding hinterland roads in a hire car is all part of the experience.

When to go Here you can top off a great meal with a swim in the sea year-round.

Burringbar This tiny hinterland village has a cheesemaker, a natural wine shop and bar, and a huge antiques store.

Festival Indulge in bespoke food experiences at the Savour the Tweed festival in October or November.

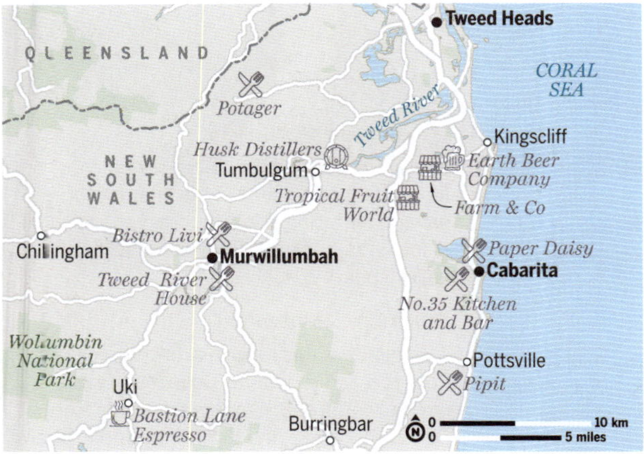

Top tables Heads began to turn in Sydney when **Paper Daisy** opened in 2015 with its creative Mod Oz dishes. Then in 2019 Paper Daisy chef Ben Devlin moved on to open **Pipit**, his own coastal fine diner in nearby Pottsville, to acclaim. Notable openings since have included 'Italian-ish' Cabarita restaurant **No.35 Kitchen and Bar**, Mod Oz/French Murwillumbah restaurant **Tweed River House**, and small European-inspired restaurant **Bistro Livi** – also in Murwillumbah – which was awarded the prestigious Good Food Guide Regional Restaurant of the Year for 2024. Deeper in the hinterland, longstanding local favourite **Potager** features produce from its own kitchen gardens on its hearty lunch menu.

Drinks Coffee shops don't get much more atmospheric than **Bastion Lane Espresso**, set in a historic Uki post office. In Tumbulgum, **Husk Distillers** offers tours and tastings of its iconic Ink Gin and agricole rums made with local sugarcane juice. On an avocado farm in Cudgen, **Earth Beer Company** serves its eco-conscious craft brews in a lovingly restored packing shed.

Farm gates Shop for farm-fresh produce at **Farm & Co** or come for breakfast or lunch overlooking the organic farm in Cudgen. Five minutes down the road, **Tropical Fruit World** has a stall brimming with everything from dragon fruit to mangoes. There's a cafe here too, and family-friendly tractor farm tours.

Left Fresh oysters
Bottom left Burringbar Natural Wine Shop

Did Someone Say Oysters?

In the Tweed you're never far away from fresh seafood, and at the **Oyster Shed** in Tweed Heads you can feast on oysters that have been farmed right in front of you.

Another fun way to sample local seafood is on a tour with **Catch A Crab**, run by the same company. Trap live crabs, go 'pumping' for yabbies and learn about the region's working oyster farms on a 2½-hour boat tour on the Tweed River. Spanner crabs, mud crabs and sand crabs are all found there at various times of the year.

Listings

BEST OF THE REST

Bakeries & Cafes

Cubby Bakehouse $

Opposite the Tweed River at Chinderah, this bakery-cafe has earned a cult following for its French baguettes.

Bruns Bakery $

This big, busy Brunswick Heads bakery does a roaring trade in pies, pastries, bread, cakes and more. Has a similarly excellent sister bakery in Suffolk Park, Byron Bay.

Supply Specialty Coffee & Bar $

The micro-roastery, espresso bar and licensed cafe in Coffs Harbour's jetty precinct is a top spot for coffee, breakfast (from 6.30am) or lunch, with creative menu options including a blue-spanner-crab omelette.

Hilltop Store $$

Housed in a restored general store in Sawtell, this charming Coffs Coast cafe is known for its simple but refined breakfast and lunch menus, with coffee by Single O.

Fredo Pies $

This pie shop in the small village of Frederickton, just off the Pacific Hwy north of Kempsey, is an institution for East Coast road trippers. The 25-plus options include a crocodile pie.

Regional Art Galleries

Tweed Regional Gallery & Margaret Olley Art Centre

The key draw of this lauded gallery, perched above the Tweed River, is the recreated studio of the late Margaret Olley, Australia's celebrated painter of still lifes and interiors.

Lismore Regional Gallery

Inland from Byron Bay, Lismore has a flourishing arts scene. After touring the gallery, featuring contemporary works in all disciplines, seek out the vibrant street-art gallery nearby.

Yarilla Arts & Museum

A highlight at this newish arts complex is the Robert & Janice Hunter Collection featuring the works of 33 Aboriginal artists from Central Australia, the Kimberley and Arnhem Land.

Glasshouse Regional Gallery

The striking Port Macquarie arts hub showcases up to 25 exhibitions per year featuring contemporary, Indigenous, historical, traditional, design and sculptural artworks, along with artist talks and workshops.

Surf Spots Beyond Byron

Duranbah (D-bah)

Neighbouring Coolangatta's Snapper Rocks is one of the world's most famous surfing beaches. But just around the headland,

TESSA PIETERSMA/GETTY IMAGES

Stone & Wood brewery

NSW's northernmost beach produces consistent A-frame beach breaks. For more beginner-friendly waves, try Cabarita, 25 minutes south.

Angourie

NSW's first dedicated National Surfing Reserve, this Clarence Valley beach has an excellent right-hand point break, and natural freshwater swimming holes on the headland.

Arrawarra

On the northern fringe of the Coffs Coast, Arrawarra has an exposed right-hand point break with pretty consistent surf, ideal in offshore winds from the southwest.

Crescent Head

Also a National Surfing Reserve, the right-hand point break at Crescent Head on the Macleay Valley Coast – which has a hip surf hotel, Sea Sea – is legendary.

Craft Breweries

Stone & Wood $

The famous Byron Bay beer brand is now owned by Asahi, but it still serves the same multi-award-winning brews in its architectural brew bar. Guided tours reveal the brewery's pioneering sustainability story, and local catering company 100 Mile Table runs the on-site canteen.

Seven Mile Brewing Co $

Next to Ballina's airport, family-run Seven Mile supports local grain growers to produce highly quaffable craft brews, including the refreshing Cali Cream ale. Food-truck fare is typically available Friday to Sunday.

Sanctus Brewing Company $$

There's plenty of indoor and outdoor seating at this large brewery, just off the Pacific Hwy near Yamba, with wood-fired pizzas also on the menu.

VISUAL COLLECTIVE/SHUTTERSTOCK

Surfing, Duranbah

Woolgoolga Brewing Co $$

In sleepy Woolgoolga (Woopi to locals), this community brewery pairs craft suds with pizzas and good times.

King Tide Brewing $$

This 250-seat suburban beer oasis in central Coffs Harbour serves up a huge range of craft brews along with European-inspired pub grub, in a nod to co-owner Lucyna King's Polish heritage.

Bellingen Brewing Co $$

This artisan brewery is an excellent reason to detour to the charming hinterland village of Bellingen, inland from Urunga on the Mid-North Coast. Also serves pizzas.

Bucket Brewery $

Next to the Macleay River in South Kempsey, the family-owned brewery is about as unpretentious as craft breweries get, with a great riverside beer garden.

SOUTH COAST NEW SOUTH WALES

COASTAL | DELICIOUS | DIVERSE

RESEARCHED BY
CAOIMHE HANRAHAN-LAWRENCE
AND SARAH REID

MARISA ESTIVILL/SHUTTERSTOCK

SOUTH COAST NSW

Trip Builder

Stretching to the very end of New South Wales (NSW), the South Coast is full of relaxed coastal towns. Far from just a haunt for surfers, the area is full of artisan foods to try, natural wonders to uncover, and locals passionate about what makes their patch uniquely theirs.

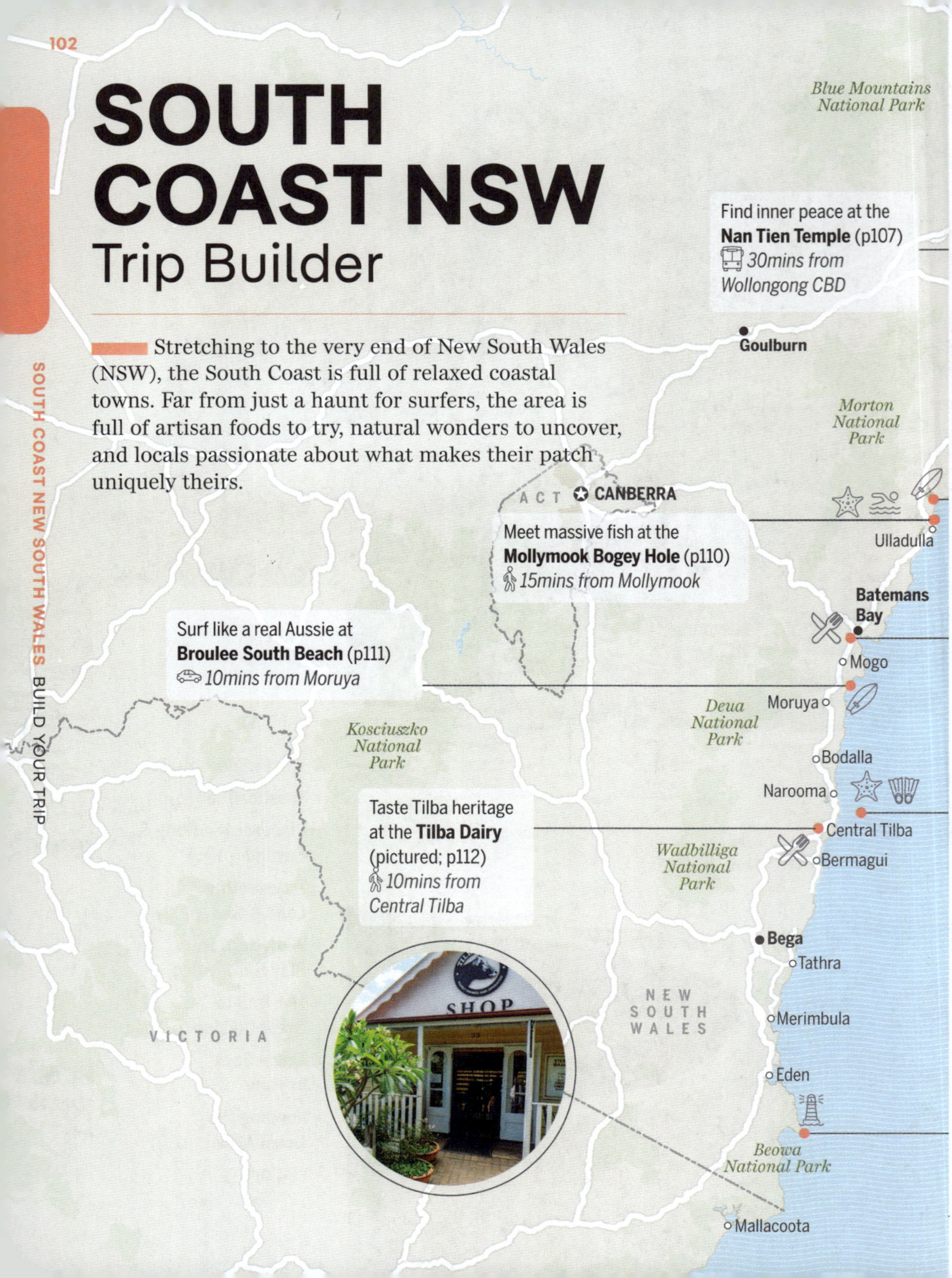

CLOCKWISE FROM BOTTOM LEFT: MARTIN BERRY/ALAMY, FRENCHIESTRAVEL/SHUTTERSTOCK, ASHTONEA/SHUTTERSTOCK, FAVELL MEDIA/SHUTTERSTOCK

Practicalities

MARTHA ALMEYDA/SHUTTERSTOCK

ARRIVING

Illawarra/South Coast Line Intercity trains run from Sydney to Port Kembla, Kiama (pictured) and Bomaderry.

Premier Motor Services Offers a daily bus service from Sydney to Eden and vice versa.

Merimbula Airport and Moruya Airport Rex and Qantas fly to Merimbula from Sydney; Rex flies to Moruya.

HOW MUCH FOR A

Local cheese
$12

Dozen oysters
$30

Unpowered national park campsite
$25–35

WHEN TO GO

JAN–MAR
Hot and dry. School holidays in January.

APR–JUN
Wet becoming cool. Fewer tourists after Easter.

JUN–AUG
Frosty. Peak whale watching, good surfing.

SEP–DEC
Cool but becoming warm and wet. Peak season from November.

GETTING AROUND

Car The South Coast is well connected by road. Between Tilba Tilba and Pambula, stick to the spectacular coastline on Bermagui Rd and the Sapphire Coast Drive. Some areas lose internet reception, so have an offline map on hand.

Bike Road biking between towns is a popular choice, but Berry and its surrounds are quite hilly.

Walking Historic towns like Milton and Central Tilba are best explored on foot.

EATING & DRINKING

The South Coast is known for its clean, sweet-tasting oysters. Pacific oysters are best from April to September, angasi oysters are available from June to August, and Sydney rock oysters (pictured right) are in season from November to March. Wines from the burgeoning Shoalhaven region profit from rich volcanic soil, and viticulturists have introduced several uncommon varietals. In the Eurobodalla region, try fresh-from-the-farm milks and cheeses.

Best winery
Crooked River Estate (pictured top right; p119)

Must-try oysters
Jim Wild's Oysters (p113)

CONNECT & FIND YOUR WAY

Wi-fi South of the Illawarra, some towns have poor internet connection. Milton/Ulladulla are relatively well connected, but expect to unplug beyond the town centres in Eurobodalla Shire.

Navigation Like much of Australia, the South Coast can be deceptively large. It consists of several regions: the Illawarra, Shoalhaven, the Eurobodalla Shire and the Sapphire Coast. By car from Sydney, take the Princes Hwy/A1 south.

WHERE TO STAY

Accommodation is plentiful on the South Coast. Holiday rentals are a great option for larger groups. Book at least a month ahead in peak seasons, when prices often inflate.

Location	Pros/Cons
Illawarra	Lively, youthful atmosphere. Plentiful accommodation. Towns are larger and harder to travel by foot.
Shoalhaven	Many beachfront hotels. Holiday parks and motor inns are common, with some holiday rentals. Family atmosphere. Fills up quickly in the summer months; can be quite expensive.
Eurobodalla	Quiet, countryside area. Smaller, boutique accommodation options. Great location for a farmstay.
Sapphire Coast	Beachfront locale. Holiday parks and motor inns are common. Often more affordable than Milton/Ulladulla.

PRIVATE LESSONS

Everyone can enjoy the local beaches, with a private surf lesson averaging about $100. For the more adventurous, Open Water Diver certification courses cost about $475.

MONEY

There are plenty of free outdoor activities in the area, from bushwalking to rock pooling to a day at the beach. Food – particularly oysters – is much cheaper on the South Coast than in Sydney, so you're likely to strike a bargain. A main meal will set you back about $25.

15 Discover the Gong & BEYOND

ENERGY | NIGHTLIFE | NATURE

Once supported by the steel and shipping industries, the Illawarra is growing in popularity among young people escaping the madness of living in Sydney. For Wollongong, affectionately shortened to just the 'Gong', the primary industry is the local university, lending the city and its surrounds a youthful energy.

LEELAKAJONKIJ/SHUTTERSTOCK

How to

Getting here and around Much of the Illawarra is serviced by the South Coast train line from Sydney. Buses run on the Opal system, and the Free Gong Shuttle runs a regular circuit in Wollongong.

When to go Beachgoers will prefer the warmer months, and cocktail connoisseurs should avoid university orientation week in late February.

Aussie music Wollongong's beloved Yours and Owls music festival takes place in early March.

GREG BRAVE/SHUTTERSTOCK

Left Nan Tien Temple
Bottom left Kiama Blowhole

Glow-worm central The **Old Helensburgh Station** first began operating in the 1880s and was decommissioned in the 1920s. Now an old railway tunnel that formed part of the station is home to a bright community of glow-worms. Their enchanting blue-green lights cover the roof and walls of the tunnel, and they're especially active during rainy periods. Glow-worms are sensitive to vibrations and external light, so keep your torch off for the best view. The ground can be wet and occasionally slippery, so do take care.

The Gong at night Spirit aficionados will find their home in **Howlin' Wolf** whisky bar, or the gin-focused **Juniper**, with over 60 types to try. Then follow the cool kids to the **Black Cockatoo**, a characterful small bar with great cocktails tucked behind a bakery. For lunchtime fare, you can't pass up the **Scarborough Hotel**, with an expansive beer garden and cliffside views over the Pacific.

Tranquil Buddhist retreat The **Nan Tien Temple** (Southern Heaven Temple) is the largest Buddhist temple in the southern hemisphere. A testament to Australia's multiculturalism, the palatial temple was designed by Australian architects. Take advantage of the regular meditation classes and retreats, or enjoy a peaceful walk through the gardens. Locals frequent the teahouse for its tasty vegetarian menu.

Spectacular Blowholes

The sea makes an impressive entrance at the **Kiama Blowhole**, known as Khanterinte by the local Dharawal people. The show is caused by waves pushing water out of a pocket in the volcanic rock that makes up the shoreline. It's most striking when there is a southeasterly wind and sea swell. Between May and November, the nearby picnic areas make a perfect whale-watching spot. Alternatively, head down to the **Blowhole Point Rock Pool** for a safe ocean swim. Just 4km south is the **Little Blowhole**, which has more consistent displays that are best when the wind and swell come from the northeast.

16 Traverse the LAND & SEA

VIEWS | WALKING | OUTDOORS

Situated within Royal National Park, the 26km Coast Track stretches between Bundeena and Otford. Cross clifftops, explore coastal heathland and take a dip in the Pacific. Hike the whole track over two days, or visit the sites as short day walks.

TRAVELLING.ABOUT/SHUTTERSTOCK

Trip Notes

Stay hydrated Be sure to carry sufficient water or water-treatment options, as there is no access to drinking water on the walk.

Check the weather Some sections are steep and exposed, so it is not advised to hike during heavy rain or high winds.

Bring proper gear Waterproof shoes are a must, as you will be walking across creeks and beaches.

Track Ecology & Views

The Coast Track (pictured left) moves through rocky clifftops, beach and coastal heathland. In springtime, the salty sea air gives way to honeyed blossoms from the abundant native flora. After the summer fire season, the lower levels of bushland regenerate quickly, demonstrating the perseverance of the Australian landscape. With elevations of over 1300m above sea level, the sea views are awe-inspiring.

01 Centring on the relationship between the Dharawal people and the orca, the **Jibbon rock carvings** were made at least 1000 years ago.

02 The **Jibbon shell midden**, a pile of shells and animal bones discarded at least 3000 years ago, indicates the traditional diet of the Dharawal.

03 Perched upon a rock shelf, the pure-white sandstone **Wedding Cake Rock** (pictured above) has deep cracks separating it from the rest of the cliff face.

04 Secluded **Wattamolla Beach** is sheltered by mountains and has a waterfall. It's perfect for a swim before you continue walking.

05 Visit the perfectly circular **Figure Eight rock pools** (pictured right and on p100) at low tide. At other times the pools are submerged and potentially dangerous.

FROM LEFT: DESTINATIONS JOURNEY/SHUTTERSTOCK, THE ESCAPE OF MALEE/SHUTTERSTOCK

17 Work Hard to PLAY HARD

SNORKELLING | SURFING | CYCLING

If the sea breeze isn't enough to get your blood pumping, plenty of experiences in Shoalhaven and the Eurobodalla Shire will help that along. Activities like snorkelling, stand-up paddleboarding and hiking provide up-close encounters with the area's wildlife and natural wonders, proving that 'relaxing' doesn't have to mean 'recumbent'.

How to

Getting around Your own car is best for getting around, but most towns are connected by daily private charter bus.

When to go Die-hard surfers will prefer the waves in winter. The warmer months bring tourists, and the beaches can get crowded. Check the tides if you're planning to visit a beach, as different water levels are suited to different activities.

Barunguba/Montague Island Only NSW Parks and Wildlife Authority–approved vessels can access the island.

SUP and fishing Stand-up paddleboarding is a unique way to tour the Narrawallee inlet and **Lake Conjola**. Several surf schools offer classes and rentals. The inlet is also a great fishing spot: expect to catch plenty of bream, whiting and flathead.

Diving and snorkelling In **Mollymook** the outer rock shelf of the Bogey Hole is a popular snorkelling location, home to some large blue gropers. Spot wobbegong sharks and maybe manta rays in **Jervis Bay**'s Little Hyams Beach and Chinamans Beach. Experienced divers can explore the SS *Merimbula*, wrecked off the coast of **Currarong** and now considered a heritage wreck site. Near **Eden**, at Twofold Bay, the *Tasman Hauler* and *Henry Bolte* are two upright wrecks scuttled in the 1980s to create dive sites.

Cycling **Berry** is a favourite with experienced cyclists

NICOLE MCLACHLAN/SHUTTERSTOCK

Snorkel with the Seals

Secluded **Barunguba Montague Island** lies off the Narooma coast. Take a day tour or stay in one of the 1880s lighthouse keeper's cottages. An important place for the local Yuin people, it was traditionally used for gathering food and conducting men's business.

The island is the breeding ground for NSW's largest little penguin colony, and many other seabirds nest here over summer. Australian fur seals are plentiful in winter and spring, and in the crystal-clear waters, snorkellers and divers can see the seals at their most playful. Between September and November, Barunguba is a great place to spot humpback whales during their migration.

for its steep descents and established cycling community. Hill-chasers will love the Block Rd ride, or reward yourself with a glass after riding to Two Figs Winery (p113). You can also ride between towns, such as Ulladulla to Milton or Nowra to Huskisson. Mountain bikers should tackle the exhilarating Deep Creek Dam Loop in **Mogo** for views of Mogo State Forest.

Surfing Beginners will appreciate Seven Mile Beach and Mollymook Beach, and **Broulee South**'s variable swells will suit many different surfers at different times of the day.

Above Seals, Barunguba Montague Island

18 The Trail to Great CUISINE

FOOD | WINE | FRESH PRODUCE

Let your stomach lead the way as you explore the fresh, complex and invigorating flavours of the South Coast in Shoalhaven and the Eurobodalla Shire. Taste the difference in your seafood when it's straight from the sea, and experience the freshness of farm-to-table eating. If you love fresh oysters, you're in the right place.

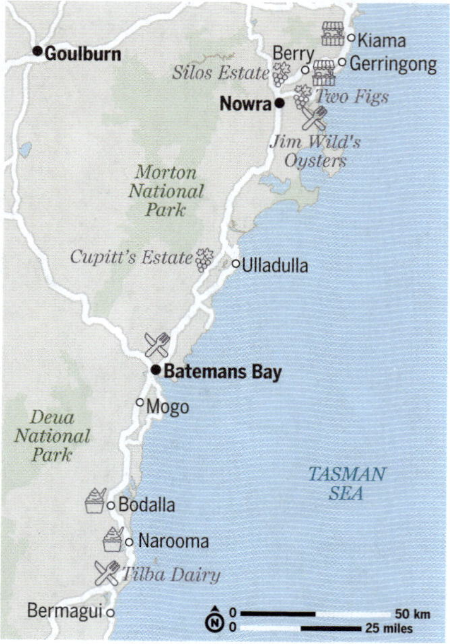

How to

Getting around Your own car is best for getting around, but most towns are connected by daily private charter bus.

When to go Foods are generally available year-round. Many cafes and restaurants are closed Monday to Wednesday, especially in low season.

Love your oysters If you're planning to follow the oyster trail, bring an Esky. This Aussie icon will help keep your purchases cool (but it won't stop you eating them all on the spot).

Slow food Many places emphasise permaculture, organic gardening and farm-to-table eating. Taste the region's best produce at weekly farmers markets in Kiama and Berry. Charming, family-run **Buena Vista Farm** in Gerringong offers classes in cooking, fermentation and organic gardening.

Top-notch dairy Milk with the cream still at the top. Ice cream churned by hand. Butter you can see the salt flakes in. Sample all this and more at South Coast dairies. **Narooma Ice Creamery**, with a diversity of flavours, is a favourite with families. Micro-dairy **Bodalla Dairy Shed** bottles all its milk in-house. Try it in milkshakes and ice creams, or sample its cheeses, many of which are flavoured with native bush tucker. For a taste of cheese history, visit the **Tilba Dairy**, housed in the 1891 ABC Cheese Factory.

Uncommon wines Though not as well known as other

STUART PERRY/SHUTTERSTOCK

Year-Round Oysters

Oysters are the essential South Coast seafood, and you can enjoy this marvellous treat in a thoroughly unpretentious atmosphere. Three varieties are farmed on the South Coast – Sydney rock, angasi and Pacific – which means that oysters are available all year. Try clean, fresh oysters from the farm at **Jim Wild's Oysters** at Greenwell Point, open since 1979, or the **Oyster Shed** on Wray St in Bateman's Bay, where you can enjoy beautiful views over the Clyde River. If you want something a bit more substantial, oysters are the stars of the show at the **Oyster Farmer's Daughter** and **Quarterdeck** in Narooma.

NSW wine regions, the Shoalhaven Coast has been producing great wines for over 40 years. Viticulturalists have taken advantage of the unique seaside terroir to explore uncommon varietals, particularly the grape of the Shoalhaven, chambourcin. **Cupitt's Estate** has a winery, craft brewery, fromagerie and restaurant. **Silos Estate** operates out of the buildings of an 1870s dairy farm, and also houses a working alpaca farm. For a more intimate experience, stop at **Two Figs**, which sources all its grapes from within the South Coast.

Above Bottle-fed calf, Bodalla Dairy Shed

19 Travel Back IN TIME

HISTORY | SCENERY | PROSPECTING

Explore some of Australia's early colonial settlements, enjoying late-Victorian and Federation-era architecture. Discover histories of gold fever and legacies of the region's enduring industries, such as 1890s dairy sheds that are still in use today. On the South Coast, you don't just learn about those who came before; you walk in their footsteps.

How to

Getting around Your own car is best for getting around, but most towns are connected by daily private charter bus.

When to go Avoid travelling from July to August if you're planning to hike, as the wind-chill can be biting. In summer, seasonal bushfires may obstruct access to some locations.

Local historians Towns such as Milton have vibrant local-history societies that are happy to share their knowledge.

Historic towns The colonial history of the South Coast dates to the late 1800s, and there are many picturesque towns if you fancy a trip back to last century.

Milton was established in the 1880s, and many of its original buildings are still in use. The main street is dotted with late-Victorian posted verandahs and corrugated roofs, and the 1930s **Milton Theatre** still hosts live music and stage productions. Drive around the country roads to spot some of the original homesteads. Heritage-listed **Central Tilba** is a prime example of early colonial architecture. Originally a gold-mining town, Tilba was kept afloat by the dairy industry. This history continues at the 1891 **ABC Cheese Factory**, now home to Tilba Dairy. At nearby **Tilba Tilba**, the town's founders are interred at the district cemetery.

FILEDIMAGE/SHUTTERSTOCK

Coastal History

Severs Beach has 3500-year-old shell middens, an indication of the traditional eating and aquacultural practices of the Yuin people.

Explore the area's whaling history at **Davidson Whaling Station**, by the Kiah inlet. In the 1890s the Davidson family hunted orcas, and this weatherboard structure was where the blubber was processed. Continue the story at the **Eden Killer Whale Museum**.

Immerse yourself in Beowa National Park's heritage during the multiday **Light to Light walk** or take a day trip to Green Cape Lighthouse. The history of Green Cape is often tragic, as you'll discover with the mysterious wreck of the *Ly-ee-Moon*.

Gold fever In **Bermagui** a short-lived gold rush began in 1880 after the discovery of alluvial gold. This history can be explored at the **Montreal Goldfield**, the only goldfield in Australia that extends to the sea. Other, less well-preserved goldfields can be seen in **Nelligen** and **Nerrigundah**. If you've caught the fever yourself, try your luck at fossicking for alluvial gold. With a fossicking licence and a gold pan, you can try to strike it rich at Yarramunmun Creek in **Yalwal** and streams around Nerriga.

Above Colonial architecture, Central Tilba

Keeping the Coast Afloat

THE INDUSTRIES THAT HAVE FORMED THE SOUTH COAST

Rich soil, clean ocean air and significant geological deposits have led to a multitude of industries on the South Coast. These industries have created the history and shaped the culture of the region, whether by bringing gold-mining hopefuls or providing the setting for improved equality.

Left Davidson Whaling Station (p115)
Middle Dairy cows
Right Fishing boats, Eden

VIRTUALEXPLORING/SHUTTERSTOCK

Whaling

Whales were very important to the Dharawal and Yuin peoples. Many rock carvings along the East Coast depict whale feasts and the specific role of orcas in the Dreaming. There is evidence that Yuin people around Twofold Bay worked with orcas to beach right whales. The whales' meat was eaten, and their bones were used for water vessels and shelters.

Begun in Twofold Bay by Thomas Raine in 1828, whaling was Australia's first primary industry. Whale blubber was processed for lamp fuel and as a base for perfume or soap, and baleen was used for corset boning and umbrella ribbing. Whaling declined in the 1840s due to gold rushes and the petroleum industry, but the Davidson family continued to hunt whales from 1857 to the 1920s. In 1979 whaling was outlawed entirely, and now the area's cetacean-based industry is whale watching.

Gold

Gold was first found in Australia in 1851, and by the late 1850s alluvial gold had been found in the South Coast region. Scores of people flocked here, hoping to make their fortune in pickaxe mining and fossicking. However, the gold rushes in places like Bermagui and the Shoalhaven area were short-lived, rarely lasting more than three years. By 1870 the region's gold rushes were over, but some pockets of industrial gold mining were active until the 1930s. Hobbyist fossickers still frequent the streams of Shoalhaven, though they tend to find themselves richer in friendship than in gold.

AUSSIEPICS/SHUTTERSTOCK

ALF MANCIAGLI/SHUTTERSTOCK

Dairy

The regular rain, plentiful rivers and sheltering mountains make the South Coast very appealing to dairy farmers, who can be assured of fresh grass for their herds. Sir Thomas Sutcliffe Mort started Bodalla's first dairy in 1860, and his vision bloomed into a thriving industry that continues in the region today. From large-scale dairy farms supplying the entire country to micro-dairies focusing on fresh-from-the-farm tastes, the South Coast plays an important role in Australia's milk production.

> Many rock carvings along the East Coast depict whale feasts and the specific role of orcas in the Dreaming.

Maritime Industry

The South Coast naturally attracted maritime industries, from shipping to industrial fishing. Many of its ports are still active, such as Eden, NSW's largest industrial fishing port, and Port Kembla, a key import terminal. Lighthouses were key in marking out the often treacherous parts of the coastline; in the 19th century Wreck Bay was infamous for trapping ships too close to the coast and, between 1805 and 1928, 26 ships were wrecked around Jervis Bay, including the convict ship *Hive*.

The docks were known for their strong union presence. In 1964 the South Coast Aboriginal Advancement League worked with the Maritime Union to enforce a series of supply bans to local segregated stores. Stores were thus forced to serve Aboriginal customers, leading to desegregation along much of the South Coast years before the official change in the law.

Oysters Through the Years

Oysters formed a key part of the diets of the Aboriginal peoples of the South Coast, as evidenced by the prevalence of oyster shells in numerous middens. Oysters were in high demand from the early 1800s, both for their meat and for their shells, the latter as a source of lime for cement production. Harvesting depleted natural oyster deposits, so commercial farming began in the 1870s. The industry peaked in the 1970s, during which time more than 150 million Sydney rock oysters were produced across the country. Today, oyster production is NSW's largest and most valuable aquaculture industry.

Listings

BEST OF THE REST

Seaside Eats

Kin Thai $$

Tops Thai food in Wollongong, including a great massaman curry.

Berry Donut Van $

Beloved by locals and visitors alike, these sweet treats are a great reason to stop in Berry.

Bangalay Dining $$$

In Shoalhaven Heads, Bangalay is renowned for its use of native ingredients. Go for the five-course tasting menu at dinnertime.

Nowra Fresh Fish & Farmers Market $

Fresh produce, great fish and chips, and amazing deli goods, all in one location.

Gunyah $$

In Huskisson, enjoy modern dining among the treetops, with possums and sugar gliders for dinner company.

Small Town Provisions $$

Wines by the glass and superb small plates highlighting provenance and quality. In Milton.

Pilgrims $$

A vegetarian institution loved by Milton locals. Try the Bliss Burger!

Milk Haus $$

Seasonal, farm-to-table meals, grown in the restaurant garden. South of Milton.

Rick Stein at Bannisters $$$

Credited with kickstarting the South Coast's food culture, Bannisters in Mollymook is a luxurious treat with top-quality seafood.

Mossy Café $

Modern cafe fare within the walls of Mossy Point's original 1939 general store.

Mimosa Wines $$$

Bermagui's gastronomic experience in a spectacular setting, with three-course lunch and six-course dinner menus.

Superette $$

Enjoy a glass of wine with a prawn roll at Merimbula's neighbourhood bar.

Craft Drinks

Reub Goldberg Brewing Machine $$

A custom-built brew machine, swap 'n' go growlers and German-inspired brews. In Tarrawanna.

Headlands Distilling Co. $

This Wollongong place keeps its spirits close to its heart, with a grain-to-glass philosophy and locally inspired infusions. Free tours on Fridays and Sundays.

Stoic Brewing $$

Father-and-son operation in Gerringong with brews and Southern-style food.

Scallops, Rick Stein at Bannisters

Dangerous Ales $

This place in Milton has been making bold moves ever since it started. Expect more than a standard lager.

Flamin Galah Brewing Co $$

Loved, frequented and founded by Jervis Bay locals, this brewpub is in Huskisson. Jervis Bay Brewing Co, the Bay's first brewery, is a block away.

Tara Distillery $$

Draws inspiration from the sea for its sea-lettuce-infused gin, and from its Irish heritage for Australia's first legal poitín (poteen). In Nowra.

North of Eden $

A Stony Creek micro-distillery producing intricately crafted gins, with only 200 bottles per batch.

More Wine?

Cambewarra Estate $$

A sunny, second-generation winery with a cellar door, high tea and a restaurant.

Coolangatta Estate $

Famed for its reds, this winery is situated in original convict-built cottages.

Crooked River Estate $$$

Regularly hosts events and festivals on its property overlooking the Gerringong area.

Lyrebird Ridge $

Makes certified organic wines and ports, taking its name from the lyrebirds heard across the Budgong property.

Mountain Ridge Wines $$

An impressive range of wines and liqueurs.

Tilba Valley Winery & Ale House $$

Overlooks Corunna Lake and produces traditional grape varieties such as semillon and cabernet sauvignon.

LEAH-ANNE THOMPSON/SHUTTERSTOCK

Greenfield Beach

Sun, Sea & Sand

City Beach

A stone's throw from central Wollongong, this beach is perfect for an afternoon dip before dinner at a nearby cocktail bar.

Port Kembla Beach

Come for the Olympic-size ocean pool, stay for the quirky 1912 changing sheds.

Werri Beach

An expansive beach in Gerringong with a swimming lagoon at one end.

Seven Mile Beach

You'll always be able to find your own spot on the sand along this seemingly endless Shoal-haven Heads beach.

Greenfield Beach

One of Jervis Bay's many beaches, Greenfield has pure white sand and water that's clear enough to see the ocean floor.

Cabbage Tree Beach

This quiet bay beach in Jervis Bay is great for ocean swimming with local wildlife as company.

Green Patch Beach

Boasts mint-green waters and a secluded Jervis Bay location.

Mollymook Beach

White-sand beach particularly popular with visiting families.

Tomakin Cove

Sheltered bay beach granting gentle waves perfect for ocean swimming.

Pebbly Beach

Docile kangaroos frequent this beach in Murramarang National Park, with nary a pebble in sight.

Blue Pool

Swim in the azure waters of this acclaimed rock pool in Bermagui.

Natural Wonders

Cathedral Rocks

These distinctive rocks in Kiama have eroded in the shape of a church steeple.

Australia Rock

Snap a photo through this rock that has worn down in the shape of Australia. In Narooma.

Glasshouse Rocks

More than 400 years older than the Twelve Apostles, these towering formations in Narooma are couched among pillow lava.

Horse Head Rock

One of the oldest rocks in NSW, this regal Bermagui formation is best viewed at low tide.

The Pinnacles

These magnificent dichromatic cliffs are composed of white sands and red clay. In the Pambula-Haycock area.

Museums & Galleries

Wollongong Art Museum

Sets the standard for regional art museums, with an impressive collection of modern Aboriginal art.

Bulli Black Diamond Museum

Shares the stories of the area's coal-mining heritage, as well as the history of Bulli.

Meroogal

This stunning example of 1880s Carpenter Gothic is now preserved as a house museum. In Nowra.

Jervis Bay Maritime Museum & Gallery

Showcases historical boats from the region and regularly hosts art exhibitions.

Bega Pioneers Museum

A time capsule housed in a former hotel built in 1857.

Eden Killer Whale Museum

Explores the great importance of the orca to the Yuin people and the settlers of Eden.

Surf Supplies

Surfpitl

For 17 years, this surf shop north of Wollongong has been locally owned, supplying the area with surf gear and streetwear.

Overboard

In Wollongong, this shop is known for its approachable, knowledgeable staff who can help you with all your surfing needs.

LEAH-ANNE THOMPSON/SHUTTERSTOCK

Cathedral Rocks, Kiama

Natural Necessity Surf Shop

A family-run venture in Gerringong. Locals know it for its catchy TV jingle.

Southern Man Surf Shop

A comprehensive surf and skate shop in Ulladulla stocking the leading sports brands.

Offshore Surf

Run by surfers since 1992, with stores in Moruya, Broulee and Narooma.

Oysters from the Source

Narooma Bridge Seafoods

Just off the Princes Hwy, this humble beach shack serves fresh-as-fresh oysters, prawns, fish and lobsters.

Wapengo Rocks Organic Oysters

Certified organic. Call ahead so you can fill your Esky guilt free.

Tathra Oysters

Open November to June, Tathra Oysters supplies many high-end Sydney restaurants.

Wonboyn Rock Oysters

These sweet and creamy oysters are farmed in a remote section of Wonboyn Lake.

Merimbula Gourmet Oysters

This place farms the native Sydney rock and angasi oysters.

Wheelers

Runs tours of its farm at 11am daily, which of course involves tasting the product. It also has an attached seafood restaurant. In Pambula.

Learn to Surf, Dive or Glide

SkySurf Paragliding

As you enter Wollongong you might see paragliders on the horizon. Join their ranks and enjoy a bird's-eye view of the coast.

UWE ARANAS/SHUTTERSTOCK

Eden Killer Whale Museum

Skydive Australia

Offers a tandem dive over Wollongong's central beach, landing near North Gong Beach.

Illawarra Surf Academy

Offers lessons for surfers of all levels, focusing on getting you out in the water and having fun.

Pam Burridge Surf School

Run by former surfing world champion Pam Burridge, who teaches paddleboarding as well as surfing in Mollymook.

Woebegone FreeDive

Living in Huskisson for 15 years, the duo who runs this outfit offers snorkelling and free-dive tours of the area.

Crest Diving

Caters to divers of all experience levels in the crystal-clear waters of Jervis Bay.

Broulee Surf School

Take on the waves at this Eurobodalla beach; among the region's best for learning.

20 Seeking Cultural INSIGHT

TRADITION | CULTURE | SPIRITUALITY

Australia is home to hundreds of Aboriginal and Torres Strait Islander nations, with rich and diverse cultural practices. The perspective of Australia's First Nations peoples will change the way you view the country, and allow you to travel to the different nations that make up this land.

MARCO TROVALUSCI PHOTOGRAPHY/ALAMY

How to

Where am I? Find the Aboriginal or Torres Strait Islander nation you are visiting with the AIATSIS *Map of Australia* or gambay.com.au/languages.

Weather patterns First Nations peoples have different calendars to the Western one, which more accurately describe the local seasons.

Bush tucker Many botanical gardens grow native plants, and may offer tasting tours.

50 Words Project Learn 50 words in the Indigenous language of the place you're visiting using an interactive map (50words.online).

KATHARINA13/GETTY IMAGES

Celebrating Indigenous Australia

Held in Sydney's Victoria Park on 26 January – Australia's national day – the **Yabun Festival** is the largest community-led one-day festival of Aboriginal and Torres Strait Islander cultures. The free event features live music, an Indigenous market, panel discussions, children's activities and more.

Held over four days in July, the **Cairns Indigenous Art Fair** celebrates the reimagining of Queensland's Aboriginal and Torres Strait Islander cultures through art in all forms, including fashion, performance art, weaves and painting. Also in Cairns is the **Shine on Gimuy** festival which illuminates Cairns Esplanade over 10 days in October with light shows, soundscapes, art installations, rich storytelling, programmed talks and music performances.

KEITMA/SHUTTERSTOCK

Take a Tour

On North Stradbroke Island (Minjerribah), **Quandamooka Coast** runs the country's only Indigenous-owned whale-watching tours. You can learn about Eora bush food in Sydney's Botanic Gardens. Melbourne's Royal Botanic Gardens are a significant cultural site, and Indigenous guides will explain the area's importance to the people of the Kulin nation.

Top left Torres Strait Islander dancers, Cairns Indigenous Art Fair
Left Royal Botanic Gardens, Melbourne
Above right Yabun Festival, Sydney

Traditional & Modern Art

Whether it be an example of traditional techniques or an expression of strength and resistance, Indigenous art is as beautiful as it is unique. Many Australian museums have collections of both traditional and contemporary work. **Queensland Art Gallery and Gallery of Modern Art (QAGOMA)** in Brisbane has significant collections of contemporary Aboriginal and Torres Strait Islander art.

Yuin Culture Immersion

Rather than simply learning about Aboriginal heritage, **Ngaran Ngaran Culture Awareness** invites you to engage with and experience Yuin culture. Dwayne Barron-Harrison, a Yuin-Ngarrugu man, founded the retreat on the NSW South Coast to maintain and strengthen connections to traditional Yuin culture. You'll get the most out of your visit if you arrive with respect and genuine curiosity. Guests are invited to walk with Dwayne and his family to

Indigenous Wares & Fare

Sydney's **Blak Markets** provide a space for Indigenous-owned small businesses to promote and sell their products. The markets are more than just a place to shop: there are smoking ceremonies, dance and music, as well as a wonderful community atmosphere drawing Aboriginal people from all over Sydney.

Experience Aboriginal gastronomy at **Midden by Mark Olive**, a fine-dining restaurant located in the Sydney Opera House. Co-owned by Bundjalung chef Mark Olive, its menu draws on Mark's heritage and celebrates Indigenous ingredients in dishes such as native rubbed kangaroo fillet and bush pavlova.

RICHARD MILNES/ALAMY

TOURISM AUSTRALIA

Far left Blak Markets, Sydney
Left Yuin retreat, Ngaran Ngaran Culture Awareness
Below Queensland Art Gallery and Gallery of Modern Art

experience traditional language, values, food and culture. Dwayne shares his culture with knowledge, passion and generosity.

First, you are invited to take part in a smoking ceremony, cleansing you of bad spirits and giving you the purest possible experience on Yuin Country. Over the course of the following 40 hours, you will experience music, dance and storytelling. You will learn about the spirits and stories that inhabit the land you stand on, and you will try bush food and bush medicine used by the Yuin people for millennia. Overnight accommodation in bell tents or private cabins is included as you travel. All meals are provided, featuring products from Mirritya Mundya Indigenous Twist.

The two-night retreat is not just a tour. It is an experience where you will immerse yourself in Indigenous culture. Previous guests speak of seeing the country in a new light and finding peace and spirituality in places they hadn't before. The Yuin retreat is a gift, and a unique insight into one of the oldest living cultures on Earth.

EQROY/SHUTTERSTOCK

By Caoimhe Hanrahan-Lawrence
Caoimhe is a Wiradjuri writer from rural New South Wales, currently living in Sydney on Wangal-Eora land.

Australia's First Nations People

CUSTODIANS OF THE EARTH'S OLDEST CONTINUOUS CULTURES

Indigenous Australian cultures date back at least 65,000 years. Prior to European invasion in 1788, there were approximately 300 distinct language groups and 500 dialects. Now, Indigenous peoples make up only 3.8% of the population. Many live in urban areas, while other communities maintain traditional lifestyles in remote regions.

Left Aboriginal tools
Middle Quandong fruit
Right Ice cream made with Indigenous ingredients

CHAMELEONSEYE/SHUTTERSTOCK

Walking the Dreaming

Aboriginal culture and spirituality revolve around Dreaming and Dreamtime. The Dreamtime tells us about how things came to be. It details the creation of the natural world – rivers, mountains, plants, animals and everything in between.

The Dreaming explains why things are the way they are, such as the birth of the first platypus, how the echidna got her spines or the meanings of certain constellations. The Dreaming is always occurring, without a defined beginning or end. It tells us about how we should behave, about our culture and families, and about living from and respecting the land.

Dreamtime and Dreaming stories differ across nations, though some nations share the same or similar stories. These stories have been passed down through oral storytelling, dance and art, and now many stories have also been written down.

An important part of the Dreaming is that First Nations people are the custodians, not the owners, of the land they live on. Instead, the relationship between the land and the people is a reciprocal one, where we care for the land because it cares for us.

Many of these Dreaming stories are connected to songlines, which are paths walked by the spirits in the Dreamtime. Songlines serve many purposes, such as preserving history, detailing agricultural practices and mapping the land.

DALLASETTA/SHUTTERSTOCK

RUIJIE/SHUTTERSTOCK

Living off the Land

For many years it was assumed that Indigenous peoples were hunter-gatherer societies prior to invasion. However, First Nations people's testimonies and recent historical research indicate that Indigenous societies employed complex aquaculture and agriculture practices. Structures such as weirs and dams still exist, and agricultural techniques and knowledges are being revived and passed on.

> The Dreaming tells us about how we should behave, about our culture and families, and about living from and respecting the land.

Many First Nations communities recognise different seasons from the ones in the Western calendar. These seasons usually align with the area's weather patterns or relate to the local flora and fauna. The Wurundjeri people of Victoria recognise seven seasons, such as Biderap, which is sunny and dry, and Warin, when the wombat and the moth are by the creek. Understanding the Indigenous calendar in the area you are visiting may help you better prepare for the specific weather of the region. Knowing when to dress for the hot and windy, the wet and windy, or the cool and dry can make a big difference to your enjoyment of your travels.

Bush tucker (food) and bush medicine are still used today. Some bush tucker, such as pepperberry, quandong and Davidson's plum, is used in fusion cooking and can be found in restaurants.

The Difficult Date

The date 26 January, when the First Fleet of settlers arrived at Sydney Cove in 1788, officially became Australia Day in 1994. For Aboriginal and Torres Strait Islander peoples, 26 January is a more sombre occasion, marking the beginning of invasion, seizure of the land and erosion of culture. It is referred to as the Day of Mourning, Survival Day or Invasion Day. For many Indigenous people and their supporters, Invasion Day is a day of remembrance and resistance rather than celebration. The issue is contentious in Australia, and calls to keep or change the date occur every year.

Countries, Clans & Cousins

Individual clans exist within Aboriginal nations. Clans within the same language group usually speak dialects that are mutually intelligible. Within these clans are individual families, though Indigenous families integrate the extended family more than most Western societies do. In some communities it is common for a person to refer to their mother's sister as Mum rather than Aunty and to call their first cousins brother- or sister-cousins. Some people may use 'cousin' to refer to anyone within their clan, skin group or language group. 'Cuz' is also a term of affection among Indigenous people even if they are from completely different nations.

Family and community ties are vital to Aboriginal culture. A person's family tells them who they are and where they come from.

Family and community ties are vital to Aboriginal and Torres Strait Islander culture. A person's family tells them who they are and where they come from. Many nations identify family ties by plant and animal totems. It is common to have a personal totem plus three further totems indicating the person's nation, clan and family ties. Sadly, much of this information has been lost due to colonisation, and it is a difficult journey for some people to find their family totems.

Aboriginal & Torres Strait Islander People Today

Across Australia, it is estimated that only 75 Indigenous languages are still spoken, but there are continuing efforts to revive languages among Indigenous communities. It is now possible to listen to music, watch TV shows or take classes in a number of Aboriginal languages. Aboriginal words are also present in the Australian vernacular. Animals such as koalas, dingoes, barramundi and galahs derive their names from Aboriginal languages, as do billabongs and boogie boards.

Similarly, Aboriginal words from different communities have spread through Australian Aboriginal English, the dialect of English spoken by many Aboriginal and Torres Strait Islander people across the country.

Around 60% of Aboriginal people in Australia live on the East Coast. This will sometimes surprise visitors to Australia, who think that they do not see many Aboriginal people in the region. Others are confused when a light-skinned person identifies as Aboriginal. It is widely accepted among Aboriginal communities that percentage of Aboriginality has

LISA MAREE WILLIAMS/GETTY IMAGES

SHIRLEY JAYNE PHOTOGRAPHY/ SHUTTERSTOCK

CHAMELEONSEYE/SHUTTERSTOCK

RICHARD T. NOWITZ/GETTY IMAGES

little bearing on identity and involvement in the community. People with light skin and blonde hair can proudly identify as Blak or Blackfullas. A common metaphor used by First Nations communities is that of a cup of tea: no matter how much milk you put in the cup, no matter how pale it becomes, it's still tea.

This also means that a lot of Aboriginal people live off-Country, meaning that they live on the land of another nation.

Since 1975 the first Sunday of July has marked the beginning of NAIDOC Week, which is dedicated to celebrating Aboriginal and Torres Strait Islander culture, history and perseverance. Communities, cities, schools and other institutions hold events that celebrate and build awareness about the rich and diverse First Nations cultures in Australia today.

Sorry Day (8 February) commemorates the day the Australian government formally apologised for its role in the Stolen Generations. From 1910 to the 1970s, First Nations children were forcibly removed from their families to integrate them into white society. First Nations people today still feel the effects of this policy through loss of culture, family ties and language. The apology was given in 2008.

Signs of Respect

An Acknowledgement of Country and a Welcome to Country are important statements that identify and thank the custodians of the land on which an event takes place. Anyone, both First Nations and non-Indigenous Australians, can give an Acknowledgement. Welcomes can only be given by Elders from that country, or a member of the community who has been given permission by their Elders.

Elders and cultural teachers are usually referred to with 'Aunty' or 'Uncle' before their first name, in the same way that respect is conferred by the use of 'Sir' or 'Ma'am'. This recognises the knowledge and experience that First Nations Elders hold.

Far left Koomurri Dance Group, NAIDOC Week, Sydney
Left Galahs
Above left Aboriginal flag, Laura Quinkan Dance Festival
Above right Boomerang carving

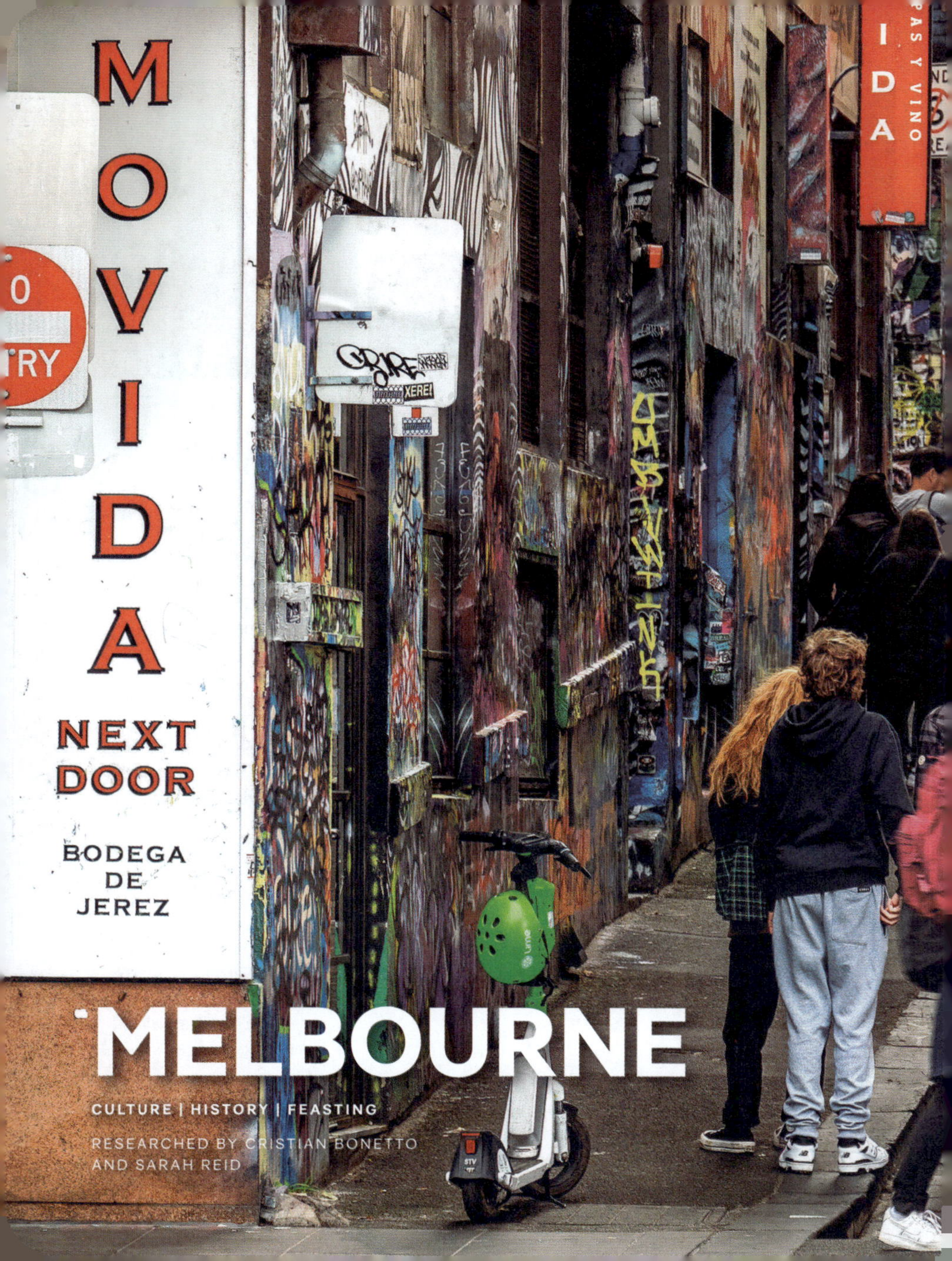

MELBOURNE

CULTURE | HISTORY | FEASTING

RESEARCHED BY CRISTIAN BONETTO AND SARAH REID

PAUL HARDING/LONELY PLANET

MELBOURNE
Trip Builder

Forget blockbuster beaches and endless sunshine: Melbourne's beauty is deeper and more complex. This is Australia's most cultured metropolis, an electrifying mix of razor-sharp art, design and dining, extraordinary architecture, sculpture-graced wineries and moody coastal landscapes made for long, pensive wanders.

Be moved at the **Bunjilaka Aboriginal Cultural Centre** (p147)
2 hours

Stumble upon studios and offbeat shops in the **Nicholas Building** (pictured left; p138)
2 hours

Hop between waves and vines on the **Mornington Peninsula** (p152)
1 day

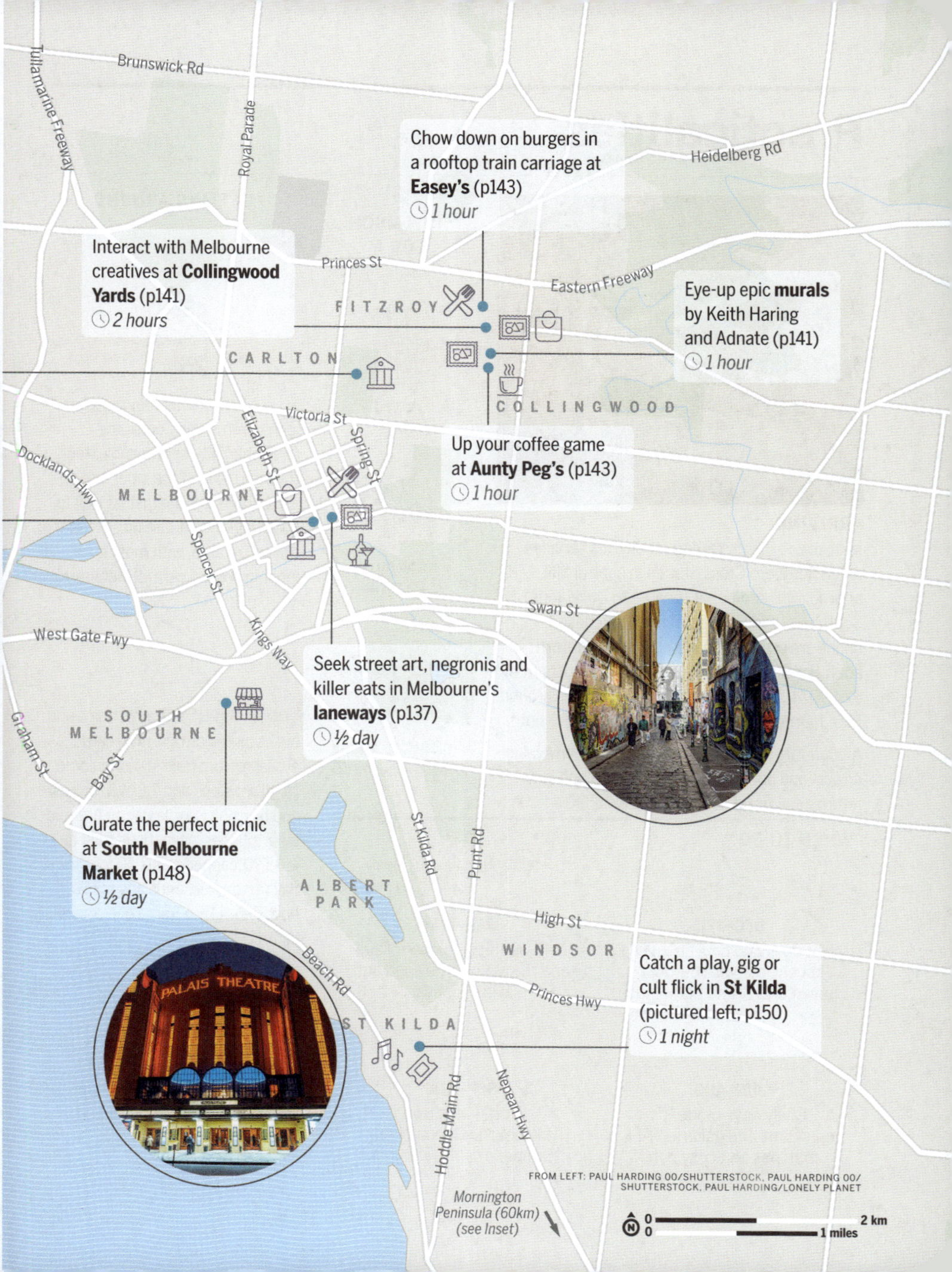

FROM LEFT: PAUL HARDING 00/SHUTTERSTOCK, PAUL HARDING 00/SHUTTERSTOCK, PAUL HARDING/LONELY PLANET

Practicalities

SHUANG LI/SHUTTERSTOCK

ARRIVING

Melbourne Airport Frequent SkyBus services reach Southern Cross Station in central Melbourne, with additional services to Docklands, Southbank and St Kilda. Tickets purchased online are usually cheaper; a one-way/return adult ticket to Southern Cross Station costs from $24.90/41.70. A taxi to the city costs from around $70. Journey time is around 25 minutes for both.

Avalon Airport SkyBus also runs between Avalon Airport and Southern Cross Station. A one-way/return adult ticket costs from $28/52.90.

HOW MUCH FOR A

Piccolo (coffee) $5

Wood-fired pizza $28

Northcote Social Club gig $20–55

WHEN TO GO

DEC–FEB
Hot days and cool changes, music festivals, outdoor cinema and Grand Slam tennis

MAR–MAY
Mild weather, golden foliage and the Melbourne Food and Wine Festival

JUN–AUG
Chilly days made for museums and galleries, AFL matches and cosy pubs

SEP–NOV
Footy-finals fever, Melbourne Cup fashion, temperamental weather

GETTING AROUND

Trams & trains Melbourne's iconic trams criss-cross the (walkable) city centre and extend through most of the inner suburbs. Trains are the fastest way to travel significant distances across the metro area, with most lines looping around central Melbourne.

Tickets & passes Trams, trains and buses use electronic myki cards, available from train stations, some city tram stops and 7-Eleven stores, and by using Google Pay on Android smartphones. A two-hour adult fare is $5.70, capped at $11.40 for the day ($8 on weekends and public holidays). A Free Tram Zone covers central Melbourne.

Driving Handy for day trips to surrounding regions, including the Mornington Peninsula and Yarra Valley.

EATING & DRINKING

Beyond Melbourne's celeb-chef restaurants is a wealth of casual, affordable eateries serving authentic global cuisines. Hit Chinatown and Swanston St (city centre) for East Asian, Carlton for Italian, Brunswick and Coburg for Middle Eastern, North Richmond for Vietnamese, Footscray for Vietnamese and Ethiopian, and, further out, Oakleigh for Greek.

The Melbourne region claims some outstanding gin distilleries, including Four Pillars (pictured right), voted 'World's Best' several years running. Other worthy makers include Melbourne Gin Company and Brogan's Way.

Must-try Asian
Lee Ho Fook (p137)

Best wine bar
Marion (p156)

CONNECT & FIND YOUR WAY

Wi-fi Free hotspots in central Melbourne include Bourke St Mall, Queen Victoria Market and Melbourne Museum; select VicFreeWiFi. Free wi-fi is common at libraries, museums, cafes and apartment rentals. Some hostels and hotels still charge.

Navigation Melbourne's largely grid-style road system makes navigation straightforward. If driving, consider that some narrower inner-city streets are one way.

WHERE TO STAY

Book well ahead if your trip coincides with major events like the Australian Open, Formula 1 Grand Prix and Melbourne Cup.

Neighbourhood	Pros/Cons
City Centre (CBD) & Southbank	World-class cultural sights, shopping, dining and entertainment. Noisy.
Carlton, Fitzroy & Collingwood	Victorian-era architecture, vibrant dining, arts and nightlife, interesting shops.
Brunswick & Northcote	Further out but Melbourne's hipster heartland. Great bars and live-music venues.
South Yarra, Prahran & Windsor	Fashionable and sceney; Windsor coolest. Buzzing eateries, bars, clubs.
St Kilda	Cosmopolitan beachside neighbourhood. Seedy in parts.

FOUR SEASONS IN ONE DAY

Melbourne's weather is infamously erratic. Bring layers of clothes you can peel off or slip on as required throughout the day.

MONEY

Halftix (halftixmelbourne.com) offers discounted theatre tickets, including to blockbuster musicals and Melbourne Theatre Company productions. Also check out todaytix.com.

Seek out Melbourne happy-hour deals on foot; liquor laws restrict overt online promotion.

21 Secrets of THE CBD

CREATIVITY | ARCHITECTURE | FOOD

Melbourne's CBD (Central Business District) holds its cards close to its chest. Here, laneways and unassuming doors lead to impeccably curated galleries and shops, architectural wonders, and rooftop drinks with sucker-punch views. Lace up your coolest kicks and seek out the city's finest assets.

ADAM CALAITZIS/SHUTTERSTOCK

How to

Getting around The CBD is relatively compact and best explored on foot. Free city trams are a handy backup.

When to go Some shops don't open before 11am and some office buildings are closed on weekends, so consider exploring on a weekday afternoon. Note that some businesses close for several weeks in January.

Melbourne Street Tours Three-hour explorations of the city's dynamic street-art scene, as well as street-art workshops. Book online.

PAUL HARDING/LONELY PLANET

Down the Laneways

Degraves St, Centre Pl, Hardware La and graffiti-drenched Hosier La may be the CBD's most Insta-famous laneways, but other alleyways harbour exceptional finds. On Warburton La, **Myrtle Wine Bar** celebrates locally sourced ingredients and Aussie wines, while nondescript Watson Pl houses **Craft Victoria**, a gallery-store championing local makers. Relics from an infamous slum punctuate Casselden Pl, where a 19th-century brothel (the only single-storey house left in the CBD) is now **Little Lon Distilling Co**, an intimate cocktail bar offering gin masterclasses. Excellent eateries and bars dot Crossley and Liverpool Sts, while gritty Duckboard La claims Steen Jones' soaring *Melbourne* mural, exceptional Chinese eatery **Lee Ho Fook** and new-school Indian **Tonka** (order the *pani puri* – filled, deep-fried flatbread shells).

Suburban House Museums

While the National Gallery of Victoria is a must for culture vultures, consider booking a guided tour of **Lyon Housemuseum** or **Justin Art House Museum (JAHM)**. Located in suburban Kew and Prahran, both showcase private collections of contemporary art, exhibited in the collectors' covetable homes.

Top left Hardware Lane
Left Lyon Housemuseum
Above right Melbourne trams

Vertical Villages

Step out of the laneways and into Melbourne's 'vertical villages': early-20th-century buildings stacked floor upon floor with independent galleries, eateries, bars and more. Legendary artist and muse Vali Myers had her studio in Swanston St's **Nicholas Building**, where subway-tiled corridors lead to one-off enterprises peddling everything from local millinery to vintage Manolo Blahnik slingbacks. Directly above the building's leadlight arcade, **Flinders Lane Gallery** showcases the work of Australian artists. You could spend all afternoon and evening in art nouveau **Curtin House**, shopping for niche streetwear at unisex PAM, leafing through design tomes at Metropolis Bookstore, or downing cocktails and jungle curry at Cookie. Hit the rooftop bar for skyscraper views, and always check the lineup at **The Toff** (anything from experimental DJs to hipster Balkan duos). The Toff's Orient Express–style private booths are hot property; book ahead to secure one.

Simone's Picks

The **Capitol** is a spectacular art deco theatre. Designed by Marion Mahony Griffin and Walter Burley Griffin, it has a flamboyantly geometric ceiling and hosts interesting cultural events. In **Guildford Lane**, residents and businesses have populated their doorstops and balconies with potted plants, turning the street into a little oasis. At the rear of NGV International, the magical **Grollo Equiset Garden** hosts the gallery's annual Architecture Commission and comes alive over the summer months. Lastly, floating, open-air bar **Ponyfish Island** is perfect for watching boats motor by.

Tips by Simone LeAmon, *designer and former advocate, and former Curator of Contemporary Design and Architecture at the National Gallery of Victoria @simoneleamon*

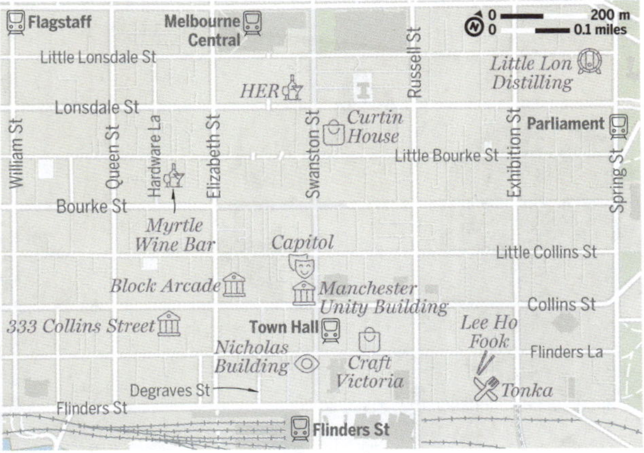

ALEX CIMBAL/SHUTTERSTOCK

On Lonsdale St, one-time cigarette factory Pacific House is now **HER**, a four-level culinary destination whose offerings include a rooftop bar and a music room inspired by Japanese listening bars.

Hidden Wonders of Collins Street

On prestigious Collins St, architectural highlights often lie hidden in plain sight. Take **333 Collins Street**, a Gotham-esque 1990s office building built over a spectacular domed banking chamber from the 1890s. Across the street, the ornate exterior of the **ANZ Bank** (1883–87) hints at the Venetian-inspired opulence inside. After fawning over the banking hall's 23-carat gold-leaf detailing, head through the doors at the rear to reach the stained-glass Cathedral Room. At mosaicked **Block Arcade** (1893), many miss Phillip Goatcher's allegorical ceiling painting (1907) in the L'Occitane store. On the northeast corner of Collins and Swanston Sts, the **Manchester Unity Building** (1932) houses Victoria's first escalator and restored lifts adorned with elegant Queensland maple. Head up the escalator to peek at what was once a glamorous art deco shopping arcade; press the buzzer to enter and head along the arcade to exit to the lifts. Monthly building tours (manchesterunitybuilding.com.au) include access to the rooftop and boardroom, the latter an internationally renowned deco masterpiece; the afternoon 'Wine and Cheese Tour' is best.

Left Capitol Theatre
Below 333 Collins Street

FILEDIMAGE/SHUTTERSTOCK

22 Collingwood off SMITH

CREATIVITY | COFFEE | BEER

Once infamous for sooty factories and working-class footy-club supporters, gentrifying Collingwood fizzes with dynamic creativity and enterprise. Veer east of its of-the-moment dining-and-retail strip Smith St to discover skyscraping street art, heritage-listed quirks, and some bloody good beer and coffee to boot.

CRAIG R F BAILEY, COURTESY CONTEMPORARY ARTS PRECINCTS LTD

How to

Getting here From the CBD it's a 15- to 20-minute ride on tram 86.

When to go Later in the week is best, with Saturday afternoons especially good for a friendly and buzzy neighbourhood vibe.

Classic dives Hazy Collingwood memories are made rocking out at indie-music pub the Tote or queer club the Peel (aka the 'Squeal').

Going Japanese Brunch on *tamagoyaki* (Japanese omelette) at factory-turned-cafe-store Cibi or book a traditional Japanese bathing experience at Ofuroya.

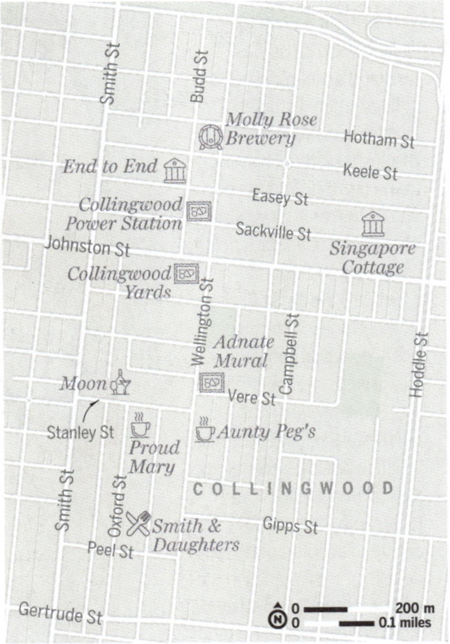

Doing the Yards

A 6500-sq-metre precinct of studios and galleries, community radio stations, one-off shops, bars and some of Australia's leading artist-run initiatives, **Collingwood Yards** is a hotbed of cultural collaborations. Before heading in (try to visit Thursday to Saturday), resident artist Emily Floyd recommends checking the Bus Projects (busprojects.org.au), Westspace (westspace.org.au), Liquid Architecture (liquidarchitecture.org.au) and Agency Projects (agencyprojects.org) websites for current exhibitions, talks and performances. Artist markets are sometimes held in the courtyard, itself flanked by **Social Studio**, selling fashion, design and accessories by Indigenous and culturally diverse creatives; check out its atelier upstairs.

JAVIER CATANO GONZALEZ/SHUTTERSTOCK

Art on the Streets

Collingwood's gritty streets are nectar for street artists. Local public-housing tenants feature in **Adnate's 20-storey mural** (corner

Top left Ceramics studio, Collingwood Yards
Left Yorkshire Brewery (p142)

of Wellington and Vere Sts). Stand further south on Wellington St to fully appreciate what is the tallest mural in the southern hemisphere. Adnate's work also features at **Collingwood Power Substation** (corner of Budd and Sackville Sts), alongside fellow Melbourne-based **Rone**. Budd St and the alleyways off it are always pimped with eye-popping works, and you'll find large-scale jaw-droppers on the side wall of nearby **46 Easey Street**. Collingwood also claims one of the world's few surviving murals by American pop artist **Keith Haring**, painted on the side of what is now Collingwood Yards' Johnston St Building.

Architectural Curiosities

Down narrow Waterloo Rd lie the heritage-listed relics of the former **Yorkshire Brewery**. Among them is a polychromatic brick brew tower, designed in the Second Empire style and Melbourne's tallest building between 1867 and 1888. If the timber abode at 136

Living History

Collingwood Yards was formerly a technical trade college where I studied. I love discovering traces of the site's material history. In the corridor outside my studio there's a beautiful blackboard used for teaching carpentry. In the leafy courtyard, **Hope St Radio** (hopestradio.community) hosts convivial gatherings; all are welcome. Yálla-birr-ang (Collingwood) has a rich history of First Peoples creative practice. For a sonic exploration, I recommend local radio station **3CR** (3cr.org.au). Favourite podcasts centring First Peoples' voices and community-led struggle include Yarra Elders Precious Memories and Thursday Breakfast Interviews.

Emily Floyd, *artist working in sculpture and public installation @emilyfloyd0*

ADNATE

Carn the Pies!

The AFL's Australian Rules football comp is Melbourne's unofficial religion and Collingwood's 'Magpies' (the 'Pies') one of its most colourful teams. While the men's team plays home games at the **MCG** (mcg.org.au), its spiritual home **Victoria Park** hosts Collingwood's women's team (collingwoodfc.com.au/teams/aflw).

NILS VERSEMANN/SHUTTERSTOCK

Sackville St looks dropped straight out of vintage Asia, that's because it is. Dubbed the **Singapore Cottage**, it's a rare example of the prefabricated abodes commonly imported to Melbourne during the 1850s gold rush. Nearby, daredevil modern engineering underscores concrete office block **End to End** (48 Easey St). Designed by Collingwood's provocative ITN Architects, the building is wildly crowned by three decommissioned train carriages. One of the carriages is home to top-notch burger bar **Easey's**.

From Brunch to Brew

South of Johnston St, brunch creatively at **Proud Mary Coffee**, whose sibling **Aunty Peg's** is practically a 'cellar door' for speciality coffee (served only black); check its socials for community cupping sessions. Rock 'n' roll chef Shannon Martinez is behind plant-based restaurant **Smith & Daughters** and the more casual **Smith & Deli**, while intimate wine bar **Moon** has a rocking selection of niche vino by the glass. North of Johnston St, **Acoffee** makes flawless lattes. A few doors down, locals kick back with IPAs and ales at craft brewery the **Mill**. For an impromptu beer crawl, roll onto **Molly Rose Brewery** to slurp Nic Sandry's out-of-the-box brews.

BEX WALTON/FLICKR/CC BY 2.0

Left Twenty-storey Adnate mural (p141)
Above top End to End office block
Above Proud Mary Coffee

CLASSIC ICONS
of Melbourne

01

02

03

04

05

01 Flinders Street Station clocks

If a local says 'Meet me under the clocks', they mean the row of vintage timekeepers at Flinders Street Station.

02 W-class trams

Ride one of Melbourne's historic W-class trams on the City Circle line.

03 Brighton bathing boxes

Brighton beach's brightly coloured Victorian-era bathing boxes are hot property. In 2019, No 15 sold for a cool $340,000.

04 Melbourne Cricket Ground (MCG)

Immortalised in Paul Kelly's song 'Leaps and Bounds', the 'G' is where footy- and cricket-mad Melburnians worship their gods.

05 Pellegrini's

It's still 1954 at this time-warped CBD espresso bar, a bastion of Italo-Melburnian life.

06 Skipping Girl

North Richmond's neon-lit Skipping Girl (Little Audrey) began life advertising vinegar in 1936.

06

07

08

09

10

11

07 St Kilda Pier kiosk

St Kilda Pier's Edwardian pavilion is an architectural phoenix, rising from the ashes after burning down in 2003.

08 American Doughnut Kitchen

A trip to the Queen Vic Market isn't complete without a bag of jam-filled doughnuts from this 1950 food van.

09 Royal Exhibition Building

This World Heritage–listed show-off features a dome inspired by Brunelleschi's cupola for the Duomo in Florence.

10 Vault

Opinion was divided when Ron Robertson-Swann's abstract sculpture was unveiled in 1980. Moved twice, it now calls Southbank home.

11 National Gallery of Victoria Water Wall

Childhood memories are made of running your fingers along the NGV's trickling Water Wall.

01 BOYLOSO/SHUTTERSTOCK. **02** LEONARD ZHUKOVSKY/SHUTTERSTOCK. **03** F11PHOTO/SHUTTERSTOCK. **04** FILEDIMAGE/SHUTTERSTOCK. **05** MICHAEL HOLLOWAY/ALAMY STOCK PHOTO. **06** DJACKMANSON, CC BY-SA 4.0, VIA WIKIMEDIA COMMONS. **07** LEONARD ZHUKOVSKY/SHUTTERSTOCK. **08** EQROY/SHUTTERSTOCK. **09** CORNFIELD/SHUTTERSTOCK. **10** WILLIAM CARAM/ALAMY. **11** 365 FOCUS PHOTOGRAPHY/SHUTTERSTOCK, JOINTSTAR/SHUTTERSTOCK, MADDYZ/SHUTTERSTOCK

23 Exploring NAARM

HISTORY | CULTURE | NATURE

Melbourne's birthday cake may still be shy of 200 candles, but the land on which the city stands has sustained the Wurundjeri and Boon Wurrung people of the Kulin nation for at least 40,000 years. To its Traditional Owners, Melbourne is Naarm, and the city's bounty of Aboriginal art, stories and knowledge offers a deep connection to place as moving as it is enlightening.

JON AUGIER/MUSEUMS VICTORIA

How to

Getting around Federation Sq faces Flinders Street Station. Melbourne Museum and the Royal Botanic Gardens are within walking distance of the CBD. Trams reach both.

When to go Aboriginal Melbourne can be experienced all year.

Barak Building Looking north up Swanston St from the Shrine of Remembrance, you'll notice a 31-storey, black-and-white building embedded with the face of Wurundjeri-willam artist, diplomat and *ngurungaeta* (clan leader) William Barak (1824–1903).

ALEX CIMBAL/SHUTTERSTOCK

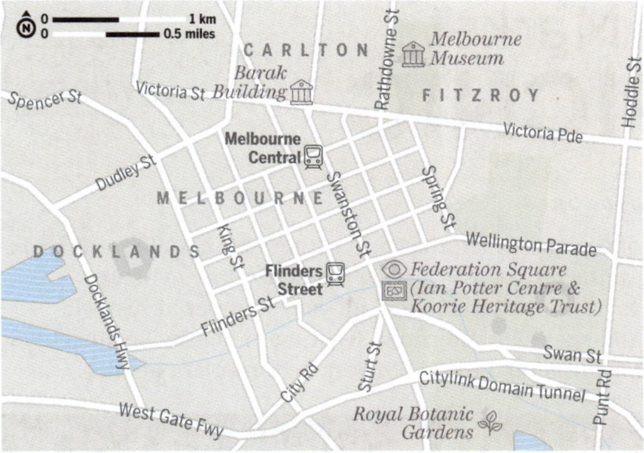

Left Bunjilaka Aboriginal Cultural Centre, Melbourne Museum
Bottom left William Barak building, Swanston Street

Journey through time The evocative Bunjilaka Aboriginal Cultural Centre at **Melbourne Museum** explores many facets of Victoria's oldest living cultures. Learn about the art of possum-skin cloaks and the ingenuity of Budj Bim's ancient aquaculture system, listen to traditional songs of mourning, and reflect on Victoria's frontier wars. From the galleries, the easily missed **Milarri Garden Walk** is a beautiful spot for quiet contemplation.

Important art On Federation Square, explore works by Victorian Indigenous artists at the National Gallery of Australia's **Ian Potter Centre**. According to Myles Russell-Cook, the NGV's former senior curator of Indigenous art, key works include William Barak's *Ceremony* (1898), Maree Clark's *Ritual and Ceremony* (2012), Destiny Deacon's *BLAK* (2020) and Brook Andrew's *Sexy and dangerous* (1996; printed 2005).

A walk in the park As eucalyptus-scented smoke billows from the *tarnuk* (wooden dish), Kulin nation ancestors are acknowledged and you are welcomed to Country. The sacred *tanderrum* ceremony forms part of the Royal Botanic Gardens' **Aboriginal Heritage Walk** (rbg.vic.gov.au). Tours lead visitors through Naarm's foremost public gardens to learn about local Aboriginal culture and knowledge, from the city's six seasons to medicinal bush tucker. Book online.

Culture Hub

A visit to the **Koorie Heritage Trust** on Federation Square is a must for any itinerary, offering a unique insight into Indigenous culture. Immerse yourself in our exhibitions from Victorian First Nations artists, and experience one of the largest collections of Koorie art and artefacts on permanent display. Our Aboriginal Walking Tours are led by First Nations guides and help you gain an understanding of how Melbourne's city centre has changed over time and the significance of the Birrarung (Yarra River) to the local Kulin peoples. Our shop supports local artists and craftspeople and all products sold are authentic and unique.

Tom Mosby, *CEO of the Koorie Heritage Trust*
@koorie_heritage_trust_inc

24 A Market PICNIC

FOOD | ARCHITECTURE | OUTDOORS

Anthony Bourdain once proclaimed that he'd rather eat in Melbourne than Paris, and nowhere are the city's gastronomic passions more evident than at its produce markets. If the weather's fine, fill your hamper at historic South Melbourne Market and spend an afternoon feasting in nearby St Vincent Gardens, surrounded by some of Melbourne's fanciest Victorian-era abodes.

PAUL HARDING 00/SHUTTERSTOCK

How to

Getting here From the CBD, take tram 12 or 96 to the market (15 to 20 minutes).

When to go The market is open Wednesday, Friday, Saturday and Sunday. The best picnic weather is generally from October to April.

Post-prandial pleasures Stroll to Albert Park village to browse boutiques and Avenue Bookstore. Alternatively, catch the 96 tram to St Kilda for a drink at the Esplanade or beachside Pontoon.

DAVID L YOUNG/SHUTTERSTOCK

Left La Central, South Melbourne Market
Bottom left St Vincent Gardens

Market provisions If possible, visit the market on Wednesday, when it's quieter and vendors have more time to chat. Ask questions, sample products. Bag some Spanish blue or Swiss Challerhocker from the magnificent Cheese Room at **Emerald Deli**, and some quiche or Peter Bouchier double-smoked leg ham from **Pickadeli**. Spanish deli-bodega **La Central** has vacuum-packed Iberian smallgoods and made-to-order grazing platters. Friday to Sunday, it also sells Basque country cheesecake, often gone by lunch. The *canelés* and lemon tea cake from **Agathé Pâtisserie** are blissful, as are the house-roasted macadamias from **Nutshoppe**. Stop by **Cobb Lane** for milk rolls and by bottle shop **Swords** for some Sailors Crave craft beer or a drop from maverick Gippsland winemaker Neil Prentice (try his Holly's Garden Überbrut or Studebaker pinot).

Picnic among belles Hamper loaded, graze and laze at **St Vincent Gardens**, a neighbourhood park graced with magnolias, Moreton Bay figs and Norfolk pines. Grand 19th-century abodes – many adorned with delicate iron lacework – circle the park. Together, they form one of Australia's most beautiful heritage-listed precincts. Montague Rd divides the park in two, with the western section (home to a playground) especially appealing given its distance from busy Ferrars St. The gardens are a 1km walk from the market, a little longer if you detour via Marshall St to admire 19th-century show-off South Melbourne Town Hall.

Chef's Picks

My picnic essentials include *jamón* from La Central, pastries from Agathé Pâtisserie, cheese and pickles from **Steve's Deli**, and ready-to-eat seafood from **Oyster Bar by Aptus**. I also love the snacks I can eat while shopping and that I can stay for a quick breakfast or lunch. Favourite on-site market eats include dumplings from **Bambu**, traditional *gözleme* at **Köy Restaurant** and a sneaky *canelé* at Agathé Pâtisserie. Beyond the market, having coffee at **St Ali** is a great way to embrace South Melbourne's culture. **Bellota Wine Bar** is my go-to for lunch or a quiet dinner with friends.

Recommended by Alejandro Saravia, *executive chef and founder of Farmer's Daughters and Victoria by Farmer's Daughters @chefalejandrosaravia*

25 St Kilda Plots & RIFFS

CULTURE | HERITAGE | COCKTAILS

Postwar Jewish enclave, red-light district, punk-rocker hub, artists' muse: bayside St Kilda has always been an eclectic bohemian at heart. While property prices may be stratospheric, there's still magic on these streets at rock 'n' roll joints, independent theatres and a Golden Age picture palace. Catch a gig, play or double feature, and let that old St Kilda energy sparkle.

PAUL HARDING 00/SHUTTERSTOCK

How to

Getting here From the CBD, trams 16 and 96 reach St Kilda (around 30 minutes). For Red Stitch and the Astor, catch a Sandringham-line train to Windsor.

When to go Year-round, but summer in St Kilda is festive.

Classic hangouts Generations of artists have brunched, slurped coffee and scribbled down ideas at Galleon Cafe, eaten Polish cheesecake at Monarch Cakes and dined Italian-style at Cicciolina; the last has an easily missed back bar.

KRZYSZTOF DYDYNSKI/GETTY IMAGES

Left Esplanade Hotel
Bottom left Astor Theatre

Cult films in a deco landmark At night there's something deliciously noir about the softly lit lobby at the **Astor**, car lights gleaming on a rainy Chapel St outside. It might be those elegant curves, the intimate bar named after the hotel in *The Shining*, or the tinkering bell of resident feline Duke (named after John Wayne). In business since 1936, this grand old cinema has a brilliant program of cult classics and double bills, best viewed with a choc-top ice cream from the bar.

Homegrown drama Watching someone unravel is intense, especially when they're within touching distance. There are only 81 seats in the converted church hall used by **Red Stitch**, and the ensemble's productions of contemporary theatre are intelligent and powerful. These include world premieres of new Australian works, developed exclusively with the company.

Theatre Works is another platform for diverse local voices. Hankering for a contemporary circus work exploring Australia's sociopolitical landscape? You'll probably see it here.

Music at the Memo Some of the biggest names in rock, jazz, blues and electronica have played historic St Kilda venues like the Palais and the Esplanade, while the summertime St Kilda Festival – a showcase for local acts – draws massive crowds. For a more in-the-know experience, catch an act at **Memo Music Hall**, a 1920s dance hall now hosting Aussie rock and jazz legends, contemporary singer-songwriters and cabaret.

A Ghost at the Espy

Everyone who's anyone in Australian music has rocked St Kilda's **Esplanade Hotel**. Singer-songwriter Paul Kelly recorded tracks in its legendary Gershwin Room, while late Daddy Cool guitarist Ross Hannaford held a long-running residency in the front bar. Built as a seaside hotel in 1878, its guests reputedly included Mark Twain and Sarah Bernhardt. Legend has it the French actress checked in with 12 pets. These days, the Espy's best-kept secret is the **Ghost of Alfred Felton**, a top-floor cocktail lounge named for the art collector and philanthropist who kept rooms here until his death in 1904.

26 Peninsula PLEASURES

BEACHES | SPAS | WINE

As good for a day trip as it is for an indulgent getaway, the Mornington Peninsula is well versed in the finer things in life, offering both wild and genteel coastlines, mind-clearing hikes and spas, stellar restaurants, wineries and sculpture gardens.

FILEDIMAGE/SHUTTERSTOCK

Trip Notes

Getting here Hire your own car to properly explore the peninsula, a 70- to 90-minute drive south of central Melbourne.

When to go Mid-December to late January is peak season, with crowds and high prices; February to mid-March offers beach weather with thinner crowds.

Dining Book notable restaurants at least a month ahead, especially if visiting in summer and on weekends; some places only open later in the week.

Top Picks

Torello Farm stocks great local produce like Cape Schanck olive oil, Main Ridge olives and sourdough bread from Mary Mother Bakes. Excellent small winery **Avani** has biodynamic estate syrah and pop-up restaurants in summer. For an interesting walk, head right of **Flinders Pier**, past the yacht club and around the cliff.

Recommended by Brigitte Hafner, *chef and owner of Tedesca Osteria @tedesca72*

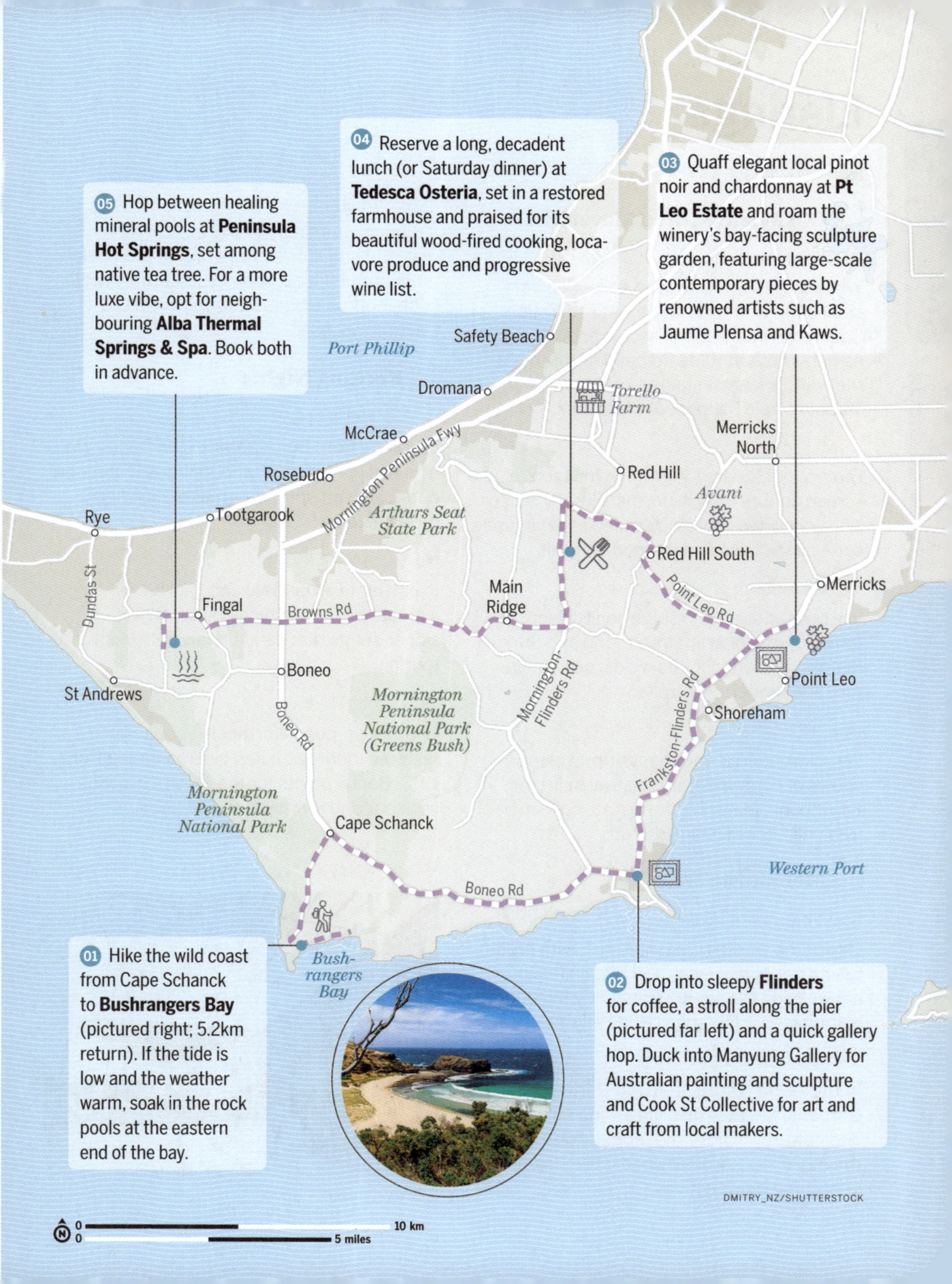

01 Hike the wild coast from Cape Schanck to **Bushrangers Bay** (pictured right; 5.2km return). If the tide is low and the weather warm, soak in the rock pools at the eastern end of the bay.

02 Drop into sleepy **Flinders** for coffee, a stroll along the pier (pictured far left) and a quick gallery hop. Duck into Manyung Gallery for Australian painting and sculpture and Cook St Collective for art and craft from local makers.

03 Quaff elegant local pinot noir and chardonnay at **Pt Leo Estate** and roam the winery's bay-facing sculpture garden, featuring large-scale contemporary pieces by renowned artists such as Jaume Plensa and Kaws.

04 Reserve a long, decadent lunch (or Saturday dinner) at **Tedesca Osteria**, set in a restored farmhouse and praised for its beautiful wood-fired cooking, locavore produce and progressive wine list.

05 Hop between healing mineral pools at **Peninsula Hot Springs**, set among native tea tree. For a more luxe vibe, opt for neighbouring **Alba Thermal Springs & Spa**. Book both in advance.

DMITRY_NZ/SHUTTERSTOCK

Listings

BEST OF THE REST

Old Masters, Mod Mavericks

NGV International

While the NGV's Australian collection occupies the Ian Potter Centre at Federation Square, its international works are housed in its behemoth St Kilda Rd building, home to the world's largest stained-glass ceiling and Tiepolo's epic *Banquet of Cleopatra*.

ACMI

Federation Square's high-tech museum of screen culture in all its forms: film, TV, video art, even video games. Dig deep at exhibitions, screenings, talks and themed festivals.

Heide Museum of Modern Art

In a bucolic setting in suburban Bulleen, the former home of art patrons John and Sunday Reed is renowned for its modernist architecture and modern Australian art.

Buxton Contemporary

Weird, wonderful and thought-provoking shows of contemporary Australian art in Southbank, featuring the private collection of avid collector Michael Buxton.

Melbourne Tales

State Library of Victoria

One of the world's great libraries, with breathtaking heritage spaces and free galleries showcasing everything from early Melbourne paintings to bushranger Ned Kelly's armour.

Melbourne Museum

In the World Heritage–listed Carlton Gardens, Melbourne's sprawling natural- and cultural-history museum delves into the city's extraordinary backstory from refreshing perspectives.

Immigration Museum

A dynamic museum exploring identity, diversity and stories from one of the world's most multicultural societies. Suitably set in Melbourne's beautifully restored Old Customs House.

Rocking Nights

Corner Hotel

Everyone from Ben Harper to the Dandy Warhols has played this rambunctious Richmond pub. Catch an up-and-comer or certified music legend.

Northcote Social Club

In hipster heartland Northcote, NSC is a great pub for fledgling and emerging singer-songwriters and bands, both local and touring.

Northcote Theatre

Another on-point Northcote venue, set in a restored, heritage-listed cinema dating from 1912. Bonus points for the on-site trattoria, wine bar and rooftop bar.

NILS VERSEMANN/SHUTTERSTOCK

Melbourne Museum

Cherry

Noel Gallagher once offered to buy this CBD dive bar – testament to its X factor. It's a come-one-come-all joint, pumping out everything from blues and punk to retro.

JazzLab

Brunswick offspring of Melbourne's late, great jazz club Bennetts Lane, serving up top local and international sax seven nights a week.

Howler

In a Brunswick warehouse, Howler has courted the likes of British singer-songwriter SG Lewis and Aussie alt-rockers Middle Kids. Expect fresh, eclectic acts.

Brunswick Ballroom

A converted hat factory with chandeliers and mirror balls, hosting live music, cabaret and comedy.

Words & Ideas

Wheeler Centre

Located at the State Library of Victoria, the Wheeler Centre runs a busy program of public talks featuring prolific minds and topics ranging from art and literature to current affairs.

Readings

With its main Carlton branch voted World's Best Bookstore in 2016, Melbourne's favourite independent bookstore chain hosts regular book launches and talks with lauded writers.

La Mama Courthouse

Playwriting greats including David Williamson cut their teeth at this intimate Carlton theatre, still a top spot to catch emerging local talent.

I. NOYAN YILMAZ/SHUTTERSTOCK

Dandenong Ranges

Great Outdoors

Main Yarra Trail

Snaking through fragrant bushland and skirting both Collingwood Children's Farm and Heide Museum of Modern Art, this scenic, 35km cycling and walking trail connects Southbank to kangaroo-speckled Westerfolds Park.

Kayak Melbourne

Take in the city skyline on a guided kayaking tour along the Yarra River. Options include a sunset tour with dinner; no prior kayaking experience necessary.

Fitzroy Swimming Pool

Featured in Helen Garner's classic novel *Monkey Grip,* this historic 50m outdoor pool is more than a much-loved hangout; it's a character in Melbourne's collective imagination.

Dandenong Ranges

These lush, cool ranges 35km east of Melbourne boast rainforest walks, elegant gardens and the thigh-busting 1000 Steps (Kokoda Track Memorial Walk).

Urbansurf

Minutes from Melbourne Airport, Australia's first surf park rolls out wave after perfect wave, from gentle white water for rookies to 2m barrels for the next Molly Picklum.

Melbourne by Design

Clementine's

Affordable, locally designed and made gifts in the CBD, from Melbourne-themed totes to ceramics, contemporary jewellery, even native skincare.

Alpha60

Statement-making threads designed by two Melbourne siblings. The label's Chapter House boutique occupies a beautiful, vaulted hall by St Paul's Cathedral.

Gertrude Street

Fitzroy's hippest strip claims some of Melbourne's edgiest fashion labels, including Leonard St, Edgeley and Handsom.

Third Drawer Down

Off Gertrude St, Third Drawer Down collaborates with prolific local and international artists to create quirky, conversation-sparking homewares, gifts and accessories.

Booze & Conversation

Marion $$

Sharp yet friendly staff, sophisticated small plates and out-of-the-box wines by the glass on Fitzroy's Gertrude St.

Carlton Wine Room $$

An understatedly refined Carlton favourite, complete with seasonally adjusted wine list and contemporary bites and mains.

Embla $$

In the CBD, congenial, intimate Embla has a New York vibe, an award-winning wine list and knockout dishes kissed by wood oven or grill.

Beermash $$

Laid-back and affable, Collingwood's Beermash pours a thrilling selection of craft brews, both draught and bottled. Niche ciders and wines add to the sense of adventure.

Vinesmith $$

Cellar door, wine bar, French-inspired bistro and wine shop rolled into a neat Flinders La package.

Commis $$

Cosy candlelit bar in Collingwood with free popcorn, interesting house cocktails and a short, smart menu.

Cafe Culture

Seven Seeds $

House-roasted speciality coffee and a short, feel-good, all-day menu underscore this Carlton classic, hidden up a side street.

Wide Open Road $

Indie vibes, comforting toasties and house-roasted beans keep northside hipsters purring at this super-local Brunswick stalwart.

Industry Beans $$

A Fitzroy-based coffee roaster revered as much for its next-level food options as for its signature blends, rotating single origins and speciality-coffee bubble cup.

Hardware Société $$

Gorgeous, Gallic-accented dishes, brunch cocktails and art by Melbourne illustrator Mads Francis, all hidden down a CBD laneway.

Gertrude Street

Brother Baba Budan $

Serves just coffee and counter food, but both are excellent. On Little Bourke St; there are only a handful of seats inside.

Florian $

Be prepared to wait for a table at this popular Carlton North cafe. The filled baguettes, sandwiches and pastries are worth it.

Foodie Hit List

Laksa King $

A casual, ever-bustling Malaysian joint in Flemington famous for its big bowls of mouth-watering laksa (spicy noodle soup).

Sunda $$

Young-gun chef Khanh Nguyen merges Southeast Asian flavours, native ingredients and new-school ingenuity to create headline-worthy dishes at his hip CBD eatery.

Anchovy $$

Critically acclaimed reinterpretations of Vietnamese cooking in Richmond. For a cheaper bite, grab a posh *bánh mì* (Vietnamese baguette sandwich) from next-door sibling Ca Com.

Savannah African Restaurant $$

Authentic Ethiopian and Eritrean home cooking in Collingwood, prepared and served by the restaurant's hospitable owner.

HuTong Dumpling Bar $$

On a CBD laneway, dexterous chefs pleat Melbourne's best *xiao long bao* (steamed dumplings filled with broth and pork). There's a second branch in Prahran.

48h Pizza e Gnocchi Bar $$

A simple menu of award-winning wood-fired pizzas, plus pillowy gnocchi and graze-friendly antipasti and olives. Two restaurant locations: South Yarra and Elsternwick.

SIAM.PUKKATO/SHUTTERSTOCK

Bowl of laksa

Attica $$$

Reserve months ahead to secure a table at Ben Shewry's world-famous Ripponlea restaurant, a bastion of contemporary Australian cooking at its most enlightened.

Farmer's Daughters $$$

A svelte ode to Gippsland produce in the CBD. Fine-dine in the restaurant, graze in the deli or sip updated cocktails on the rooftop.

Osteria Ilaria $$$

Thoughtful, modern Italo-Australian cooking in the CBD, with clever twists, house-cured meats and surprising wines.

Maha $$$

Chef Shane Delia puts an innovative spin on Middle Eastern cooking at his plush CBD restaurant. For something more casual, hit wine bar Maha East in Windsor.

Gimlet $$$

Contemporary European cuisine in a CBD heritage space reminiscent of a Viennese cafe.

27 Great Ocean Road EXPLORER

BEACHES | WILDLIFE | GOURMET

Stretching from Torquay to Allansford, the Great Ocean Road is Australia's most fabled coastal drive, a 240km route where bracing southern waters meet luxuriant forests, emerald fields and salty beach towns. Stay a while and let its secrets, legends and flavours bewitch you.

JEFFERYHAMSTOCK/SHUTTERSTOCK

How to

Getting here The route's eastern gateway is Torquay, 103km southwest of Melbourne via the M1. Rent a car for maximum freedom.

When to go February and March are warm, with fewer crowds than December and January. Winter is whale-watching season.

Go west Drive from the east for the best views and easy access to lookouts.

Accommodation Book well ahead in summer, at Easter and in school-holiday periods, especially in Lorne, Anglesea and Apollo Bay.

MICHAEL XIAOS/SHUTTERSTOCK

Forest Secrets

Much of the Great Ocean Road lies within **Great Otway National Park**, which sprawls from Torquay to Princetown and north through the Otway Ranges in a sweep of rugged beaches, lush fern gullies and towering mountain ash. While some of its highlights are well known – koala spotting in Kennett River, hiking to Hopetoun Falls (especially beautiful in late winter and spring), wandering through the rainforest canopy at **Otway Fly Treetop Adventures** – others are less familiar. Few know that just outside Forrest, tranquil **Lake Elizabeth** is one of the best places in Australia to spot platypuses, particularly when canoeing with local experts **Otway Eco Tours** (platypustours.net.au). Another mysterious local creature is the fungus gnat larva (native glow-worm), which

YMGERMAN/SHUTTERSTOCK

Making Waves

At the eastern edge of the Great Ocean Road lies surfing mecca **Bells Beach**. Head there early in the morning to watch pros ride its world-famous right-hand breaks, at their peak in autumn and winter. Inspired? **Go Ride a Wave** (gorideawave.com.au) runs lessons along the Great Ocean Road.

Top left Otway Fly Treetop Adventures
Left Great Ocean Road aerial view
Above Koala, Great Otway National Park

inhabits particularly cool, wet sections of the rainforest. As darkness falls, wrap up warm and take a walk along the **Maits Rest Trail** (800m) near Cape Otway or **Madsens Track Nature Walk** (1.5km) at Melba Gully (west of Lavers Hill). Eyes adjusted to the darkness, you will see them, their delicate blue-green threads glowing ethereally in the dark.

Apostles, Shipwrecks & Treasure

Rising out of savage, shipwrecking waters, the **Twelve Apostles** make for a grand finale at the western end of the Great Ocean Road. The monumental limestone stacks are especially spectacular juxtaposed against the setting sun, shortly after which little penguins begin waddling out of the ocean on their way home (bring binoculars). Further west, **Loch Ard Gorge** is where the sole two survivors of the *Loch Ard* – a British iron clipper wrecked nearby in 1878 – swam to safety. Washed-up cargo included the *Loch Ard Peacock*, a life-size majolica sculpture bound for Melbourne's

Where Whalers Once Slumbered

While many wrap up their Great Ocean Road drive at the Twelve Apostles, it's worth continuing west to spend a night or two in the old whaling town of **Port Fairy**. There's a haunting quality to the place, with its pine-graced streets flanked by snug cottages and stoic stone inns fit for a period coastal drama. Consider slumbering at impeccable **Drift House** and make a dinner reservation at cosy **Merrijig Kitchen**, located in Victoria's oldest inn. If you're visiting during the popular **Port Fairy Folk Festival** (portfairyfolkfestival.com) in March, note that accommodation can book out a year ahead; plan accordingly.

LKONYA/SHUTTERSTOCK

Left Moyne River, Port Fairy
Below Childers Cove

Great Exhibition of 1880. Valued at over $4 million, the exquisite Minton piece is now on display at Warrnambool's **Flagstaff Hill Maritime Museum**. Further west still lies **Childers Cove**, a beautiful, solitary beach that's one of the Great Ocean Road's best-kept secrets.

Savour the Region

Don't just see the Great Ocean Road; taste it. Feast on next-level fish and chips at **Fish by Moonlite** in Anglesea and sip native-botanicals gin at Torquay's **Great Ocean Road Gin**. Down by Apollo Bay's harbour, **Apollo Bay Fishermen's Co-op** both sells and cooks off-the-boat local fish and southern rock lobsters, caught sustainably by local skipper 'Frosty' and his crew. Inland from the Twelves Apostles, Josh Walker crafts elegant single-malt whisky at his **Timboon Railway Shed Distillery**, which also stocks local artisanal comestibles. North of the Otway Ranges, in sleepy Birregurra, you'll need to book a few months ahead for a table at Dan Hunter's internationally acclaimed farmhouse restaurant **Brae**, where extraordinary tasting menus might include a guided walk through the produce garden.

GREG BRAVE/SHUTTERSTOCK

28 The Great OCEAN WALK

WILDLIFE | RAINFOREST | BEACHES

The Great Ocean Road may be one of the world's most famous coastal drives, but that doesn't mean you need a car to enjoy its exhilarating landscapes. On the spectacular, six- to eight-day Great Ocean Walk, you can venture deep into the region's verdant rainforest, camp by wild beaches and traverse dramatic clifftops.

MARCELLA MIRIELLO/SHUTTERSTOCK

How to

Getting here Apollo Bay is 196km southwest of Melbourne. V-Line has a daily train–bus connection via Melbourne and Geelong.

When to go March–June and September–November are the best times weather-wise, but check school-holiday dates in June and September.

Tour operators Though many hikers complete the walk independently, tour operators can arrange guided and self-guided trips, shuttle transfers, food drops and camp set-ups. Consult greatoceanwalk.info or greatoceanroadshuttle.com.au.

IMOGEN WARREN/SHUTTERSTOCK

IAN CROCKER/SHUTTERSTOCK

Far left top Cape Otway Lighthouse
Far left bottom Echidna
Left Great Otway National Park

The Walk

Starting in the seaside hamlet of Apollo Bay, the epic, 110km (one way) Great Ocean Walk is wondrous from the get-go. You'll journey across coastal clifftops and onto the sands of rugged, remote surf beaches, and hike through verdant temperate rainforest. Winding through glorious **Great Otway National Park**, you'll pass tree ferns, grass trees and towering eucalypts before returning to the beach, punctuated by **Cape Otway Lighthouse**. Along the way you'll hear tales of shipwrecks, spot koalas in the trees, and feast your eyes on sublime natural attractions. The climax awaits at the finish line: there before you is the unforgettable sight of the **Twelve Apostles**, rising majestically from the sea.

Indigenous History

As you walk along the sands and forests of Great Otway National Park, reflect on the legacy of the Gadubanud people who've lived on these lands for tens of thousands of years. A good place to learn about their ancient culture is at Cape Otway Lighthouse, which has guided walks, bush-tucker tours and a keeping place displaying artefacts.

Camping & Wildlife

Dedicated hiker campsites add another layer of appeal to this memorable journey. You'll encounter plenty of wildlife, from koalas at Cape Otway to eastern grey kangaroos, wallabies and echidnas. From June to August you might see migrating southern right whales off the coast. Book via bookings.parks.vic.gov.au.

Perfect Detours

Crayfish Bay With water under 2m deep, and protected by a reef, this is Australia's number-one beach. Even on a 'crowded' day there are never more than six people here.

Ryan's Den Lights. Camera. Action. Sit and wait while you enjoy the view, keeping your camera on standby for that ultimate shot.

Melanesia Beach Hike to the Great Ocean Walk's strangest beach to see 'cannonballs' embedded in the rockfall. Pack a picnic and take a friend to enjoy its magic.

Recommended by Mark Brack, *local Otway expert and retired tour guide*

THE GIPPSLAND COAST

COAST | WILDERNESS | FOOD

RESEARCHED BY TRENT HOLDEN AND SARAH REID

THE GIPPSLAND COAST

Trip Builder

Stretching out across Victoria's far east is this verdant expanse of coastal wilderness that mixes remote beaches with outdoor adventure and artisanal produce. In between exploring national parks, you'll visit laid-back towns that entice with breweries, distilleries and wineries, among other epicurean temptations.

LKONYA/SHUTTERSTOCK

Practicalities

ARRIVING

Melbourne Airport From here it's a 1½-hour drive to South Gippsland's coast.

Southern Cross Station Has buses to South Gippsland and a train to Bairnsdale Station for bus connections throughout East Gippsland.

FIND YOUR WAY

Tourist info centres in Gippsland's coastal towns have maps, brochures and helpful staff (visitgippsland.com.au).

MONEY

Free campsites are located along the dunes of Ninety Mile Beach, the perfect spot to reel in your own dinner.

WHERE TO STAY

Location	Features
Tidal River	The visitor hub for Wilsons Promontory National Park has an excellent mix of safari tents, cabins and campsites.
Lakes Entrance	This tourist town is filled with family-friendly accommodation.
Mallacoota	A super-chilled, old-school coastal destination that's all about relaxed caravan parks, waterfront camping and houseboats.

GETTING AROUND

Car Hiring a car is by far the best way to explore the region, and it's the only way to access Wilsons Prom.

Bus Services run to most townships throughout the region, but not the national parks.

Train Services run from Spencer Street Station to Bairnsdale Station, from where buses run to East Gippsland destinations.

EATING & DRINKING

If you like to keep things local, sustainable, organic, experimental, rustic, scenic and, above all, delicious, then you've definitely come to the right place. With its huge coastline of fresh seafood and rolling green dairy farms, Gippsland offers gourmet produce that'll be the highlight of your visit.

Best winery
Lightfoot Wines (p169)

Must-try seafood
Sardine Dining (p169; pictured bottom left)

JAN–MAR
Peak season, with perfect beach weather

APR–JUN
Mixed bag weather-wise, but ideal for hikes and camping

JUL–SEP
Cold, blustery conditions add to the coastal romance

OCT–DEC
Delightful weather and fewer visitors

29 Epicurean GIPPSLAND

FOOD | DRINK | LOCAL

In recent years Gippsland has attracted acclaimed chefs, respected winemakers and artisanal producers, all here to capitalise on the region's gourmet bounty. Their work is showcased across cellar doors, high-end restaurants and local farmers markets. From seafood and speciality cheeses to breweries and distilleries, there are plenty of ways to indulge along Gippsland's food-and-wine trail.

PAUL HARDING/LONELY PLANET

How to

Getting here and around Some attractions can be reached by public transport, but for the most part a car is necessary. Otherwise, join a tour with **Gippsland Food Adventures** (gippslandfoodadventures.com.au).

When to go Year-round; reservations are required during peak periods.

Wineries One of Australia's up-and-coming wine destinations, the area has soil ripe for viticulture. Pinot noir and chardonnay are the region's specialities; see winegippsland.com.

HOGGET

Left Loch Brewery & Distillery
Bottom left Charcuterie, Hogget Kitchen

Seafood

Unpretentious fine-dining restaurant **Sardine Dining** in Paynesville, serving sublime contemporary and seasonal dishes, is one of the best places to sample delicious seafood. You won't get classic fish and chips any fresher than at **Port Albert Wharf Fish & Chip Co**. Here it comes straight off the boat, as it does at the floating Lakes Entrance restaurant **Sodafish**.

Farm Produce

Gippsland is famous for its rolling green paddocks, so dairy and farm produce is another reason to visit. **Hogget Kitchen** in Warragul is well worth the inland detour for its award-winning menu of paddock-to-plate dishes and estate-grown wines. **Long Paddock** in Lindenow is run by a husband-wife team with a wealth of experience in some of the world's finest restaurants.

Cellar Doors

Gippsland boasts an array of top-shelf booze produced by talented locals. For a fine single malt look no further than **Loch Brewery & Distillery**, which also makes artisanal gins and ales. **Sailors Grave Brewing** in Orbost is one of Australia's most respected microbreweries, producing experimental beers using local, seasonal ingredients. Fans of traditional cider should stop by **Gurneys Cider** just outside Wilsons Prom, where an expat family of Brits makes the real thing. And for wonderful cool-climate maritime wines, **Lightfoot Wines** delivers the goods with award-winning pinot noir and chardonnay.

Sips, Treats & Eats

Gurneys Cider Stunning views of Wilsons Prom and some of the best ciders in Australia.

Lightfoot Wines Has an amazing cellar door and makes some of our favourite local wines.

Gippsland Jersey After a lot of road testing we can confirm the butter here is the best. We eat it like cheese on fresh baguettes from **Seasalt Sourdough Bakery** in Swan Reach.

East Gippsland Coffee Roasters A must-stop if you're passing through Orbost, this hole-in-the-wall place is also known as the Bean Hive.

Marlo Hotel We always take visitors here. Overlooking the mouth of the Snowy, it's excellent for a fresh Sou'East Draught on the deck.

Recommended by Gab and Chris Moore, *Sailors Grave Brewing, Marlo @sailorsgravebrewing*

30 Adventures in the OPEN AIR

PADDLING | CYCLING | DIVING

Immerse yourself in Gippsland's natural beauty as you hike, cycle or stand-up paddleboard (SUP) along its stunning landscapes. Most visitors are here to get out on the water: the sparkling lakes and alluring beaches are perfect for swimming, surfing, kayaking and snorkelling. Fishing is the other big lure, providing the perfect way to unwind from the stresses of modern life.

QUINCY LEE/SHUTTERSTOCK

How to

Getting here and around Lakes Entrance can be reached by train–bus connection from Melbourne via Bairnsdale Station. From Lakes Entrance, local buses go further afield, including to Mallacoota.

When to go The shoulder seasons (March to June and September to November) bring lovely weather and fewer crowds.

Surf's up! From monster breaks to learner waves, Gippsland is blessed with surf spots to suit all levels. Newbies can get in touch with **Surf Shack** (surfshack.com.au).

NOELIA RAMON · TELLINGLIFE/GETTY IMAGES

Heli-SUP A collaboration by **Venture Out** and **Lakes Entrance Helicopters**, these exhilarating trips take you up in a chopper for a memorable coastal flight before landing on **Ninety Mile Beach**, from where you return via guided SUP tour along the sparkling **Gippsland Lakes**. Helicopters depart from Lakes Entrance.

Diving and snorkelling The Gippsland coast is part of the Great Southern Reef, an interconnected system of rocky temperate reefs stretching across Australia's underbelly and teeming with a rich diversity of fish, weedy dragons, kelp forests and shipwrecks. **Bunarong Marine National Park** and **Cape Conran Coastal Park** have good snorkelling and shore diving. You might also be lucky enough to swim alongside long-nosed fur seals on Gabo Island. Wilderness Coast Charters in Mallacoota (03 5158 0701) can take you there.

Houseboats Fishing, swimming, reading, drinking – life doesn't get much more relaxed than a few days spent lazing on a houseboat. In East Gippsland, **Mallacoota Wilderness Houseboats** kits out boats with all the mod-cons, ensuring you enjoy nature in style. No boat licence required.

Cycling With a mix of bike paths, rail trails and MTB parks, coastal Gippsland is a wonderful destination to explore on two wheels. A highlight is the **Great Southern Rail Trail**: pedal along a 131km path that follows the old train line past some of Gippsland's less-visited coastal hamlets and country towns, surrounded by beautiful bushland. The shorter **Bass Coast Rail Trail** (23km) is another great option for exploring South Gippsland's beaches and countryside.

Left Great Southern Rail Trail
Bottom left Ninety Mile Beach

East Gippsland Rambles

Ninety Mile Beach If you like long walks on the beach you're gonna love this one – all 94 miles (151km) of it! Stretching from Port Welshpool to Lakes Entrance, this wild and remote stretch of surf beach can be tackled as individual walks.

Raymond Island Koala Walk A memorable 3km walk loops around tiny Raymond Island (koalaislandfoundation.com.au), allowing you glimpses of its koala population, along with echidnas, kangaroos, wombats and plenty of birds.

Entrance Walk A stunning 5km coastal trail rewards with dramatic views over Lakes Entrance, where the Gippsland Lakes empty into the ocean.

31 Wilsons Prom WONDERS

WALKS | WILDERNESS | BEACHES

Turquoise waters and bone-white sands meet pristine bushland at Wilsons Promontory (affectionately known in Victoria as 'the Prom'). A very popular place for hiking and camping, this is one of Australia's most spectacular swathes of coastal wilderness.

NICO FARAMAZ/SHUTTERSTOCK

How to

Getting here and around Tidal River is 224km southeast of Melbourne. You'll need your own vehicle, as there's no public transport. Otherwise, **Hike & Seek** (hikeandseek.com.au) runs day tours.

When to go August to November is ideal, with spring wildflowers, whale watching, temperate weather and lighter crowds.

Wildlife From inquisitive wombats at your campsite to kangaroos and emus along the **Prom Wildlife Walk** (2.3km return), this is a destination rich in native fauna.

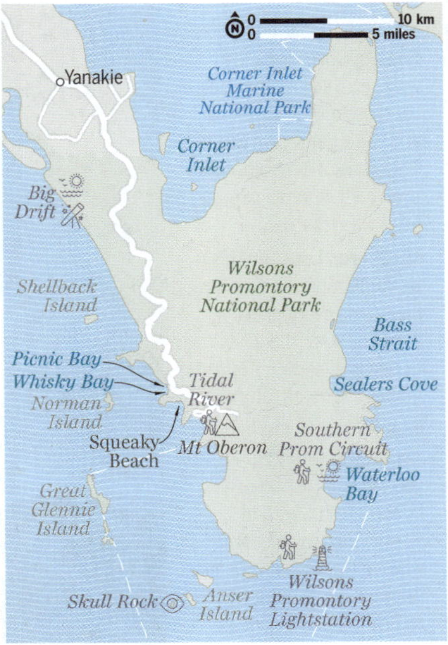

Skull Rock

Emerging from the sea like a villain's lair in an Indiana Jones film is the remote and enigmatic island known as Skull Rock. This monolith used to be off-limits to tourists, but thanks to **Wanderer Adventures**, you can cruise close to its 130m-wide cave. Getting here is half the fun: cool amphibious boats pick you up from the sands of **Norman Beach** for a memorable 2½-hour tour of the Prom's unique coastal wilderness. This is Victoria's largest marine protected area, so you'll pass islands home to seals, penguins and mutton birds. Keep an eye out for bottlenose dolphins and, from May to October, southern right whales.

Southern Prom Circuit

One of the best ways to experience the Prom is to strap on your boots and set out on a long walk through part of its vast wilderness. Hikes last anywhere from 30 minutes to a week, and there are all kinds of trails depending on your time and energy. Stretching over

AUTHORLINYT PHOTOGRAPHY/SHUTTERSTOCK

Top left Skull Rock
Left Seal colony

36km, the **Southern Prom Circuit** is the park's signature trek: a three-day, two-night camping adventure showcasing the Prom's stunning biodiversity. The route takes in eucalypt-scented forests, fern gullies and mountaintop lookouts before concluding at blissful white-sand beaches where you can camp overlooking calm azure waters.

Big Drift

Though there's no shortage of golden beaches across Wilsons Prom, there's nothing else quite as monumental as the sands found at the Big Drift. These spectacular inland dunes rise from the encroaching woodland in a surreal and unexpected sight: it feels as though you've landed on another planet as you wander across the evocative landscape,

Best Prom Hikes

Sealers Cove Along the walk you'll see multiple forest types and ecosystems, and you'll get to visit Sealers Cove (one of Australia's best beaches!). Approximately five hours return.

Mt Oberon Lookout This is an unmissable, world-class panorama overlooking Wilsons Prom. The best time to visit is at sunset. Approximately 2½ hours return.

Beach trifecta Starting at Tidal River campground, you can walk to Squeaky Beach, Picnic Bay and Whisky Bay via coastal walking tracks and beaches. Approximately three hours return, but you'll want to spend longer on the beach.

Recommended by Bill Gurnett, *former Parks Victoria ranger and current co-owner of Gurneys Cider @gurneyscidery*

Wilsons Prom Lightstation

You can sleep in a 19th-century cottage at mainland Australia's most southerly lighthouse. Mind you, you'll earn your rest: to get here you must walk 20km (one way) through the Prom's beautiful hinterland. Climb to the top of the windswept beacon for views over Bass Strait.

GREG BRAVE/SHUTTERSTOCK

GREG BRAVE/SHUTTERSTOCK

admiring views over the expansive Vereker range bushland and the distant ocean. For the best photos, come at sunrise or sunset, when the sands glow rose gold. If you're into stargazing, come back at night to witness a spectacular galactic light show. Sandboarding is also a thing here, so if you've got an old boogie board, bring it along to surf the Big Drift's sandy swells.

Walks from Tidal River

If you're not sold on a multiday wilderness hike, you'll be happy to learn that many of the Prom's iconic attractions are only a short stroll from the park's headquarters at Tidal River. If you have time for just one walk, make it the trip up **Mt Oberon**. At the summit you'll be treated to all-encompassing, life-affirming vistas across the entire national park. A beach walk is also a good choice. The most well known of these is the walk to the aptly named **Squeaky Beach**, which makes sounds like a dog toy as you stroll across its powdery quartz sands. Equally spectacular is nearby **Whisky Bay**, with its chalky white sands, sparkling aquamarine waters and photogenic lichen-splattered boulders.

KEVIN WELLS PHOTOGRAPHY/SHUTTERSTOCK

Left Views from Mt Obern
Top right Squeaky Beach
Above Blotched blue-tongued lizard

Listings

BEST OF THE REST

National Parks

Croajingolong National Park

One of Australia's finest swathes of coastal wilderness, this UNESCO Biosphere Reserve features untouched beaches, towering dunes, great fishing and oceanfront camping. The region was badly hit by the 2020 bushfires, so check access ahead of your visit.

Cape Conran Coastal Park

This protected area in East Gippsland is perfect for blissful summers of swimming, surfing, fishing, camping, reading and long walks along its beautiful beach.

The Lakes National Park

Mixing Ninety Mile Beach with the serene Gippsland Lakes is this biodiverse marine park that's all about unwinding by the water.

Coastal Pubs

Kilcunda Ocean View Hotel $

The well-loved 'Killy' enjoys 180-degree ocean views. A popular stop for a beer and a feed on the journey from Melbourne to Gippsland, it's also accessible along the Bass Coast Rail Trail.

Metung Hotel $$

Overlooking the yacht-filled waters of the Gippsland Lakes, this Metung institution has been drawing tourists and locals alike for over 100 years for pub meals and drinks with a view.

Lake Tyers Beach Tavern $$

Offering a low-key alternative to its more famous neighbour Lakes Entrance, Lake Tyers has a ripper coastal pub across from Ninety Mile Beach. Enjoy local craft beers and tasty food on the deck.

Marlo Hotel $$

Sitting at the confluence of the Snowy River and the ocean, this East Gippy fave lures in farmers, fishers and just about everyone else for cold drinks, bistro meals and the relaxed atmosphere on its deck.

Loch Sport Marina Hotel $$

Life doesn't get more relaxed than sitting at a lakeshore table on a sunny day with a cold drink in hand.

Fish Creek Hotel $$

Gateway pub to Wilsons Promontory, this art deco hotel has long served as the pride of Fish Creek, offering a quality Gippsland wine and beer menu to go with its pub-grub classics.

Archies Creek Hotel $$

A 10-minute drive from the beach, the Archies Creek Hotel offers a rock-and-roll vibe, with live gigs to go with a quality menu of local produce.

Fresh Local Food

Farmers Markets

From Koonwarra and Korumburra to Meeniyan and Mirboo North, Gippsland is known for its farmers markets, which take place across its rural townships on a rotating schedule.

Prom Country Cheese

When it comes to Gippsland produce, dairy is king – cheese especially! Drop by this farmhouse to taste an array of gourmet sheep's- and cow's-milk cheeses, or enjoy a platter accompanied by local wine. Check the website for stockists.

Lakes Entrance Fishermen's Co-op

While many visitors come to Gippsland to reel in their own dinner, don't despair if you didn't bring your fishing gear. Located on Bullock Island, the Lakes Entrance co-op is a popular spot to stock up on some of the local catch to cook up back home.

Prom Coast Ice Cream

With all that dairy it'd be a shame if you couldn't get local ice cream. Fortunately, Prom Coast whips up the likes of salted-caramel ripple and various fruit sorbets, all made using Gippsland cream. Look for it at cafes, wineries and fine food outlets across the region.

Lighthouses

Point Hicks Lighthouse

Hidden away in remote East Gippsland's Croajingolong National Park is this secluded 1880s lighthouse. Take the 162 steps to the top for dramatic views over the place where Captain Cook sighted mainland Australia in 1770. You can spend a night in its lighthouse keeper's cottage. Access may be limited due to bushfire impacts.

Gabo Island Lighthouse

Accessible only by boat or chartered flight, Gabo Island is home to Australia's second-tallest lighthouse (47m). You can spend the night in its assistant lighthouse keeper's cottage, dating to 1862, alongside your neighbours: penguins and seals, as well as dolphins and whales further out at sea.

Cape Liptrap Lighthouse

Guarding South Gippsland's rocky coastline is Cape Liptrap's octagonal 1950s lighthouse, reached via a clifftop trail that offers astounding coastal vistas.

Ancient Sights

Bataluk Cultural Trail

Running from Sale to Cape Conran, this road trip takes in Aboriginal cultural sites across East Gippsland. Stops include sacred caves, coastal middens, hunting areas and wooded wetlands. For more, see batalukculturaltrail.com.au.

GREG BRAVE/SHUTTERSTOCK

Croajingolong National Park

Krowathunkooloong Keeping Place

Located in Bairnsdale, the Krowathunkooloong Keeping Place (gegac.org.au/keepingplace) is a must-see for those who want to learn about Aboriginal history and culture. The focus is on the Gunaikurnai people, the Traditional Owners of the East Gippsland area, who've lived here for at least 30,000 years.

East Cape Boardwalk

A featured stop along the Bataluk Cultural Trail, this coastal boardwalk in Cape Conran (batalukculturaltrail.com.au/cape_conran.php) tells the story of the Gunaikurnai people who came to Salmon Rock to feast on seafood.

Dinosaur Traces

Predating humans by some 130 million years, South Gippsland's dinosaurs roamed across what is now Inverloch's Bunurong Marine National Park. Many fossils have been found in the region, and remarkably you can even observe a dinosaur footprint embedded in the rock pools and visible only at low tide.

BRISBANE & SOUTHEAST QUEENSLAND

WILDLIFE | BEER | BEACHES

RESEARCHED BY TRENT HOLDEN AND SARAH REID

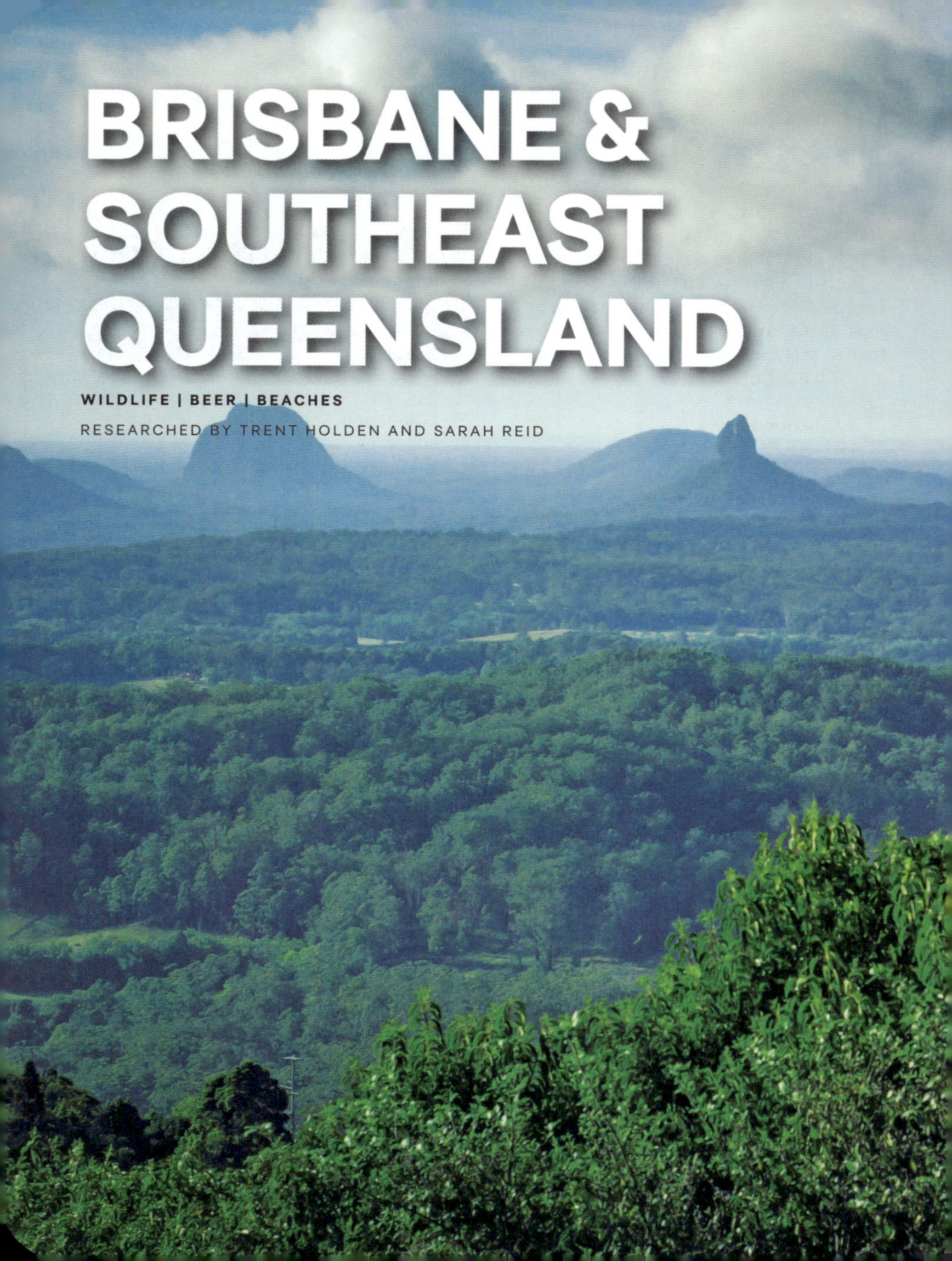

JEMMA OKAPIE SMITH/SHUTTERSTOCK

BRISBANE & SOUTHEAST QUEENSLAND
Trip Builder

Just call it 300 days of summer. That's how many days of annual sunshine you can expect in southeast Queensland (SEQ), which stretches from the NSW border through the Gold Coast's theme parks to the Sunshine Coast's surf breaks and inland to wild rainforest.

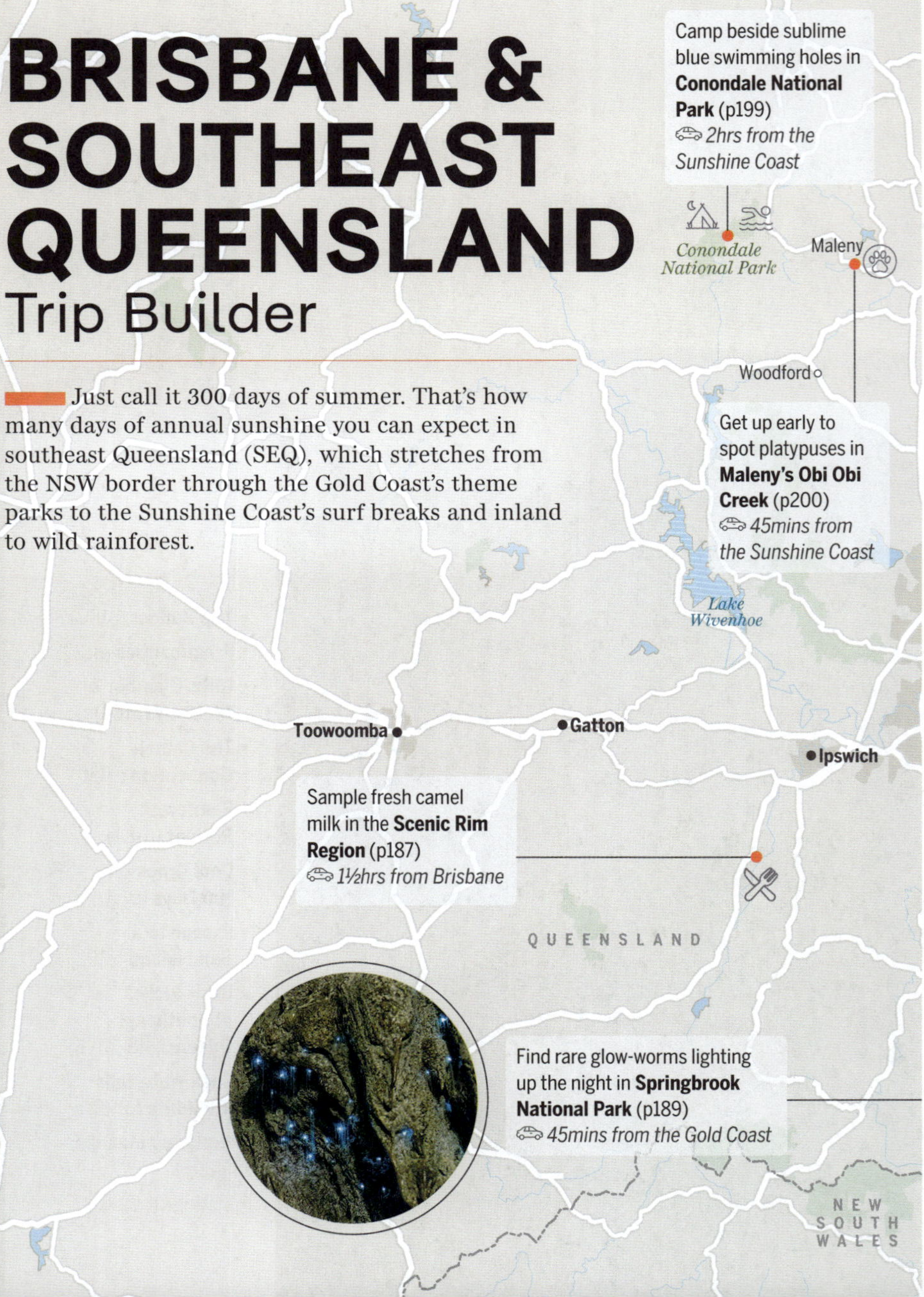

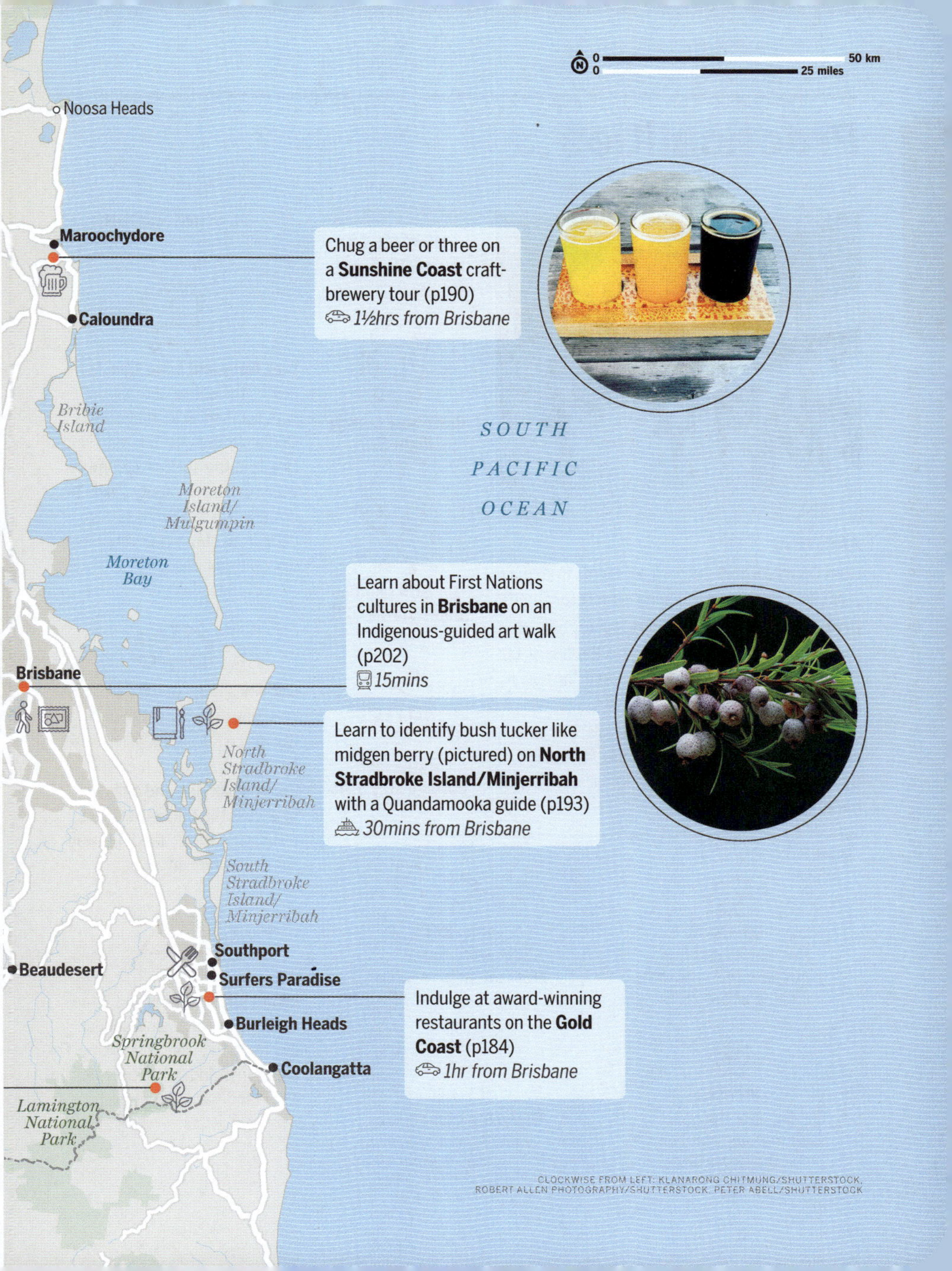

Chug a beer or three on a **Sunshine Coast** craft-brewery tour (p190)
1½hrs from Brisbane

Learn about First Nations cultures in **Brisbane** on an Indigenous-guided art walk (p202)
15mins

Learn to identify bush tucker like midgen berry (pictured) on **North Stradbroke Island/Minjerribah** with a Quandamooka guide (p193)
30mins from Brisbane

Indulge at award-winning restaurants on the **Gold Coast** (p184)
1hr from Brisbane

CLOCKWISE FROM LEFT: KLANARONG CHITMUNG/SHUTTERSTOCK, ROBERT ALLEN PHOTOGRAPHY/SHUTTERSTOCK, PETER ABELL/SHUTTERSTOCK

Practicalities

CHAMELEONSEYE/SHUTTERSTOCK

ARRIVING

Gold Coast Airport Catch direct flights from major Australian cities to this regional airport (pictured).

Brisbane International Airport Halfway between the Gold and Sunshine Coasts, this is the largest, busiest and most centrally located airport in the region. It's about a 20-minute drive to the city.

Sunshine Coast Airport In Marcoola, this small airport has daily flights to Adelaide, Melbourne, Sydney, Cairns and Canberra, plus several international destinations.

HOW MUCH FOR A

Craft-beer tasting flight $15

1hr SUP paddle-board rental $25

Hinterland cottage stay $185

WHEN TO GO

JAN–MAR
Hot, humid and rainy, with temperatures that climb above 25°C

APR–JUN
Clear skies and pleasant, mild weather

JUL–SEP
Mild near the coast; chilly mornings and nights in the hinterlands

OCT–DEC
Blooming jacarandas herald spring; warm, sunny days

GETTING AROUND

Bus, ferry and train Translink covers the entire SEQ region, with services extending from Coolangatta in the south to Noosa Heads in the north. A commuter train runs from Varsity Lakes to Gympie North. Purchase a 'go card' from stations or retailers for discounted fares.

Car While most of the Gold Coast, Brisbane and destinations along the Bruce Hwy are well serviced by public transport, it can be time-consuming and difficult to access the Sunshine Coast coastline or hinterland this way. For flexibility, rent a car.

Island ferry SeaLink and Stradbroke Flyer car and passenger ferries go to Stradbroke Island. For Moreton Island, Micat operates on a demand-based timetable.

TOP: THPSTOCK/SHUTTERSTOCK
BOTTOM: JACKSON STOCK PHOTOGRAPHY/SHUTTERSTOCK

EATING & DRINKING

Like the rest of Australia's East Coast, SEQ is known for its seafood, including Moreton Bay bugs (pictured top right). Named after the bay near Brisbane, they're not insects but a type of slipper lobster.

On menus at many fine-dining restaurants you may see bush-tucker (native food) ingredients. These indigenous animals, insects and plants were traditionally used as meals or medicine by Aboriginal peoples.

Feeling thirsty? Choose from dozens of craft brewers and distillers.

Best craft beer
Brouhaha brewery (p191)

Must-try bush honey
Yura Tours on Stradbroke Island (p194)

CONNECT & FIND YOUR WAY

Wi-fi Few cafes offer free wi-fi; try a library or one of the public networks found at many major public spaces, including parks and beaches.

Navigation The M1 highway runs along the entirety of the coast but can slow to a snail's pace during peak hour. The inland routes are less direct, but less hectic and considerably more scenic.

WHERE TO STAY

Brisbane has accommodation options for all budgets and tastes. Elsewhere, the further you are from the coastline, the more limited your choices become.

Location	Options
Gold Coast strip	Motels, apartments, midrange hotels and luxury accommodation, all within easy walking distance of the beach.
Gold Coast hinterland	Camping, glamping and luxury health retreats surrounded by native bush.
Brisbane CBD, South Bank, West End & Fortitude Valley	Four- and five-star hotels in the centre of the action.
Sunshine Coast	Primarily tourist apartments and private rentals, with views of the coastline.
Montville & Maleny	B&Bs, cottages and boutique family-owned inns high in the hinterland.

DISCOUNTS

The official regional tourism organisations – visitbrisbane.com.au, visitsunshinecoast.com and experiencegoldcoast.com – feature discount codes and exclusive deals on accommodation and activities.

MONEY

Passion fruit, pineapples, avocados: you name it and you'll probably find it being sold roadside. Most farm-gate stalls are unstaffed and cash only, operating on the honour system; have gold ($1 and $2) coins and $5 notes handy.

32 Glitz, Glamour & GLUTTONY

CAFES | COCKTAILS | DINING

Not long ago, food on the Gold Coast was synonymous with greasy takeaway designed to sop up hangovers. But over the last decade the place has been transformed into a five-star foodie destination, with top chefs from Sydney and Melbourne decamping to the stretch between Broadbeach and Burleigh. Family-friendly beachside venues, award-winning cafes and glitzy cocktail bars are all on offer.

THE MILKMAN'S DAUGHTER @THEMILKMANSDAUGHTER_GC

How to

When to go Cafe kitchens close as early as 2pm; dinner service starts around 6pm.

What's in a hat? 'Hats', indicating culinary excellence, are awarded annually by the Australian Good Food Guide. Confusingly, the *Good Food Guide*, a different entity, also awards hats to restaurants in NSW and Victoria.

Pace yourself Free-flowing drinks aren't restricted to weekends: bottomless brunches can be found up and down the coast on any day of the week.

MAYA SCHOLZ/PADDOCK BAKERY

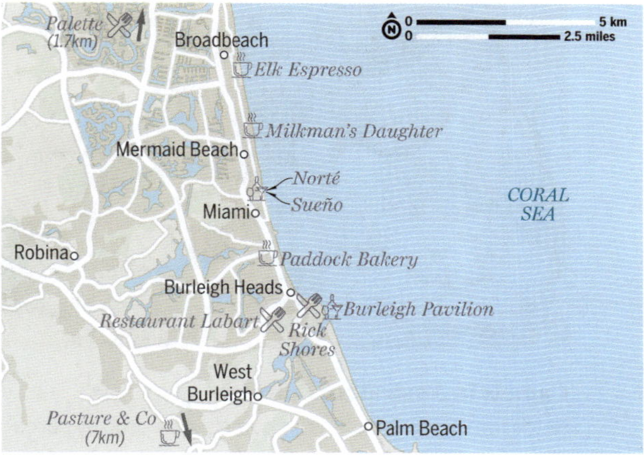

Early-morning indulgence Arrive early to score a seat in the garden at **Paddock Bakery** in Burleigh Heads, set in a 1950s cottage. Inside, watch pastry chefs at work whipping up Nutella cruffins or Paddock's trademark *crème brûlée* doughnuts. Or head to **Pasture & Co** in Currumbin Village: surrounded by 100-year-old fig trees, the cafe caters to every dietary need imaginable, including paleo, vegan, nut-free and gluten-free. For a boozier brunch, there's **Elk Espresso** in Broadbeach, where bottomless mimosas are served daily from 10am to 1.30pm.

Afternoon tipple The mandate is endless summer at casual, beachside **Burleigh Pavilion**. Jugs of Pimm's, freshly shucked oysters and resident DJs are ensuring it meets its goal. To guarantee a seat with ocean views, make a reservation at the **Tropic**, the Pavilion's full-service establishment.

Dine beachside The mandate is endless summer at casual, beachside **Burleigh Pavilion**. Jugs of Pimm's, freshly shucked oysters and resident DJs are ensuring it meets its goal. To guarantee a seat with ocean views, make a reservation at the **Tropic**, the Pavilion's full-service establishment. Just up the road in Mermaid Beach, rooftop **Sueño** serves Latin-inspired cocktails and small plates. For a more substantial feed, head downstairs to **Norté**.

Get glammed up The Gold Coast has nearly two dozen hatted restaurants, including **Rick Shores** in Burleigh Heads, where the Moreton Bay bug roll is a perennial must-order, and **Palette** at HOTA in Surfers Paradise, where the menu names the farmer, producer, hunter or fisher behind every dish, from the Gold Coast prawns with scampi caviar to Waroo kangaroo with Davidson's plum.

Left Milkman's Daughter
Bottom left *Crème brûlée* doughnut, Paddock Bakery

From Dawn to Dessert

For brunch: Milkman's Daughter, Mermaid Beach This vegetarian cafe serves coffee with a conscience, which you can sip among an urban oasis of greenery.

For afternoon drinks: Rosella's Bar, Burleigh Heads Enjoy innovative cocktails and a fun environment.

For dinner: The Collective, Palm Beach A great spot for group meals, and the rooftop bar is perfect for a sunset dinner.

For dessert: Scoop Gelati, Burleigh Heads It always has interesting flavour combinations, such as mango macadamia.

Tips by Alex Munoz Labart, *chef and owner of Restaurant Labart*
@restaurantlabart

The Camel Connection

SOUTHEAST QUEENSLAND'S CAMEL DAIRIES REVEAL AN UNTOLD HISTORY

There will never be an animal more synonymous with Australia than the kangaroo, more beloved than the koala or more feared than the crocodile. Yet camels – despite not being an indigenous species – have managed to cement their place in the country's iconography.

Left Camel calf
Middle Camel, wombat and kangaroo road sign
Right Camel ride, Stockton Beach, New South Wales

BERIT KESSLER/SHUTTERSTOCK

Camels in Australian Culture

At the turn of the 20th century, camels were used by police officers to patrol rural areas, in Australia's very own version of the mounted police. In 1977 camels were the pack-animal companions to adventurer Robyn Davidson when she spent nine months trekking from Alice Springs to the Western Australian coast (a journey she wrote about in her 1980 book *Tracks,* the basis of the 2013 movie of the same name). Every year thousands of people descend upon Yulara in the Northern Territory to watch jockeys racing astride the ungulates, and as a tourist you can ride around Uluru on one.

Camel Milk

In southeast Queensland, entrepreneurial farmers are milking the invasive species for what they're worth – literally.

Some of the biggest camel dairies in the world are located just outside Brisbane, selling a product that's gaining superfood status. Camel milk is a low-lactose option that's touted as a cure for everything from eczema to diabetes. It's also arguably a more ethical animal milk. Unlike a dairy cow – which must be separated from her calf when it's born in order to give milk for just six to nine months – a camel can share her milk with the farmer and her calf for up to 18 months. Domesticating and milking the feral animals also saves them from being culled. With an estimated two million camels roaming freely through the outback, Australia is said to have the largest camel herd in the world.

But a visit to one of SEQ's camel dairies isn't just a chance to learn about the burgeoning industry – it's also an opportunity to understand a piece of Australian history that could otherwise easily be missed.

JOHN WHITE PHOTOS/SHUTTERSTOCK

POMINOZ/SHUTTERSTOCK

Cameleers

The one-humped dromedaries were introduced to Australia in the 1840s. Identified for their suitability for the outback landscape, they were imported en masse, and became the primary means for transporting goods through the centre of the country. They didn't come alone, though – they were accompanied by camel drivers from what are now Afghanistan, Pakistan and India.

> With an estimated two million camels roaming freely through the outback, Australia is said to have the largest camel herd in the world.

These cameleers and their steeds played a critical role in opening up the interior of Australia. In addition to hauling supplies, they helped build railways and the Australian Overland Telegraph Line between Adelaide and Darwin. But by the 1930s the introduction of the motor vehicle had rendered their services obsolete. Faced with hostility – including discriminatory government policies that prevented them from obtaining citizenship – many cameleers were forced to pack up and return home.

Yet you can still see traces of their impact on Australia. In Brisbane's Holland Park, for example, you'll find the site of Queensland's first formal mosque. Dating back to the 1880s, it's also home to Queensland's Muslim Museum, where you can learn about the cameleers' early contributions to the country. But one of the biggest marks they left on the landscape is the intelligent and resilient animals they had to leave behind.

Camel Cuddles

In the Scenic Rim Region, 65km southwest of Brisbane, **Summer Land Camels** is the largest commercial camel dairy outside the Middle East, and the third largest of its kind in the world. At its cafe you can look out onto the paddocks as you sample camel-milk cheese, camel-milk gelato or a latte made with camel milk, and slather your hands with camel-milk beauty products. Family-friendly farm tours and camel rides are also available.

The award-winning **QCamel Milk Dairy** in the Glass House Mountains offers a similar experience, with meet-the-herd tours every Saturday and on school holidays. Bookings are essential.

33 Rainforest RETREAT

BUSHWALKING | GLOW-WORMS | SPAS

With its casinos, nightclubs and theme parks, the Gold Coast is renowned for being a little bit extra. But go inland and you'll find excess of an entirely different sort. With a geological history dating back more than 225 million years, the Gold Coast hinterland is home to around 500 waterfalls, 390 wildlife species and hundreds of kilometres of bushwalking tracks.

JESSICA WYNNE LOCKHART

How to

Getting here Budget ample time. The road to Lamington National Park is single lane at times, with hairpin turns and monster potholes. Southern Cross Tours offers day trips.

When to go At an elevation of 1000m, the hinterland is 5°C to 8°C cooler than the coast. For gushing waterfalls, visit between November and March.

What to pack Wear long pants to ward off leeches, and bring a torch (flashlight) with a red light for nocturnal wildlife spotting.

JESSICA WYNNE LOCKHART

Bushwalking Although **Tamborine Mountain** has long been the go-to, many prefer the tranquillity of **Springbrook National Park** and **Lamington National Park**.

There are really only two spots to stay in Lamington: Binna Burra Lodge on the eastern side and O'Reilly's Rainforest Retreat in the western Green Mountains section. Both offer glamping tents and lodge rooms, as well as guided tours and direct trail access. The 21.4km **Border Track** – part of the longer **Gold Coast Hinterland Great Walk** – connects the two, with shuttles making it possible to walk one way. However, there are trails for all skill levels, such as the 90-minute walk to 80m Morans Falls – listen for the mewling call of green catbirds and look for golden regent bowerbirds.

With limited accommodation, Springbrook is better tackled on a day trip, although spending the night allows you to see pademelons, which emerge at dusk, and rare glow-worms. Both parks have few amenities, so fuel up before you leave.

Adrenaline Opened in **Beechmont** in 2025, the Happitat 'cliff park' has two cliffside zipline tours, a via ferrata course, cliffside viewing platforms and bushwalking trails.

Spas You're in Australia's spa capital, with some of the most luxurious hidden in the hinterland. **Gwinganna Lifestyle Retreat** in Tallebudgera Valley is a celebrity favourite; its award-winning spa is open only to guests. The same goes for treatments at the five-star **Eden Health Retreat** in Currumbin Valley. For day treatments, try the **Bathhouse at Ground** in Currumbin, with massages and cedar hot tubs. Or find your Zen at **Sol Elements**, a Japanese-inspired day bathhouse surrounded by a serene pond at Tamborine Mountain.

Left O'Reilly's Rainforest Retreat
Bottom left Gwinganna Lifestyle Retreat

Glow Bright

Glow-worms – the larvae of *Arachnocampa* fungus gnats, and typically found in damp cave environments – are renowned for producing a blue-green bioluminescence, and this is one of the only places in the world to see it.

Australia's largest colony is under Springbrook National Park's **Natural Bridge**. In Lamington National Park, **O'Reilly's Rainforest Retreat** offers a glow-worm tour. If you're not a night owl, visit Tamborine Mountain's purpose-built caves during the day.

Fun/gross fact: it's the glow-worms' excrement that glows – but that doesn't make this experience any less ethereal. For the best viewing, avoid the use of torches and keep noise low.

34 Cool Drops for HOT DAYS

BEER | FOOD | MUSIC

Holding the title of Australia's Craft-Beer Capital, the Sunshine Coast claims the most craft breweries per capita. The region's 20-plus labels are known for their award-winning beers, busy gastropubs and live music events. Here are five taprooms to tap into.

RILEY JUDD

Trip Notes

Getting around If you plan to visit more than one brewery – or sample more than one beer – sign up for a tour with Sunshine Coast Craft Beer Tours.

Beer Trail Use the **Craft Beer Trail Map** (visitsunshinecoast.com/craftbeer capital) to uncover 24 breweries and eight distilleries on the Sunshine Coast.

Bring an Esky Many seasonal beers are only available direct from the breweries. Arrive prepared to take home a growler, or forever live with regret.

Surf Club Suds

Southeast Queensland's surf clubs are great places to enjoy craft beers with ocean views. Just around the corner from Noosa, the **Sunshine Beach Surf Club** stocks local craft beer and spirit brands including Heads of Noosa, Boiling Pot and Sunshine & Sons.

01 **Moffat Beach Brewing Co** (pictured far left) is the expert in classic pale ales. The original beachside location has the ocean views, while its production outpost hosts music and comedy events.

02 The name says it all: Warana's **Your Mates** is a meeting spot (complete with playground) for friends and families. Try the easy-drinking Larry Pale Ale, which ticks all the boxes on a hot day.

03 **Brouhaha**, which champions the hinterland's producers, has taprooms in Maleny and Baringa. Don't miss the not-too-sweet Strawberry Rhubarb Sour, made with local strawberries and Maleny Dairies' yoghurt.

04 With food trucks, live music and even a petting zoo, **Terella Brewery** in North Arm is made for Sunday sessions. Pack a picnic rug and settle in on the large grassy area.

05 Although it has experimental and sessionable beers on tap, Cooroy's **Copperhead Restaurant Brewery** is just as well known for its kitchen, with offerings such as homemade linguine with local seafood. Bookings recommended.

RAWPIXEL.COM/SHUTTERSTOCK

35 Escape to a Sand ISLAND

BUSH TUCKER | WHALES | CULTURE

Fondly known as 'Straddie', North Stradbroke Island/Minjerribah is the world's second-largest sand island. Swim in freshwater lakes, stroll along empty beaches, watch humpback whales from the shore and immerse yourself in Indigenous culture – it's all here, just 45km from Brisbane's CBD.

CHRIS BRAY VISIONS/SHUTTERSTOCK

How to

Getting here Ferries leave from Toondah Harbour in Cleveland (one hour by train from Brisbane's Roma St Station) and arrive in Dunwich.

When to go Whale season runs from May to November.

Getting around A car is handy but not necessary. A cash-only bus runs from Dunwich to Myora, Amity Point and Point Lookout, and tour operators pick guests up from the ferry terminal. Scooter and bicycle rentals are available.

Take It Slow

Straddie is southeast Queensland's answer to K'gari (formerly Fraser Island), except it's arguably more accessible (you don't need a 4WD), making it possible to experience on a day trip. But if your schedule allows, don't rush your visit – this is the kind of place where time slows and folds in on itself in the best possible way.

NEIL BOWMAN/SHUTTERSTOCK

Quandamooka Country

The Quandamooka (people of the bay) – including the Nughi, Nunukul and Gorenpul – have continuously occupied Minjerribah and neighbouring Moreton Island/Mulgumpin for tens of thousands of years. A visit to Straddie is an opportunity to learn about their history, including at the **Myora Mission Site**. Now a place for contemplation, it's also where you can find an award-winning bush-tucker garden trail.

Top left Cylinder Beach (p195)
Left Koala

Yura Tours takes visitors to key cultural and historical sites on the island. On the three-hour cultural excursion, Quandamooka woman Elisha Kissick shares her family's stories and helps guests identify and taste bush tucker, including honey produced by native stingless bees.

For another contemporary perspective, make an appointment to visit **Delvene Cockatoo-Collins' art studio** in Dunwich. Using techniques passed down from her grandmother, the Quandamooka artist produces ceramics, clothing and homewares with prints of *bunbiya* (turtles), *jalaman* (native bees) and *yalingbilla* (humpback whales). Delvene also offers an art walk and workshop.

Thar She Blows

Straddie is the easternmost point in Queensland, so thousands of humpback whales pass by during the winter months as they migrate north from their Antarctic feeding grounds to mate and give birth. The best vantage point to watch for them is from the 1.2km **Gorge Walk** boardwalk at Point Lookout, which sits about 30m above sea level. You might also see dolphins, sea turtles and manta

Waterway Warnings

If you see ripples or waves on the surface of **Brown Lake/Bummiera**, proceed with caution. According to Quandamooka stories, it's a sign that the rainbow serpent has travelled from her home in **Blue Lake/Karboora** to play in its waters.

Like Bummiera, Karboora (meaning 'deep, silent pool') is a site of spiritual significance. To respect that, visitors are asked not to swim in Blue Lake regardless of the conditions. Instead, stick to the 5.2km walking track around its edges, and keep your eyes peeled for rare golden swamp wallabies, endemic to the island.

THP CREATIVE/SHUTTERSTOCK

Ask an Elder

The **North Stradbroke Island Aboriginal and Islander Housing Co-Operative** is a 10-minute walk from the ferry terminal in Dunwich. Drop in to meet some of the Elders, and see the display of historical community photos, newspaper clippings and artefacts.

Elisha Kissick, *owner of Yura Tours* *@yura_tours*

THP CREATIVE/SHUTTERSTOCK

rays in the waters below, and koalas, eastern grey kangaroos and swamp wallabies in the surrounding bush.

Pure Shores

For many, the appeal of Straddie is having a wide stretch of sea and sand all to yourself. **Main Beach** is the spot for surf, patrolled **Cylinder Beach** is safe for swimming, and **Frenchman's Beach** is ideal for picnics.

But the freshwater lakes, perfect for a dip, are what truly set Minjerribah apart. **Brown Lake/Bummiera** may sound unappealing, but its waters are actually an inviting warm amber owing to tannins from the surrounding paperback eucalypts. It's not uncommon to see a koala on its shores. Or visit the freshwater **Myora Springs** at high tide, when seawater flows through the mangroves. Traditionally a favoured camping place of the Quandamooka people, the banks host large shell middens. You'll need a 4WD to access local favourite the **Keyholes**, just off Main Beach, or book a tour with 'barefoot' Dave from **Straddie Kingfisher Tours**. If you want to drive onto the beach in your own 4WD, you must purchase a permit online from Minjerribah Camping (minjerribahcamping.com.au).

PETER UNGER/GETTY IMAGES

Left Blue Lake/Karboora
Top right, above Frenchman's Beach

BUSH TUCKER
of Southeast Queensland

01 Davidson's plum

Only distantly related to European plums, *Davidsonia johnsonii* is too sour to be eaten raw. Instead, it's used in jams, wines and ice cream.

02 Native ginger

The rhizomes, young shoots and blue berries of this plant all have an earthy ginger flavour.

03 Native raspberry

Found in sunlit rainforest areas, these prickly bushes produce sweet red berries, which can be eaten raw or made into jam or tea.

04 Lemon myrtle

The leaves of this fragrant and flavourful herb also have handy mosquito-repelling properties.

05 Pigface

The salty leaves, fruit and flowers of this succulent – which grows on sand dunes – can be eaten raw or boiled.

06 Australian finger lime

This prized fruit is known as 'citrus caviar' for good reason. Squeeze out the segments for a burst of flavour.

06

07

08

09

10

11

07 Macadamia nut

Most of the world's macadamias are grown in Hawaii, but they're indigenous to Australia. Scientists believe they may originate from a single Queensland tree.

08 Bunya nut

Growing up to 50m, this tree produces a seed that can be eaten raw, roasted or ground into flour for cakes.

09 Saltbush

An ingredient on menus at Australia's top restaurants, the salty leaves of this shrub are best fried.

10 Blue tongue

Not to be confused with the lizard of the same name, this evergreen has sweet blue fruit that will stain your mouth.

11 Native honey

This rare and intense sweet treat is produced by tiny stingless native bees, which are also called sugarbags.

37 Seek Waterfalls & WILDLIFE

ROAD TRIP | PLATYPUSES | SHOPPING

The Sunshine Coast hinterland is only 30km from the ocean, but the region is a world apart from the hum of coastal activity. Ascend high into the Blackall Ranges to be rewarded with lush rainforests, green pastures, eclectic mountain towns and made-for-postcards views.

PHOTOGRAPHY BY ROB D/SHUTTERSTOCK

How to

Getting around It's a 23km drive from Mapleton to Maleny, but plan for plenty of stops. To extend your exploration, make it a circuit by taking Hwy 22 from Maleny to Kenilworth, taking Obi Obi Rd to Mapleton, and then returning to Maleny via Hwy 23.

When to go During the summer months the hinterland is cooler than the coast – and the waterfalls should be full and flowing.

While you're out here Conondale National Park has great bushwalks and creekside campgrounds.

ALEX CIMBAL/SHUTTERSTOCK

Fill Your Belly & Your Bags

At the heart of the Sunshine Coast hinterland region are the townships of Maleny and Montville.

Appealing little **Montville** is known as the Blue Mountains of Queensland. Its buildings have a European Alps aesthetic, with storefronts mainly catering to visitors – which isn't necessarily a bad thing. There are numerous cafes, a chocolatier, a clockmaker, a tea shop and a handful of art galleries to explore.

Maleny is where locals from the surrounding area do their shopping – which is part of the reason you'll have a hard time finding parking. (Try behind the IGA.) Grab a coffee or a gelato at **Maleny Food Co** to enjoy while wandering up the main street. Leave enough time to do the 900m walk to the **Playtpus**

ALEX CIMBAL/SHUTTERSTOCK

Mountain Views

Maleny's Mountain View Rd has unparalleled views of the Glass House Mountains, particularly from **Mountain View Cafe**, located near the entrance to the Mary Cairncross Scenic Reserve. Breakfast, lunch, coffees and local craft beers are available seven days a week. There's another good lookout spot 1.2km west.

Top left Kondalilla Falls (p200)
Left Montville Clock Shop
Above right Riverside boardwalk, Maleny

Viewing Area, which can be found along the accessible boardwalk starting behind the Riverside Shopping Centre.

Further down the road is the village of **Mapleton**. Its pub, built in 1910, isn't known for its food but rather for its position – sitting at nearly 400m in elevation, it has a wrap-around verandah with clear views down to the coast and beyond.

Dive In

The ocean might be a half-hour drive away, but hinterland residents are spoilt for choice when it comes to wild swimming. One of the most accessible spots is at **Gardners Falls**, about 5km east of Maleny. From the car park, head downstream to find shady spots and rope swings. Another option is **Kondalilla Falls**, just southwest of Flaxton. For the best vantage point of the 90m drop, follow the

Platypus Whispers

You can find platypuses in the Mary River, in Peachester's Creek and in Nambour, behind the train station. The national average is two platypuses for every kilometre of creek – but in **Maleny's Obi Obi Creek**, there are up to 10 per kilometre.

It's a misconception that platypuses are only active at dawn and dusk: they need to forage for up to 16 hours a day.

To spot them, look for a ring of low ripples on the water's surface that take a long time to dissipate. (By contrast, eastern water dragons produce very sharp ripples that dissipate quickly.)

Neil Andison, *photographer, tour guide and platypus whisperer*
facebook.com/platypuswhisperer1

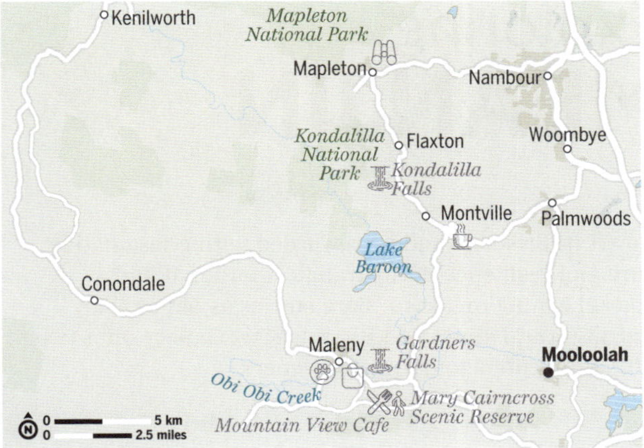

Left Platypus
Below Mary Cairncross Scenic Reserve

WORLDSWILDLIFEWONDERS/SHUTTERSTOCK

4.7km-circuit bushwalk to the bottom of the falls – but note that the best swimming is in the rock pools at the top.

If you have ample time, the 58.8km **Sunshine Coast Hinterland Great Walk** takes about four days to complete. Starting from the dammed **Lake Baroon**, it passes by Kondalilla Falls, Baxter Falls, Mapleton Falls and Gheerulla Falls. Along the way, keep an eye out for yellow-tailed black cockatoos, snakes, goannas and, if you're lucky, koalas.

Ancient Remnants

When settlers arrived on the Sunshine Coast in the 1870s, they quickly set to work logging the area's red cedar and beech trees. The bush you see today is largely regrowth, with one notable exception: the 55-hectare **Mary Cairncross Scenic Reserve** outside Maleny. A remnant subtropical lowland rainforest, its trees have stood for hundreds of years, sheltering endemic species that you're unlikely to see elsewhere. The fully accessible trails provide an opportunity to spot red-legged pademelons, squirrel gliders, paradise riflebirds and rare plant species. Entry is by gold-coin donation, with interpreters on site to help you identify birdlife in the canopy.

ALEX CIMBAL/SHUTTERSTOCK

38 Exploring MEANJIN

ART | CULTURE | HISTORY

Seek out Indigenous art in Brisbane and be rewarded with a fascinating window into the rich culture and resilience of Australia's Aboriginal and Torres Strait Islander peoples. Leaning on art to share stories as old as time, Indigenous-owned BlackCard Cultural Tours and Birrunga Art Gallery offer two of the city's most memorable Indigenous tourism experiences.

EQROY/SHUTTERSTOCK

How to

When to go Any time's a good time to visit, but summer can be hot. BlackCard Cultural Tours run year-round.

Getting around Translink buses, trains and ferries offer convenient transport around the city.

Preparation Wear comfortable shoes on tours and bring a reusable water bottle.

Original name The area occupied by Brisbane is known to the local Jagera and Turrbal peoples as Meanjin, meaning 'place shaped as a spike', in reference to a bend in the Brisbane River.

EQROY/SHUTTERSTOCK

Left Gallery of Modern Art
Bottom left State Library of Queensland

Art Walk

Start your Indigenous art expedition in South Bank's Kurilpa Point and Cultural Precinct, where **BlackCard Cultural Tours**' dedicated Indigenous guides will lead you on a 90-minute excursion. Outside the **Gallery of Modern Art**, you'll see a bronze sculpture by Indigenous artist Judy Watson. Called *tow row,* the sculpture is a recreation of a traditional fishing net used by the Aboriginal people of the area. In the **State Library of Queensland**, Dr Lila Watson's *Kurilpa Country* is a large-scale illuminated mural that tells the story of the habitat of the native water rat. Along the way, your guide will also tell you about the Indigenous Australians behind the city's public murals and share some of the area's lesser-known Aboriginal backstory.

Gallery Stop

Central Brisbane's **Birrunga Gallery**, an Indigenous-owned and -operated art space, houses contemporary art pieces by Aboriginal and Torres Strait Islander artists at all stages of their careers. Be sure to check out the 32m-long Rainbow Serpent, depicting the great life-giver of the Dreaming, which runs through several rooms. Some artwork is by students in Birrunga's Cultural Creative Development Program, which helps nurture Indigenous artists. Tiesha Martin's acrylic canvas *True* represents her totem, the kookaburra, a symbol of joy and fertility. There's also an on-site cafe showcasing native ingredients.

Look Deeper

Indigenous history is all too easily unseen by visitors as they move around contemporary Brisbane. Cultural art tours encourage you to analyse and reflect on the significance of First Nations experiences through art: history, politics and culture are intertwined in the narrative of each of the installations you'll see. For instance, the State Library of Queensland hosts a work by Aboriginal artist Fiona Foley called *Black Opium,* which refers to the *Aboriginals Protection Act 1897,* under which Indigenous people received opium as wages. Engaging with artworks such as these will give you fresh eyes for when you visit other places in the river city.

Mundanara Bayles, *managing director and co-founder of BlackCard @blackmagicwomanpodcast*

Listings

BEST OF THE REST

Local Markets

HOTA Farmers & Artisan Markets

One of the Gold Coast's biggest and most popular weekly farmers markets takes over the Home of the Arts precinct in Surfers Paradise on Sunday mornings.

Collective Markets

Held Friday through Sunday on Little Stanley St in Brisbane's South Bank, these markets run into the evening hours, with food, live music and artisan fare.

Saturday Fresh Market

One of Brisbane's longest-running fresh-food markets, this Saturday-morning market has over 200 stalls with an emphasis on produce, baked goods, meat and flowers. Held in the covered unloading area of the Brisbane Produce Market in Rocklea.

Yandina Country Market

Best known for its massive selection of indoor and outdoor plants, this Saturday-morning market is where you can eyeball bush tucker and nosh on food from local vendors.

Eumundi Market

This legendary market is said to be the biggest artisan market in the country. It's open on Saturday and Wednesday, but head there midweek to avoid the crowds.

Sand & Surf

Greenmount Beach

This beautiful blond beach in Coolangatta is great for surfing (or learning to) and swimming.

Tallebudgera Creek

With 70km of golden sand, there's no lack of swimming spots on the Gold Coast. This estuary, a local family favourite, provides calm, warm waters for splashing, SUPing and kayaking.

Streets Beach

Brisbane may not be located on the ocean, but that doesn't mean it lacks a beach. This artificial inner-city beach is fringed by white sand and subtropical plants.

Woorim Beach

The closest patrolled swimming and surfing beach to Brisbane, Bribie Island's family-friendly area has barbecues, picnic areas, playgrounds and a skate park nearby.

Mudjimba Beach

Seemingly endless, this unpatrolled stretch of sand is favoured by dog walkers. Wander through the Foreshore Conservation Reserve, which connects the ocean to the mouth of the Maroochy River.

Tea Tree Bay Beach

Located in Noosa National Park (a 15-minute walk from the car park), this little bay has shady trees, rock pools and a surf break. It's less crowded than Noosa's main beach, but it isn't patrolled by lifeguards.

Family Fun

Bim'bimba Park

This award-winning nature-based park in Pimpama has a 14m-high play tower, outdoor table tennis, and 3km of walking and cycling trails.

QAGOMA

The Queensland Art Gallery and Gallery of Modern Art are housed in two buildings in

Brisbane. At the Kids' Art Centre, young artists can get their hands busy creating. Entry is free.

Moreton Island/Mulgumpin

Delight bigger kids with a day trip from Brisbane to Moreton Island/Mulgumpin to snorkel the Tangalooma Wrecks. Tours are operated by Tangalooma Island Resort.

Buderim Ginger Factory

Set in 9 hectares of subtropical garden, this place offers factory tours and tastings. Kids will love jumping aboard the 100-year-old sugar-cane train.

Mary Valley Rattler

Departing from Gympie Station, this refurbished steam train travels through the Mary Valley to the cute country communities of Dagun and Amamoor.

Distilleries & Drinks

Wild Flower

Distilling what it calls 'Burleigh in a bottle', the Gold Coast's Wild Flower produces gins and spirits, including speciality blends such as lamington-flavoured vodka. Sourdough pizzas are available on Friday and Saturday.

Howard Smith Wharves

Nestled under Brisbane's Story Bridge, along the historic wharves on the banks of the Brisbane River, are cocktail bars, restaurants and a brewery with wood-fired pizzas.

Piggyback

Run by Tony Kelly, known for Sunshine Coast institutions such as Rice Boi, Piggyback in Palmwoods serves up Asian street food and creative cocktails.

DARREN TIERNEY/SHUTTERSTOCK

Tallebudgera Creek

BeachTree Distilling Co.

Infusing native botanicals with organic and traditional ingredients, this Caloundra distillery makes animal-themed spirits, such as its Quokka native berry gin. Its cellar door is open Tuesday to Saturday.

Handmade Souvenirs

Artisan

Since 1970, Artisan has been the home of art and design in Queensland. Head to the store in Brisbane's Bowen Hills for Aboriginal textiles, opal jewellery, and ceramics painted with native wildflowers.

Pottery Classes

Learn to shape clay by hand, throw pottery on a wheel, glaze your work and fire up the kiln. Classes in its Maroochydore studio include the 90-minute Make a Platter workshop.

David Linton Furniture & Timber Works

Showcasing the work of local artists, this expansive shop in Maleny sells beautifully carved objets d'art made from Australian woods, such as Huon pine and bunya pine.

CAIRNS & THE QUEENSLAND COAST

REEF ADVENTURES | ANCIENT RAINFOREST | TROPICAL VIBES

RESEARCHED BY SARAH REID

T.VISUAL/SHUTTERSTOCK

CAIRNS & THE QUEENSLAND COAST
Trip Builder

The key gateway to the Great Barrier Reef and the Daintree Rainforest, tropical Cairns is an unmissable stop on any East Coast traveller's itinerary. But the fun doesn't end here, with waterfalls, reef adventures, Indigenous experiences and more dotted all the way along the coast.

CLOCKWISE FROM TOP LEFT: MARK HALDING/SHUTTERSTOCK, MIKE WORKMAN/SHUTTERSTOCK, MATHIAS BERLIN/SHUTTERSTOCK, KRYSSIA CAMPOS/GETTY IMAGES

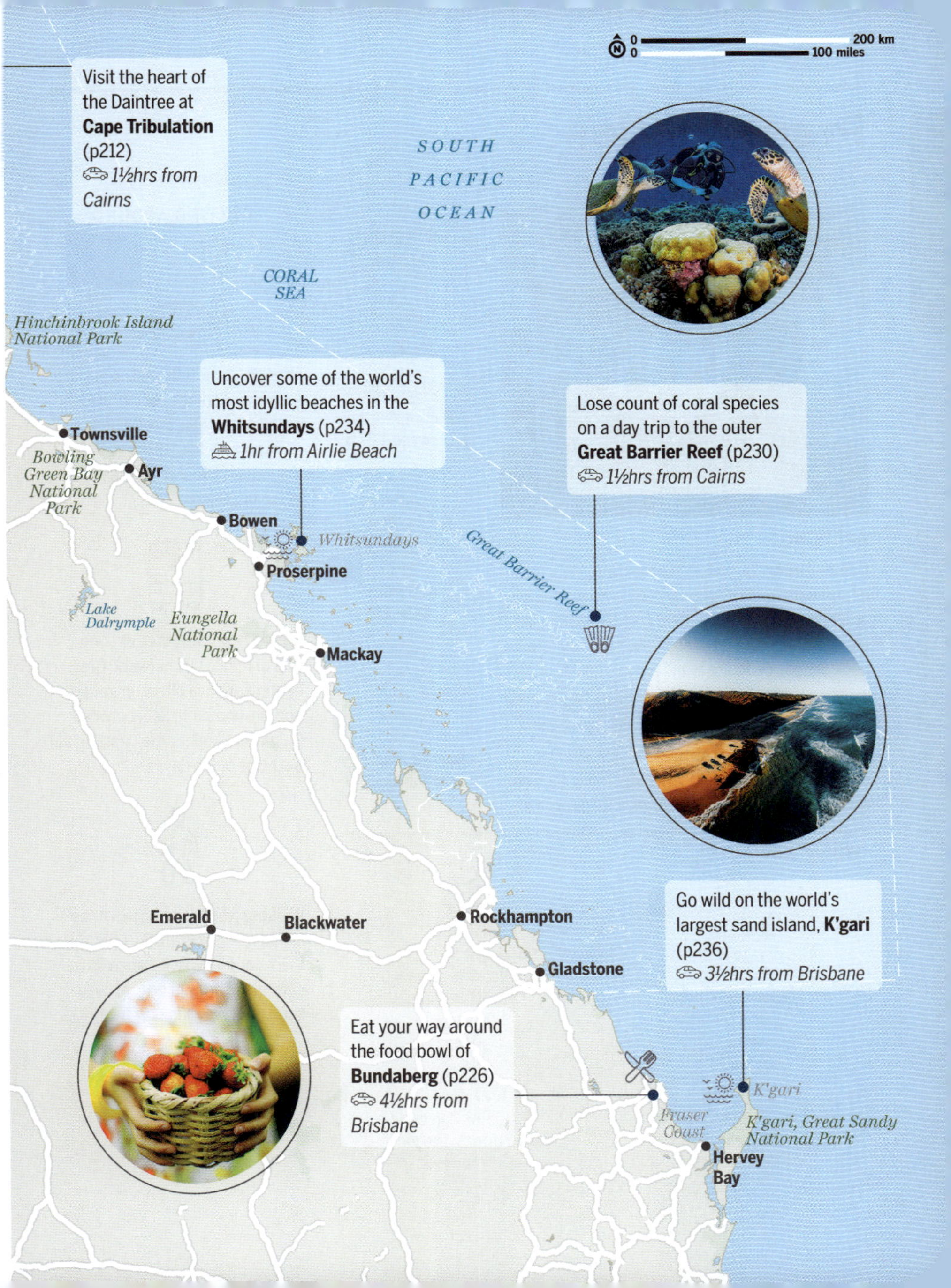

0 200 km
0 100 miles
Visit the heart of the Daintree at **Cape Tribulation** (p212) 1½hrs from Cairns
SOUTH PACIFIC OCEAN
CORAL SEA
Hinchinbrook Island National Park
Uncover some of the world's most idyllic beaches in the **Whitsundays** (p234) 1hr from Airlie Beach
Lose count of coral species on a day trip to the outer **Great Barrier Reef** (p230) 1½hrs from Cairns
Townsville
Bowling Green Bay National Park
Ayr
Bowen
Whitsundays
Proserpine
Great Barrier Reef
Lake Dalrymple
Eungella National Park
Mackay
Go wild on the world's largest sand island, **K'gari** (p236) 3½hrs from Brisbane
Emerald
Blackwater
Rockhampton
Gladstone
Eat your way around the food bowl of **Bundaberg** (p226) 4½hrs from Brisbane
K'gari
Fraser Coast
K'gari, Great Sandy National Park
Hervey Bay

Practicalities

CHAMELEONSEYE/SHUTTERSTOCK

ARRIVING

Cairns Airport Busy domestic and international airport 5km north of the city centre. An Uber costs around $20. Transfers to Cairns and Port Douglas are available with Excellence Coaches and more; book ahead or enquire at the arrivals hall desk.

Townsville Airport Receives domestic flights from major Australian cities and regional Queensland.

Bundaberg Regional Airport Serviced by Qantaslink, Link Airways and Virgin Australia. Pick up a hire car, or take a shuttle (book ahead) or taxi.

HOW MUCH FOR A

NP camping site per person $7.50

Pub meal $15–25

Barrier Reef day trip $200–350

WHEN TO GO

JUN–OCT
The dry, cool season offers ideal weather for outdoor activities

OCT–DEC
You might be lucky to catch the annual coral spawning

NOV–MAR
See marine turtles nest and hatch on Great Barrier Reef beaches

NOV–MAY
Bargains can be found during the wet, humid season

GETTING AROUND

Hire car A car is by far the easiest way to explore the region, where many attractions lie off public transport routes. Check your insurance coverage before heading along unsealed roads.

Bus All major towns have some sort of public bus network. Greyhound Australia offers unlimited hop-on, hop-off tickets between Cairns and Melbourne (starting at $309 for seven days).

Walking Northern tourism hubs including Cooktown, Port Douglas, Cairns and Townsville are relatively easy to get around on foot. Wear sun protection and stay hydrated.

EATING & DRINKING

The further north you travel, the more likely you are to find barramundi (a tender, white-flesh fish; pictured top right) on menus. Many coastal pubs offer a different $15 meal special each night. And while fine dining is less common, there are several standouts to be discovered. Craft beers, along with boutique spirits, now have a foothold in northern Queensland, but it's a rite of passage to try a schooner of XXXX. Good coffee is now easier to find, particularly in Cairns.

Best cocktails
Three Wolves (p217)

Best food market
Rusty's Market (p239; pictured bottom right)

TOP: CHRIS OTTO PHOTOGRAPHER/SHUTTERSTOCK
BOTTOM: BEN WEHRMAN/SHUTTERSTOCK

CONNECT & FIND YOUR WAY

Wi-fi Complimentary at most accommodation, but less commonly available at cafes. The best way to stay connected is to purchase a digital SIM; reception can be patchy to non-existent outside cities and larger towns.

Navigation Download offline maps to save your mobile data. Free offline maps app Organic Maps tends to have good walking-trail coverage. The Queensland National Parks & Wildlife Service has downloadable trail-map pdfs.

WHERE TO STAY

Road-trippers will find plenty of waterside holiday parks and scenic national park campgrounds along the coast. Resort bargains abound in Cairns and Port Douglas during the wet season.

Location	Accommodation options
Cairns & Port Douglas	Resorts galore, with more hotel and hostel options in Cairns.
Cassowary Coast	Camping, motels and B&Bs.
Townsville	Hotels, holiday apartments and a few hostels.
Whitsundays	Flash island resorts; affordable resorts, hotels and hostels on the mainland.
Capricorn Coast, Bundaberg & Fraser Coast	Family-friendly resorts and holiday parks, B&Bs and small hotels.

STINGER SAFETY

Marine stingers are present along the northern Queensland coast (down to around K'gari) from November to May; protective stinger suits are provided by activity operators.

MONEY

Cash is more readily accepted up here than it is further south – handy when Eftpos machines drop offline in bad weather or in remote locations. Smaller towns may not have ATMs.

38 Escape to CAPE TRIB

DAINTREE RAINFOREST | ROAD TRIP | SWIMMING HOLES

When you drive off the ferry that shuttles vehicles across the Daintree River, it feels like you've entered another realm. The Daintree Rainforest and the Great Barrier Reef meet at Cape Tribulation ('Cape Trib'), a magical place dotted with rainforest trails and freshwater swimming holes. Most visitors only come for a day, but it's worth carving out three to connect more deeply with this off-grid wonder.

AUSTRALIANCAMERA/SHUTTERSTOCK

How to

Getting here and around The Daintree Ferry is a 1½-hour drive north of Cairns. Once across, it's about an hour to Kulki Lookout at the northern end of Cape Trib (if you don't stop).

When to go Avoid (most of) the rain during the May–November dry season.

Where to stay More than a dozen guesthouses (some with their own natural swimming holes) dot Cape Trib. Several camping spots include a basic national park campground at Noah Beach.

ANGIE TANK/SHUTTERSTOCK

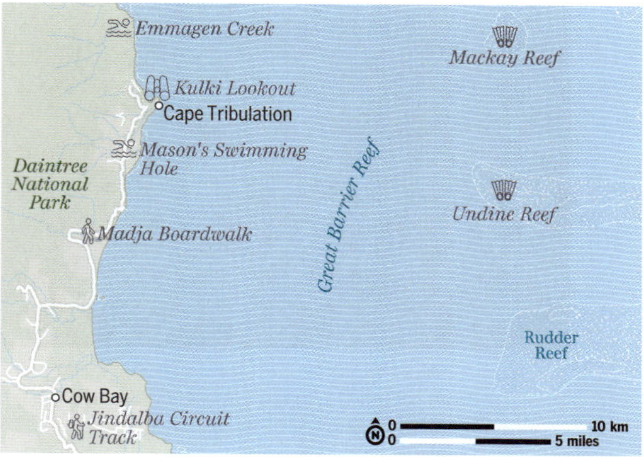

Nature's Playground

Rainforest trails Overnight stays allow for tackling Cape Trib's longer walks, including the lush **Jindalba Circuit Track** (3km) and the 7km-return slog up Mt Sorrow for spectacular views (allow six hours). Weaving through coastal mangroves, the elevated **Madja Boardwalk** (1.2km) is one of the world's most scenic wheelchair-accessible trails. Learn more about this ancient ecosystem on a walk with long-time local Neil Hewett (coopercreek.com.au). Cassowaries are spotted on most of his tours.

Next-level snorkelling If you only do one Great Barrier Reef snorkelling tour, make it this one. It only takes 25 minutes on Ocean Safari's inflatable boat to reach **Mackay** and **Undine Reefs**. Part of the Great Barrier Reef, these neighbouring reefs teem with marine turtles, tropical fish and some of the most beautiful, untouched corals accessible to snorkellers in the entire World Heritage Site. Gin-clear waters and shallow reef systems create ideal conditions for underwater photography.

Magical waterholes Cape Trib's beautiful beaches are off-limits for swimming due to 'salties' (saltwater crocodiles), but some of Australia's best (and croc-safe) freshwater swimming holes are found here. Don't miss **Emmagen Creek** (3.5km along the Bloomfield Track) and **Mason's Swimming Hole** (behind Mason's Cafe; gold-coin – $1 or $2 – donation). There's another beautiful waterhole you may hear about but won't find signposted, and for good reason: it's a sacred site for Kuku Yalanji Traditional Owners, so you should not attempt to access it

Left Boardwalk, Daintree National Park
Bottom left Saltwater crocodile

4WD Adventure

One of Australia's most legendary 4WD trails, the **Bloomfield Track** links the northern end of Cape Trib to the Aboriginal community of Wujal Wujal, from where a sealed road runs to Cooktown. The Bloomfield is only 30km long, but it's a famously challenging drive, with creek crossings, ultra-steep hills, and potholes the size of people. An extra 40km past Wujal Wujal (don't miss its Indigenous arts centre), the historic **Lion's Den Hotel** is an obligatory post-Bloomfield stop. If one celebratory beer turns into a few – which can easily happen here – you can camp on the property. The pizzas are excellent.

Daintree Dreaming

FEEL THE ANCIENT ENERGY

An ecosystem so spectacular that Sir David Attenborough called it 'the most extraordinary place on Earth', the Daintree Rainforest is a real-life Jurassic Park, home to descendants of plants and animals from the era of the dinosaurs. This biodiversity powerhouse is not only ecologically significant but also culturally important to its Traditional Owners, the Eastern Kuku Yalanji people.

Left Daintree Rainforest
Middle Magnificent tree frog
Right Southern cassowary

Covering more than 1200 sq km between Mossman Gorge and the Bloomfield River, the otherworldly Daintree is estimated to be around 180 million years old. So it's no wonder that visiting this verdant corner of Queensland feels like stepping (a long way) back in time.

Part of the Wet Tropics World Heritage Area (WTWHA), the ancient rainforest is also protected by Daintree National Park, which has two sections: Mossman Gorge and Cape Tribulation. Just 20 minutes from Port Douglas, the Mossman Gorge Centre at the national park's southern end is the most accessible section. Here you can take self-guided or Indigenous-led walks and swim in the idyllic Mossman River, which tumbles between huge granite boulders. On the northern side of the Daintree River, accessed by a car ferry, the Cape Tribulation section (p212; 110km north of Cairns) feels even more wild, but like Mossman Gorge it also has a handful of easily accessible walking trails, as well as accommodation and ecotours.

Historic Handback

In 2021, more than 160,000 hectares of land in Tropical North Queensland, including the Daintree Rainforest, was officially handed back to Eastern Kuku Yalanji people.

Central to the culture and spirituality of the Eastern Kuku Yalanji, who have an intimate knowledge of the rainforest passed down through generations, the handback means that Daintree National Park is now jointly managed by Traditional Owners and the Queensland government. At the time of research, construction was underway on

ANDREJ BLAGOJEVIC/SHUTTERSTOCK

TORSTEN PURSCHE/SHUTTERSTOCK

the Eastern Kuku Yalanji Bamanga Muruku Tourism Hub at Kulki on Cape Tribulation (p212), which will offer visitors new ways to engage with this ancient landscape.

Heritage Under Threat

Having survived for so long, the Daintree might seem pretty resilient. But research has found that the WTWHA, home to 36% of Australia's mammal species alone, is highly susceptible to climate change. Current modelling predicts that global warming of just 1°C – which science suggests has already been reached – could decrease the distributional range of the region's endemic vertebrate species by 60%. At 3.5°C, approximately 65% of endemic vertebrates are projected to disappear from the WTWHA, leading to a likelihood of mass extinctions, beginning with frogs and possums.

> The otherworldly Daintree is estimated to be around 180 million years old. So it's no wonder that visiting this verdant corner of Queensland feels like stepping back in time.

Additional threats to the rainforest identified by the Wet Tropics Management Authority include invasive species such as feral pigs and yellow crazy ants, increased demand for infrastructure, and a significant decline in research and investment due to a lack of government funding. And while tourism, too, has the potential to create negative impacts, it's impossible to visit this special place without being inspired to help protect it.

Daintree Experiences

Croc cruise Operating on the Daintree River, **Solar Whisper** (solarwhisper.com) boats are both ecofriendly and super quiet, so you can glide up to salties and other wildlife without scaring the animals.

Daintree Discovery Centre In the Cape Tribulation section, this attraction has a treetop walkway that immerses you in the canopy – look out for cassowaries down below.

Rainforest lodges Immerse yourself in the rainforest by staying at a rainforest lodge at Cape Tribulation or near Mossman Gorge. Treat yourself to a stay at Silky Oaks Lodge.

Indigenous experiences See p222 for more information.

39 Sundowners in CAIRNS

CRAFT COCKTAILS | SEA VIEWS | GOOD TIMES

With year-round balmy weather, the buzzy Tropical North Queensland holiday hub of Cairns was made for sunset drinks by the sea. The city's bar scene has exploded in recent years, with craft breweries joined by slick rooftop bars and moody laneway speakeasies.

OCHRE RESTAURANT AND CATERING

Trip Notes

Getting around The bars of central Cairns are all within easy walking distance.

Don't miss Near Cairns Airport, the Stratford neighbourhood is an emerging drinking hub; here Barrier Reef Brewing Co. was recently joined by the Fox Small Bar and Narrow Tracks Distilling, which opens its tasting room on Friday and Saturday afternoons.

Happy hour Cairns' bars offer great happy-hour deals, but Queensland law prohibits advertising them externally. Contact venues for current deals.

Dinner Time

Ochre Restaurant (pictured left) Cairns' best waterfront fine dining, with creative uses of native ingredients.

Tokyo Dumpling Serves the best Japanese curry outside Japan.

NuNu This Palm Cove fine diner also serves the best beachfront breakfast around.

Tips by Darren Barber, *co-owner of the Hospo Group @darrenjbarber*

01 Start on a high – literally, at Cairns' most elevated bar. Perched on the 12th-floor rooftop of the Crystalbrook Riley hotel, Mediterranean-inspired **Rocco** calls for an Aperol spritz (or two).

02 Soak up more epic Coral Sea sunset views at **Whiskey & Wine**, on level two of the Riley's sister hotel Flynn, where you can choose from more than 80 local and imported whiskies.

03 With a prime location on Cairns' marina, swanky **Salt House** (pictured left) is a superb spot to watch the sun go down with a cocktail in hand.

04 When only a craft beer will do, **Hemingway's Brewery** is the place to pair a frothy one with views across Chinaman Creek towards the forested peaks of the Great Dividing Range.

05 You won't be able to see the sunset from **Three Wolves**, but you'll be happy you found this Prohibition-inspired laneway bar when you sample its theatrical cocktails.

FROM TOP: PAUL KINGSLEY/ALAMY STOCK PHOTO, CLAUDINE VAN MASSENHOVE/SHUTTERSTOCK

WILDLIFE OF THE
Wet Tropics World Heritage Area

01

03

02

05

06

04

01 Ulysses butterfly

Seen throughout the region, particularly in Cape Tribulation, the star of the Wet Tropics' insect world has huge, electric-blue wings.

02 Amethystine python

Named for the irides-cent sheen on its scales, Australia's largest snake is as beautiful as it is docile.

03 Spotted-tailed quoll

The famously elusive ground-dwelling predator is mainland Australia's second-largest native carnivore, after the dingo.

04 Lace monitor

Known to skulk around campgrounds looking for an easy snack, these beautifully patterned lizards can grow up to 1.5m long.

05 Boyd's forest dragon

Look for these colourful, myth-like 'dragons' clinging to tree trunks along the pathways of Mossman Gorge.

06 Herbert River ringtail possum

Affectionately known as 'Herbie', the nocturnal emblem of the Queensland Parks & Wildlife Service is found at highland altitudes.

07

08

09

10

11

12

07 Mahogany glider

Increasingly threatened by land clearing, this endangered sweet-toothed glider is one of six glider species found in the Wet Tropics.

08 Tree kangaroo

Two arboreal kangaroo species live in the Wet Tropics. Try your luck spotting the Lumholtz's tree kangaroo in the Atherton Tablelands.

09 Southern cassowary

The dinosaur-like icon of the Wet Tropics faces an uncertain future, with fewer than 4400 estimated to remain in the wild.

10 Musky rat-kangaroo

This adorable pint-sized roo is diurnal, meaning it can often be seen foraging on the forest floor during the day.

11 Platypus

Sit quietly by Peterson Creek in Yungaburra in the Atherton Tablelands at dawn or dusk for good chances of observing these monotremes.

12 Saltwater crocodile

The world's largest living reptile patrols the rivers and beaches of the Wet Tropics and beyond.

40 Townsville Island HOPS

ISLAND HIKING | BEACHES | INDIGENOUS CULTURE

The only Great Barrier Reef island with wild koalas, Magnetic Island offers a unique escape. It's a great base for exploring the Museum of Underwater Art (MOUA) at John Brewer Reef. But it's not the only island you can visit near Townsville, which is preparing to open its showpiece Great Barrier Reef Aquarium in 2029.

PAULINE MONGARNY/SHUTTERSTOCK

How to

Getting here and around Magnetic Island Ferries (which takes cars) and SeaLink run daily services from Townsville to Magnetic Island (25 to 40 minutes). SeaLink runs to Palm Island Wednesday to Monday (one hour 45 minutes). Miniature 'Barbie Cars' can be rented on Magnetic Island.

When to go May to September, when the humidity's lower and stinger suits aren't required.

Snorkel Great options at Magnetic Island beyond MOUA include the snorkel trails at Nelly Bay and Geoffrey Bay.

LISA HOLMEN PHOTOGRAPHY/SHUTTERSTOCK

Magnetic Island Laid-back 'Maggie' boasts palm-fringed beaches, good snorkelling, scenic hiking trails and a robust koala population. Taking you to WWII fortifications with epic views (with koala-spotting on the way), the 4km-return **Forts Walk** is the island's top trail. Pack a picnic and continue from Forts Junction around to Horseshoe Bay via Radical Bay, a 7.5km trail linking the island's most beautiful beaches. Come for the day or stay longer, with plenty of holiday accommodation options.

Orpheus Island Well-heeled guests are helicoptered to the island national park's luxurious **Orpheus Island Lodge**, the only place to stay. But mere mortals can also visit on a day trip from Townsville with SeaLink, with three hours to swim, snorkel impressive reefs and tackle the island's only trail, the 450m-return **Yanks Jetty Walking Track**.

Palm Island Known for its troubled history, the former Aboriginal mission of Palm Island (Bwgcolman) is now looking to tourism to future-proof its economy. A major project to develop 70km of walking trails is underway. Until its completion, local Indigenous guides can take you on walks to cultural sites and remote snorkelling spots.

Left WWII fortification, Magnetic Island
Bottom left Orpheus Island

Plan Your Palm Island Visit

Etiquette For independent visits, it's best to contact the local council to let them know you're coming. They can connect you with guides and provide information about visiting respectfully.

Whale watching In July and August you can often spot migrating humpback whales on the boat trip to Palm Island from Townsville. If the whales are close, the boat stops for a while to let you watch.

Culture Start your visit at the Bwgcolman Indigenous Knowledge Centre, near the jetty, for a primer on local culture. We have lots of celebrations during NAIDOC Week in July, so that's a good time to come to experience culture.

■ **Vicki Saylor,** *Manbarra Traditional Owner and cultural adviser @vickeranne*

41 Through Indigenous EYES

TOURS | BUSH TUCKER | CULTURE

More than 70 Aboriginal and Torres Strait Islander groups have lived alongside the Great Barrier Reef for millennia. There have never been more opportunities to explore the region with Indigenous guides, particularly in the following tourism hubs.

LIANNE B LOACH/WOMEN WHO DRONE/GETTY IMAGES

How to

Etiquette Always ask before taking photos on an Indigenous-led tour, as it may not be allowed for cultural reasons. And remember that most questions are acceptable if asked respectfully.

Tours Discover and book more Indigenous experiences via the Discover Aboriginal Experiences website (discoveraboriginal experiences.com).

Eat Enjoy a sumptuous tropical feast featuring native ingredients at the Indigenous Culture Experience, run by Aboriginal-owned Flames of the Forest, near Port Douglas.

Cooktown

The first recorded act of reconciliation between Indigenous and non-Indigenous people in Australia occurred in Cooktown. This is just one fascinating fact you'll learn on a self-guided tour of the **Cooktown Museum**, which recounts Captain Cook's landing here in June 1770 from an Aboriginal perspective. Just south of Cooktown, interpretive panels offer insights into the cultural significance of the unusual **Kalkajaka** (Black Mountain) boulder field. Nearby, at **Rossville Retreat**, Kuku Nyungkul Elder Harold Tayley, or 'Mooks', leads popular bush food and medicine walks on his traditional homeland. It's a two-hour drive west from Cooktown to Laura, the jumping-off point for Kuku Yalanji man Johnny Murison's highly regarded two-day **Jarramali Rock Art Tour**.

CHAMELEONSEYE/SHUTTERSTOCK

Cairns & Daintree

Cairns' first Indigenous-led Great Barrier Reef tour, **Dreamtime Dive & Snorkel**, weaves Indigenous storytelling, music and dance throughout its outer-reef day trip. On

Top left Kalkajaka (Black Mountain)
Left Cooktown Museum

a half-day experience with **Mandingalbay Authentic Indigenous Tours** you'll cruise from Cairns Marina to the East Trinity Wetlands to connect with culture on the homelands of the Mandingalbay Yidinji people.

Nearby, in the Daintree region – the traditional home of Eastern Kuku Yalanji people – there are a number of Indigenous experiences. On a Ngadiku Dreamtime Walk, organised by the Indigenous-run **Mossman Gorge Centre**, your guide will tell you about the special relationship their people share with the unique tropical environment during a meandering rainforest stroll. You can also explore the Daintree region with Kuku Yalanji guides from **Walkabout Cultural Adventures**. Or take a cultural walk along Cooya Beach near Mossman with brothers Linc and Brandon Walker of **Kuku Yalanji Cultural Habitat Tours**. Feeling creative? Sign up for an art class with renowned Aboriginal artist Brian 'Binna' Swindley at **Janbal Gallery**.

First Nations Must-Reads

Dark Emu, by Bruce Pascoe (2014) Re-examining colonial accounts of Indigenous people in Australia, this ground-breaking non-fiction tome challenges long-held perceptions of Australia's First Peoples.

Welcome to Country: A Travel Guide to Indigenous Australia, by Marcia Langton (2018) Cultural etiquette tips, plus insights into Aboriginal and Torres Strait Islander languages, customs, art and more.

The Yield, by Tara June Winch (2019) Evocative, Miles Franklin Literary Award–winning novel about a man's determination to preserve his people's language and culture.

Australia Day, by Stan Grant (2019) Excellent backgrounder on First Nations Australia, with uncomfortable truths about the country's colonial history.

Indigenous Art

The mid-year **Cairns Indigenous Art Fair** (ciaf.com.au) offers an unrivalled opportunity to purchase Indigenous art and handicrafts directly from artists. Throughout the year, northern Queensland's Indigenous art centres such as the Yarrabah Art Centre, near Cairns, as well as the Cairns Art Gallery, host excellent exhibitions.

MOSSMAN GORGE CENTRE

CHRIS ALLAN/ALAMY

Townsville

A central theme in Indigenous culture, caring for Country (traditional lands) is woven into each instalment of the Townsville region's **Museum of Underwater Art** (MOUA). On dry land, **Gudjuda Tours** runs a bush-tucker and rock-art tour in the Townsville region. Its owners, the Gudjuda Reference Group Aboriginal Corporation, have been conducting marine-turtle tagging and monitoring for more than 20 years. Contact them for more information about upcoming turtle rescue tours.

Fraser Coast

Walk in the footsteps of a Butchulla man on the **Djinang Cultural Walking Tour** in Hervey Bay. Learn more about significant sites to the Butchulla people in Hervey Bay and nearby K'gari (formerly known as Fraser Island), sample local bush tucker, and get creative using natural materials. The tour is run in partnership with Hervey Bay Eco Marine Tours, which also runs a cultural sunset cruise with a Butchulla guide on board.

MARCO TROVALUSCI PHOTOGRAPHY/ALAMY

Left Ngadiku Dreamtime Walk, Mossman Gorge Centre
Top right Mandingalbay Authentic Indigenous Tours boat
Above Torres Strait Islander dancers, Cairns Indigenous Art Fair

42 Bundaberg's BOUNTY

FOOD TRAILS | DRINKS | FARM GATES

Australia's food bowl, Bundaberg grows 25% of Australia's fresh produce. And there are more opportunities than ever to sample the bounty of this friendly farming region directly from the source, from fresh fruit to rum and spirits crafted with local sugar cane and botanicals.

ALEX CIMBAL/SHUTTERSTOCK

How to

Getting here and around Bundaberg is a 4½-hour drive (or a longer bus ride) north of Brisbane. The more scenic Queensland Rail Tilt Train takes 4½ hours. You'll need your own wheels to visit farm gates; hire-car options are plentiful.

When to go Year-round; Bundaberg Tourism's produce calendar (bundabergregion.org) details what's in season.

Stay Recently opened Splitters Farm offers camping and glamping, and a menagerie of rescued farm animals to meet.

THE POCKET STOREHOUSE

Distilleries & Drinks

Producing liquid gold since 1889, **Bundaberg Rum** is a local icon. Even if you're not a 'Bundy' drinker, the distillery tour is fascinating, particularly the museum, with each section housed in a retired 75,000L vat. There's also a blend-your-own-rum experience.

But Bundaberg Rum is no longer the only distillery in town. Artisanal distiller **Kalki Moon** offers customised tastings – gin is its key tipple, but there is also rum, vodka and liqueurs. Learn more on a free tour or kick back with a cocktail in the huge bar or gin garden.

You can also sample locally brewed Bargara Brewing Company craft beers at city-centre brewhouse **Ballistic Bargara**. Pair your suds with a tasty pizza.

LEEROY TODD

Early Riser

Open 9am to 2pm Wednesday to Friday and 7am to noon Saturday, teeny bakery the **Pocket Storehouse** turns out some of the finest sourdough you'll ever sample. The fermentation process of its authentic, organic sourdough renders the bread essentially gluten-free, making it popular among coeliacs (though not officially recommended).

Top left Bundaberg Rum Distillery
Left Kalki Moon gins
Above Sourdough loaves, Pocket Storehouse

Housed in a giant barrel, **Bundaberg Brewed Drinks** produces premium soft drinks from Queensland ingredients, from ginger to mango. Taste your way through the range and create your own six-pack as part of the self-guided gallery tour.

Farm-Gate Experiences

Learn about the sustainable farming practices of family-run **Macadamias Australia** and sample its premium nuts at its visitor centre, which has an attached boutique and cafe overlooking a macadamia orchard. Tours are also available.

Pick your own strawberries at **Tinaberries** from June to August, or pop by at any time of the year to sample the farm's gourmet real-fruit ice creams (a dairy-free sorbet option is also available). You can also shop for a wide range of fresh produce at farm gates including **Alloway Farm Market**, the **Lettuce**

Indigenous Food

Before Bundaberg's modern farmers arrived, Taribelang people fished, hunted and farmed the region's natural bounty. Learn more on a 2½-hour tour of Taribelang Country with **Taribelang Bunda Cultural Tours** (bundaculturaltours.com.au).

'We've always eaten a lot of seafood here, from fish to pipis,' says tour guide Rebecca Domaille. 'But also kangaroo, which is usually cooked on hot coals, and goanna, which we might steam in paperbark.'

The cultural tour includes a taste of local bush tucker in the form of fresh damper (bush loaf made from flour and water) with bush tomato relish or lilly-pilly and lemon myrtle jam.

■ With Rebecca Domaille, *Taribelang woman and tour guide* *@taribelangbundatours*

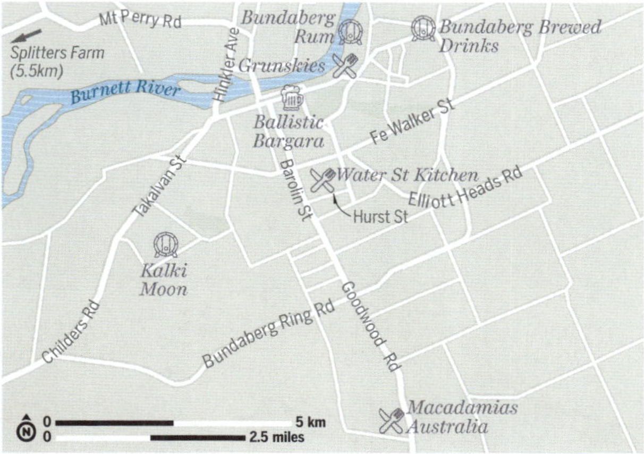

TY LIM/SHUTTERSTOCK

Left Bundaberg Brewed Drinks beverages
Below Freshly harvested macadamias

Patch and **One Little Farm**. The latter also sells delicious salads and frittatas, making it a great light lunch option.

Paddock-to-Plate Dining

Fresh Bundaberg produce is championed at local restaurants and cafes, with must-visits including the **Windmill Cafe** in the satellite suburb of Bargara, arguably one of Queensland's best brunch spots (tip: the açai bowl with local dragon fruit will feed two). Come dinnertime, chef Alex Cameron whips up Bundaberg's finest produce into modern Australian dishes that look as good as they taste at **Water St Kitchen**, hidden in a residential neighbourhood.

Bundaberg's fresh produce also includes seafood, which is hauled off the trawlers at **Grunskies'** own wharf. This Bundaberg institution has a seafood market attached to its restaurant overlooking the Burnett River, where you can feast on locally caught prawns, reef fish and more.

BARMALINI/SHUTTERSTOCK

43 Discovering THE REEF

DIVING | ISLANDS | CONSERVATION

With 2300km of the Great Barrier Reef (GBR) to explore, where does a traveller begin? Hint: the outer reef is generally the best place to snorkel and dive, from top to bottom. Pinpoint your perfect base with this quick guide.

MARCOBRIVIOPHOTOGRAPHER/SHUTTERSTOCK

How to

Getting here It takes around 90 minutes to reach the outer reef on a motorised catamaran from Port Douglas and Cairns, and around two hours from Townsville and Bundaberg.

When to go The comfortably warm May–October dry season proffers the best conditions for diving and snorkelling, though many operators run trips year-round.

Reef-safe sunscreen Protect the reef by using sunscreens that contain only mineral UV-blocking ingredients such as oxide and titanium dioxide.

Northern Great Barrier Reef

Stretching from the Torres Strait to **Hinchinbrook Island**, north of Townsville, the Northern GBR is typically accessed from the holiday resort hubs of Cairns and Port Douglas, with smaller operators running trips from Cape Tribulation and Mission Beach. Or base yourself on luxe **Lizard Island**, reached by plane.

Visitors are spoilt for choice when it comes to reef operators. While bigger boats offer a smoother ride, they also hold more people. Day and overnight trips to Green and Fitzroy Islands are also available from Cairns.

Northern reefs are more susceptible to extreme weather events, including cyclones and ocean warming (which causes coral bleaching), yet these reefs tend to have more vibrant corals than the southern, more temperate end of the reef. Tourist boats visit some of the healthiest corners of the marine park.

Top left Great Barrier Reef aerial view
Left Clownfish and anemone

Central Great Barrier Reef

The Central GBR runs from the Townsville region down to Mackay, with outer-reef day trips available from Townsville, Orpheus Island, Magnetic Island, Airlie Beach, the Whitsundays and Mackay.

The Townsville region is home to the Museum of Underwater Art (MOUA) as well as the **SS Yongala**, Australia's best wreck dive. There's decent snorkelling around the islands of the Central GBR, but this region doesn't compare to the quality of outer-reef locations like John Brewer Reef (accessed from Townsville) and Hardy Reef in the Whitsundays area. Visited by Cruise Whitsundays day trips from Airlie and the Whitsundays, **Hardy Reef's Reefworld Pontoon** also has two underwater hotel rooms (Reefsuites) and an upper-deck camping experience (Reefsleep).

Southern Great Barrier Reef

Ending at **Lady Elliot Island**, home to the reef's foremost eco-resort, the lesser-visited

Give Back to the Reef

Get involved with citizen science. Every visitor can help to safeguard the reef by uploading data via the Eye on the Reef app.

Visit the reef with a High Standard Operator (see gbrmpa.gov.au); many have a Master Reef Guide on board.

Support reef-friendly businesses; most are Advanced Ecotourism certified by Ecotourism Australia.

Join the Citizens of the Great Barrier Reef by making an online pledge to take reef-friendly actions at home.

Follow the Reef Authority's motto: See the Reef, Love the Reef, Protect the Reef.

■ **David Wachenfeld,** *Research Program Director, Australian Institute of Marine Science @australianmarinescience*

Meet Turtles on Dry Land

Mon Repos Turtle Centre From November, nightly ranger-led tours observe marine turtles coming ashore near Bundaberg to lay their eggs. Hatchlings appear from January to late March.

Cairns Turtle Rehabilitation Centre This Fitzroy Island centre cares for sick and injured turtles. Book a turtle tour to meet the patients.

NICO FARAMAZ/SHUTTERSTOCK

southern fringe of the GBR has much to offer. Anchored near uninhabited **Lady Musgrave Island** on the outer reef, Lady Musgrave HQ is a pontoon that's used as a base for day and overnight trips from Bundaberg. The calm, shallow surrounding lagoon is fantastic for families.

Lady Musgrave Island day trips are also available from Seventeen Seventy, while overnight stays on Heron Island and nearby Wilson Island depart from Gladstone. Closer to the mainland yet still within the Great Barrier Reef Marine Park, the **Keppel Islands** can be visited from Yeppoon.

While the coral tends to be slightly less colourful than in the north, the Southern GBR, which has the highest percentage of hard coral cover, is widely regarded to be in better health overall, making for some epic diving and snorkelling. Enjoy manta ray sightings galore at Lady Elliot Island, and plenty of turtle action around Heron and Lady Musgrave Islands.

MARCUS DORADO/SHUTTERSTOCK

COLIN BAKER/GETTY IMAGES

Left Coral, SS *Yongala* wreck
Top right Manta rays, Lady Elliot Island
Above Green sea turtle, Lady Musgrave Island

44 Retreat to the WHITSUNDAYS

ISLAND-HOPPING | TROPICAL HIKES | ROCK ART

From living it up at luxury island resorts to slamming down drinks in the backpacker bars of Airlie Beach, there are plenty of ways to 'do' the Whitsundays. A day trip to the mesmerising swirl of powder-white sand and turquoise water known as Whitehaven Beach is obligatory. But there's plenty more to do. Here's a taste.

PRODESIGN STUDIO/SHUTTERSTOCK

How to

Getting here Flights land at Hamilton Island Airport and Whitsunday Coast Airport, 30 minutes from Airlie Beach.

When to go Join in the Airlie Beach and Hamilton Island Race Week yachting festivities in August, or beat the crowds during the April–May and November–December shoulder seasons.

Sunset There's only one place to be on Hamilton Island (affectionately known as 'Hamo') as the sun goes down, and that's hilltop bar One Tree Hill.

BEN CALLAHAN/SHUTTERSTOCK

DAVID PRUTER/SHUTTERSTOCK

Far left Airlie Beach
Bottom left Sunset, Hamilton Island
Left Sailing, Whitsunday Islands

Airlie Beach The mainland hub of 'Airlie' is the most affordable base for exploring the 74-island Whitsundays archipelago, part of the Great Barrier Reef Marine Park, with outer-reef and island-hopping excursions available daily. While there's no shortage of backpacker bars and hostels, you'll find family-friendly resorts here, too. For one of the best views in the Whitsundays, make the 8.2km return hike to **Honeyeater Lookout**; allow three hours.

Hamilton Island hikes The largest inhabited island of the Whitsundays is laced with more than 20km of scenic trails to explore. Leading you to a blissfully secluded cove with a giant timber hammock to laze on, the 5.1km-return **Escape Beach Trail** is the perfect excuse to stretch your legs. Allow two hours to complete the return hike from the Scenic Trail entrance, or loop back via South East Head, which adds an additional hour of walking.

Island-hopping Bounce between Airlie, Daydream Island and Hamilton Island with **Cruise Whitsundays** (cruisewhitsundays.com) or sign up for one of the many Whitsundays day cruises on offer. More adventurous travellers can join a multiday sailing adventure, or skipper your own barefoot charter. This is one of the world's only sailing destinations that don't require you to have a boating licence – a half-day training session is all you need to set sail.

Ancient Trail, New Hike

The Whitsundays is the traditional home of the Ngaro people, whose connection to the archipelago dates back some 9000 years. Learn more about Ngaro history and culture via interpretative signage and artworks on the **Ngaro Track** (ngarotrack.com.au), a 32km, three-day hiking trail weaving across uninhabited Whitsunday Island. Opened in 2026, the trail was developed in partnership with Ngaro knowledge holders to showcase the natural beauty and rich stories of Ngaro Country. Hikers can tackle the trail independently or book a guided adventure with **World Expeditions** (worldexpeditions.com) – stay on the trail to avoid disturbing sacred places.

45 Go Off-Grid on K'GARI

4WD ADVENTURE | FRESHWATER FUN | WILD CAMPING

Once known as Fraser Island, K'gari is the world's largest sand island – and one of Australia's greatest adventures. Join an organised tour or tackle the island's 4WD-only trails in your own vehicle in search of waterholes, historical traces, dingoes and more. There are guesthouses and two resorts, but bush and beach camping is a highlight of the K'gari experience.

ALEXANDRE.ROSA/SHUTTERSTOCK

How to

Getting here Take a ferry or barge from River Heads (south of Hervey Bay) to the western side of K'gari, or the barge from Inskip Point to Hook Point at the island's southern tip.

When to go K'gari is a year-round destination, but the summer months are ideal for swimming.

Hot showers Bring $2 coins to operate the showers at Central Station, Dundubara and Waddy Point Top camping areas.

LOUIELEA/SHUTTERSTOCK

CAM LAIRD/SHUTTERSTOCK

Far left Lake McKenzie
Bottom left Dingo
Left SS *Maheno* wreck

Swimming spots K'gari's beaches are among the world's most dangerous due to strong currents and sharks, but its idyllic freshwater lakes and seaside rock pools make up for it. Chief among them are **Lake McKenzie** and similarly azure **Lake Birrabeen**. Strolling the 200m **Eli Creek Boardwalk**, then floating back downstream, is another K'gari must-do. Just north of Indian Head, the **Champagne Pools** 'fizz' as seawater spills into the rock pools. And after the 4.1km bushwalk to **Lake Wabby**, you'll be ready for a dip there, too.

Drives and walks Days on K'gari are best spent exploring by car or on foot. Four scenic inland driving routes offer hours of bumpy fun; allow extra time for bogged-vehicle traffic jams.

Part of the Great Sandy National Park, the island's 40-odd marked walking trails immerse you in surreal landscapes, from tall rainforest to striking sand blows. Look out for cute Krefft's river turtles on the **Lake Allom Circuit** (1.4km).

Cultural and historical sites The history of the Butchulla people goes back at least 5000 years. Sharp-eyed visitors may spot middens, artefact scatters and scarred trees that bear witness to the first inhabitants' deep and continuing connection to K'gari.

The rusting wreck of the **SS Maheno**, which ran aground in 1935 just north of Eli Creek, is one of K'gari's best-known sights. Learn more about the island's maritime incidents and WWII history on the **Sandy Cape Lighthouse Walk** (4.8km return) at the island's northern tip.

Dingo Safety

Around 200 dingoes are thought to roam K'gari in about 30 packs. To ensure a safe encounter (for you and for the sandy-hued wild native dogs), the Queensland National Parks and Wildlife Service advises the following for visitors:

- Never feed dingoes.
- Always stay within arm's reach of children.
- Walk (never run) in groups and carry a stick.
- Camp in fenced areas when possible.
- Keep food stores locked and never store food or food containers in tents.
- Secure all rubbish. With limited rubbish bins on the island, it's best to pack it out with you, too.

Listings

BEST OF THE REST

Wondrous Waterfalls

Barron Falls

Take the elevated, wheelchair-accessible Barron Falls Lookout Track (1.2km return) for a front-on view of this dramatic waterfall near Kuranda. Or view it from the Skyrail Rainforest Cableway or Kuranda Scenic Railway.

Millaa Millaa Waterfall

Arguably the most photogenic waterfall in the Atherton Tablelands, near Cairns, surrounded by lush rainforest.

Josephine Falls

The crystal-clear pool at the bottom of this cascade in Wooroonooran National Park, an hour's drive south of Cairns, is one of Queensland's most idyllic freshwater swimming spots. It's a 1.2km return walk from the car park.

Wallaman Falls

Southwest of Ingham in Girringun National Park, the highest permanent single-drop waterfall in Australia plunges 268m into the gorge below. There's a viewing platform on the edge of the gorge, from where you can hike down to the base of the falls.

Little Crystal Creek

Cascading under a heritage-listed stone arch bridge, this series of small waterfalls is a picturesque spot to cool off in Paluma Range National Park, near Townsville.

Finch Hatton Gorge

Hike alongside a turquoise cascade tumbling through Finch Hatton Gorge in Eungella National Park, an hour's drive west of Mackay. There are natural swimming pools at the ends of the Wheel of Fire Track (4.2km return) and the Araluen Cascades Track (2.8km return).

Seaside Pubs

Court House Hotel $$

Housed in a gorgeous old Queenslander on Wharf St, the 'Courty' in Port Douglas oozes old-school Aussie pub charm. The premium location has prices to match.

Mission Beach Tavern $$

A block from Mission Beach, this relaxed neighbourhood pub serves good-value classic pub grub, from mackerel and chips to chicken parmigiana. It's just a 200m stroll from Mission Beach Camping & Caravan Park.

Dingo Beach Hotel $$

Right on Dingo Beach, a 40-minute drive north of Airlie Beach in the Whitsundays, this relaxed, unassuming pub is a choice spot to while away an afternoon with a coldie in hand.

Eimeo Pacific Hotel $$

Perched at the edge of a cliff in Mackay's northern suburbs with cracking views towards the Cumberland Islands, this historic pub is a fantastic lunch spot.

JASON PATRICK ROSS/SHUTTERSTOCK

Barron Falls

1770 Beach Hotel $$

Ease into the relaxed vibe of Seventeen Seventy at this rustic pub, just paces from the peaceful 1770 Inlet Beach.

Bargara Beach Hotel $$

Tucked behind the esplanade on the Bundaberg coast, the recently renovated Bargara Beach Hotel has a sweeping deck, craft brews and an extensive pub-grub menu.

Quirky Attractions

Historic Village Herberton

With more than 50 restored period buildings, this outdoor museum is an unmissable Atherton Tablelands attraction.

Paronella Park

This tropical pleasure garden, south of Cairns, has a Spanish castle built by emigrant José Paronella in the 1930s.

Big Mango

You can't miss the 10m-high mango statue on the Bruce Hwy in Bowen. The next-door Bowen Visitor Information Centre sells tasty mango ice cream.

Capricorn Caves

Just 30 minutes north of Gladstone, this series of beautiful limestone caves can be visited on three types of guided tour.

Hidden Beaches

Etty Bay Beach

Cassowaries are often spotted foraging on this small beach surrounded by rainforest near Innisfail. Has a popular campground.

Horseshoe Bay Beach

Linked to similarly pretty Rose Bay and Murray Bay beaches by the stunning 2.5km Cape Edgecumbe Walking Trail, this tiny curve of golden sand fringed by turquoise water is a gorgeous place for a swim in Bowen.

MATHIAS BERLIN/SHUTTERSTOCK

Wallabies, Cape Hillsborough Beach

Coral Beach

Take the 1.1km rainforest track in Conway National Park, east of Airlie Beach, to this secluded coral rubble beach.

Cape Hillsborough Beach

It's famous for its kangaroos and wallabies that gather on the beach at dawn, attracted by roo food provided by the local council, but this remote beach is a beautiful spot for a stroll at any time of day. For great views, hike up the Andrews Point Track at the southern end of the beach (5.2km return).

Springs Beach

Enjoy a dip at picturesque Springs Beach, just south of Agnes Water, or head south along the trail linking it to Red Rock Beach to find a series of small coves and rock pools.

Top Markets

Rusty's Market $

Cairns' iconic tropical fresh produce market (Friday to Sunday) is surrounded by street-food stalls.

Yungaburra Markets $

On the fourth Saturday of each month, local growers, producers and artisans gather in the historic Atherton Tablelands village, with up to 260 stalls.

GARY YIM/SHUTTERSTOCK

Practicalities

Right Sea Cliff Bridge, New South Wales

EASY STEPS FROM THE AIRPORT TO THE CITY CENTRE

Located 8km south of central Sydney, Sydney Airport (officially Sydney Kingsford Smith Airport; pictured below) is Australia's busiest air hub. The international (T1) and domestic (T2 and T3) terminals are 4km apart on either side of the runways. Each has a train station. Melbourne, Brisbane, and Perth Airports are also major international gateways.

AT THE AIRPORT

SIM CARDS
Available from the Optus and Vodafone stores in the T1 arrivals hall. Major supermarkets like Woolworths often have better-value options, or purchase a digital SIM. If you're travelling through rural Australia, Telstra offers the best coverage.

CURRENCY EXCHANGE
Booths operate in the arrivals hall of Sydney Airport (and other major Australian airports), but airport ATMs offer better rates; choose one belonging to your home bank's global ATM network for fewer fees.

EQROY/SHUTTERSTOCK

FREE WI-FI Connect to Free SYD Wi-Fi, then follow the prompts. Connectivity is reasonable, with coverage reaching taxi and Uber stands.

ATMS Located in the arrivals hall; stick to ATMs belonging to major banks (ANZ, Commonwealth Bank, Westpac), not exchange bureaux.

CHARGING STATIONS Found throughout T1, including wireless charging stations. Cables are provided for both Android and Apple phones.

ENTRY FORMALITIES

Duty free Limits per incoming passenger include 50 cigarettes and 2.25L of alcohol (for passengers aged 18 and over) and general goods up to the value of $900 ($450 for people aged under 18).

Biosecurity Quarantine regulations are strict, so declare all goods of animal or vegetable origin. Flowers and fresh food (including meats and cheeses) are prohibited.

GETTING TO THE CITY CENTRE

Train Connect the international and domestic terminals to central Sydney (around $22) in 15 minutes. Trains run every six to 22 minutes from 4.22am (4.42pm weekends) to around midnight.

Cheap alternative Bus 420 connects the terminals to nearby Banksia train station, from where regular trains run to Central. Download the TripView app for planning.

Shuttle bus Airport shuttles head to hotels and hostels in the city centre, and some reach surrounding suburbs and beach destinations. There are numerous airport-to-downtown operators, some with desks in the arrivals hall – expect to pay $15 to $25 to the centre.

HOW MUCH FOR A...

Train
$20
15 minutes

Shuttle bus
from $15
20–30 minutes

Taxi
$45–55
20 minutes

Taxi $60 flat fee ($80 for maxi taxi) and takes around 20 to 40 minutes. Pickup is from the front of the terminals.

Rideshare There is a dedicated Uber pickup zone at the end of the taxi rank at T1. T2/T3 domestic terminals use the Priority Pick-Up Zones; follow the signs.

Opal Sydney's public transport network runs on a ticketing system called Opal (opal.com.au). Rechargeable, 'tap-on, tap-off' Opal cards for adults and children are available from WH Smith (international terminal), NewsLink and Relay (domestic terminal), and both airport train stations. Minimum credit load is $10/5 per adult/child ($35 at airport stations).

OTHER POINTS OF ENTRY

Melbourne Airport Australia's second-busiest international gateway, with daily non-stop flights to New Zealand, the Pacific, Gulf countries, Asia and the Americas.

Brisbane and other Queensland airports Brisbane serves numerous non-stop international flights, as well as an extensive network of flights within Queensland. It also has good ground connections to the Gold Coast and Sunshine Coast. A handful of non-stop international flights also reach Gold Coast, Sunshine Coast and Cairns airports.

International cruises Dock at one of two terminals in Sydney: the Overseas Passenger Terminal in Circular Quay (right in the city centre) or the less convenient White Bay Cruise Terminal in inner-city Rozelle. The latter is roughly a 5km taxi or Uber ride from central Sydney.

In Melbourne, international cruise ships dock at Station Pier, Port Melbourne, a 4km tram, taxi or Uber ride from the city centre. Other international cruise-ship terminals on Australia's East Coast include Brisbane, Cairns, Newcastle and Eden.

TRANSPORT TIPS TO HELP YOU GET AROUND

Australia is huge, so getting from A to B requires some thought. While driving offers the freedom to travel at your own pace and explore more remote areas poorly serviced by trains and buses, the country's affordable internal flights will save you some long travel days when moving between distant locations.

CAR OR CAMPERVAN HIRE

Most car-rental companies in Australia require drivers to be over the age of 21; some add a surcharge for drivers under 25. When booking, check if unlimited kilometres are included; it's almost essential in Australia, as extra kilometres can add to your costs considerably.

AUTOMOBILE ASSOCIATIONS

Every state and territory has its own automobile club, among them NSW's NRMA (mynrma.com.au), Victoria's RACV (racv.com.au) and Queensland's RACQ (racq.com.au). All are handy resources for road rules and driving tips, as well as insurance and holiday information.

DRIVING COSTS

Car rental per day from $120

Petrol approx $1.98/litre

Harbour Bridge/ Tunnel toll from $2.76

Respect the rules Road rules are strictly enforced. Red-light and speed cameras are common, and being just a few kilometres over the limit can land you a hefty fine. High-tech cameras can now also detect motorists handling mobile phones while driving, which is illegal and subject to heavy fines. At roadside tram and light-rail stops, always stop behind the tram until the doors have closed and any disembarking passengers are safely off the road.

DRIVING LICENCES To drive in Australia you'll need to hold a current driving licence issued in English from your home country, or, if the licence isn't in English, you'll also need to carry an International Driving Permit, issued in your home country.

ROOS AHEAD Kangaroos sometimes jump onto country roads, especially at night, dawn and dusk. Avoid driving at these times. If a roo does leap out in front of you, brake in as straight a line as possible to wipe off speed, and only then swerve if safe.

DRIVING ESSENTIALS

KEEP LEFT

Drive on the left; the steering wheel is on the right.

60

Speed limit is 100km/h or 110km/h; 50km/h in urban areas unless otherwise posted.

0.05%

Blood-alcohol limit is 0.05% (0% for drivers on a learner's or provisional licence).

Seat belts are mandatory for all passengers; small children must be belted into an approved safety seat.

Give way to the right at intersections and roundabouts.

FLYING Time pressure, combined with the scale of the Australian continent, can make air travel a convenient option. The country's flight network is extensive, safe and generally competitive. Qantas (qantas.com) is the flag carrier, with Virgin Australia (virginaustralia.com) the nation's other full-service airline. Other carriers include Rex (rex.com.au) and low-cost carrier Jetstar (jetstar.com).

BUS & TRAIN Buses are handy for budget travellers. Greyhound Australia (greyhound.com.au) operates an especially extensive network along the East Coast. Long-distance train travel in Australia is comfortable and affordable but slow, with no high-speed connections.

BICYCLE Cycling around Australia is possible, but distances can be gruelling. In the major cities, kerbside bike lanes and off-road trails are increasingly common; invest in a heavy-duty lock to avoid theft. Bike helmets are compulsory nationwide.

KNOW YOUR CARBON FOOTPRINT A domestic flight from Sydney to Melbourne would emit about 196kg of carbon dioxide per passenger. A car carrying four would emit around 75kg of carbon dioxide per person, while a train would emit about 76kg of carbon dioxide.

There are a number of carbon calculators online. Try MyClimate: co2.myclimate.org/en/calculate_emissions.

ROAD DISTANCE CHART (KMS)

	Wilsons Promontory	Melbourne	Sydney	Newcastle	Byron Bay	Brisbane	Noosa	Bundaberg	Airlie Beach
Melbourne	211								
Sydney	968	879							
Newcastle	1118	1029	170						
Byron Bay	1714	1626	766	618					
Brisbane	1868	1665	924	782	164				
Noosa	2013	1811	1067	919	314	148			
Bundaberg	2105	1903	1265	1123	526	360	239		
Airlie Beach	2588	2385	1871	1729	1263	1097	987	769	
Cairns	3049	2818	2416	2291	1845	1678	1568	1351	619

SAFE TRAVEL

Australia is one of the safest travel destinations in the world. That said, it pays to use common sense and be aware of the few but real risks you may encounter by the water, in the bush and on city streets.

SWIMMING Hazards include rips, sharks, jellyfish and, in northern Queensland, crocodiles; heed safety signs and swim between the flags where surf lifeguards are on beach patrol. There's also sunburn: wear SPF50+ sunscreen, a broad hat and sunglasses, particularly in the warmer months.

BUSHFIRES Bushfires can be fast moving and unpredictable, especially in spring and summer. Check the fire danger rating, which ranges from Low–Moderate to Catastrophic, for the district you're in. If fires are in your area, pay attention to the news and follow any orders to evacuate. One of the best apps for monitoring wildfires is Fires Near Me.

URBAN SAFETY While crime rates are relatively low, avoid walking alone late at night and never leave valuables in a parked car, especially within sight. Keep an eye on your belongings in public places and be cautious if someone offers you a drink in a bar; drink spiking is not unheard of, especially for women.

Snakes You're very unlikely to encounter snakes in the city. In bushland, urban or rural areas, stick to trails and avoid long grass. If you see a snake, leave it alone. If bitten, call 000 for an ambulance.

GALEXIA/SHUTTERSTOCK

OLGA KASHUBIN/SHUTTERSTOCK

Bushwalking Always choose a trail within your realm of fitness and experience, and check with local authorities for weather and track updates. Also, tell someone where you are going and when you will be back.

INSURANCE
Essential for all travellers. Some policies specifically exclude activities such as scuba diving, skiing and even bushwalking. Make sure the policy you choose fully covers you for your planned activities and interests.

HITCHHIKING
Despite the general friendliness of Australians, hitching a ride is dangerous and never recommended, whether you're in the city or the country. This applies to both solo travellers and those travelling in pairs.

QUICK TIPS TO HELP YOU MANAGE YOUR MONEY

CREDIT CARDS Visa and Mastercard are widely accepted for accommodation, activities, meals and drinks, and are also essential when renting a car. Contactless payment is the norm, and Apple Pay and Google Pay are also increasingly popular. Credit cards can be used for cash advances at ATMs and banks, but transaction charges apply. Diners Club and American Express (Amex) are not as widely accepted.

CHEAPER TRAVEL
In major cities, using an electronic, rechargeable transport card is often cheaper than buying single-trip tickets.

PAYING THE BILL
While most cafes have table service, it's common to pay at the counter when you leave. You may also need to order at the counter.

CURRENCY

Australian dollar

HOW MUCH FOR A...

Flat white
$6

Pint of craft beer
$14

Cafe lunch for two
$55

MONEY CHANGERS Foreign currency can be changed at most Australian banks and licensed money changers like Travelex, but the exchange rate for cash withdrawals from an ATM will always be superior.

ATMS & EFTPOS
ATMs are widespread throughout Australia, including in smaller towns. Eftpos terminals – usually offering contactless transactions – are ubiquitous at retailers and hospitality venues and used for even very small transactions.

BARGAINING
Bargaining or haggling is not common practice and generally only acceptable at market stalls, garage sales and in online communities such as Gumtree or Facebook Marketplace. If bargaining, keep it polite and good-humoured.

TAXES & REFUNDS A flat 10% goods and services tax (GST) is applied to most items and experiences for sale and is included in the price quoted. If you purchase goods with a total minimum value of $300 from any one supplier no more than 60 days before you leave Australia, you are entitled to a refund of any GST paid under the Tourist Refund Scheme (TRS). For details, search TRS on the Australian Border Force website (abf.gov.au).

TIPPING

While tipping is not obligatory in Australia, many locals leave a modest tip (usually around 10% of the total bill) at restaurants where service has been exceptional. At cafes with great table service, leave the change or tip a dollar or two. In taxis, round up the fare to the nearest dollar.

UNIQUE & LOCAL WAYS TO STAY

From lo-fi camping by wild ocean beaches to living it up in art-crammed, inner-city boutique hotels, Australia's slumber options offer a gamut of experiences. Disconnect from the world in a designer eco cabin, realign your chakras at a holistic spa retreat, or hire a campervan and hit the highway for an epic road trip along Australia's dazzling eastern shores.

HOW MUCH FOR A...

Basic campsite $7–35+

Dorm bed $27

Tiny house $300

TARAS VYSHNYA/SHUTTERSTOCK

CAMPERVAN CRUISING

Spectacular scenery and well-maintained roads make Australia prime road-trip territory. If time is on your side, hiring a campervan offers maximum independence. Private holiday-park chains like G'day Parks (gdayparks.com.au) and Big4 (big4.com.au) have locations across Australia, and most are well equipped with family-friendly perks like swimming pools, playgrounds and laundry facilities. If you plan on numerous stops, consider joining one of the chains, which offer member discounts. Bookings for popular national-park camping spots are often handled online by state departments, so plan ahead.

ART HOTELS

The closest thing to a gallery sleepover, art hotels lure with their caches of striking contemporary art. Among them are the Art Series (artserieshotels.com.au) suite of properties: midrange hotels in Melbourne, Brisbane, Adelaide and Perth named for (and featuring the work of) a particular modern Australian artist. Free collection tours are offered to guests.

ELISE HASSEY

SPA RETREATS

If the budget allows, retreat to one of Australia's seductive spa resorts, where luxurious digs, holistic treatments and sustainable dining are set in lush surrounds. Top choices include Gaia (gaiaretreat.com.au) near Byron Bay and Daintree Eco Lodge (pictured left; daintree-ecolodge.com.au) in Tropical North Queensland. The latter offers Indigenous-inspired spa treatments and accommodation in rainforest-canopy cabins.

@CABN.LIFE/@RILEYS_TRAVELS

TINY HOUSES

To unplug sustainably and fully immerse yourself in Australia's natural beauty, consider spending a few nights in a 'tiny house'. Also known as wilderness or eco cabins, these pocket-size holiday abodes are often set in a secluded corner of a farm or private land. Depending on the cabin, you might find yourself based beside a gurgling river, overlooking mountain ranges or the ocean, or within a stone's throw of a photogenic vineyard.

While these tiny houses may be off the grid, there's nothing rudimentary about many of them. Queen- or king-size beds and kitchen facilities are standard, along with higher-end compostable toilets and bathrooms with (hot) showers. Many also come with a firepit, while others crank up the luxe factor with a sauna, an outdoor bath or edibles from local artisan producers and winemakers.

For standout options, check out Unyoked (unyoked.co), Cabn (pictured left; cabn.life), Shacky (shacky.com), In2TheWild (intothewildescapes.com) and Salty Cabins (saltycabins.com), which together cover destinations across eastern and southern Australia. Just remember to book well ahead: word is out and these petite sanctuaries are a big hit with frazzled city slickers.

BOOKING

Booking accommodation in advance is highly recommended, especially for beach destinations during the Australian summer (December to February), at Easter and over long weekends. Booking ahead is also recommended during winter (June to August) in popular Queensland destinations like the Gold Coast, the Sunshine Coast, the Whitsundays and Port Douglas, when holidaymakers from the chillier southern states head north to thaw.

Lonely Planet (lonelyplanet.com/australia/hotels) Find independent reviews and recommendations on the best places to stay, and book them online.

Airbnb (airbnb.com) Wide range of options, from city apartments to beach houses.

Green Getaways (greengetaways.com.au) Beautifully curated selection of stylish, ecofriendly accommodation across Australia.

Great Small Hotels (greatsmallhotels.com) Boutique hotels, inns and resorts.

Luxury Lodges of Australia (luxurylodgesofaustralia.com.au) High-end accommodation, often with a focus on gourmet dining and natural beauty.

Hostelworld (hostelworldgroup.com) Find and book hostels across the country.

G'day Parks (gdayparks.com.au) Caravan and holiday parks throughout Australia.

CAMPING APPS

The free Campermate app (campermate.com) is great for finding campsites and facilities around Australia. Other useful resources include Camps Australia Wide (campsaustraliawide.com) and Hipcamp (hipcamp.com).

POSITIVE-IMPACT TRAVEL

Tips to leave a lighter footprint, support local and have a positive impact on local communities.

ON THE ROAD

Report injured wildlife If you come across an injured native animal, contact the relevant state's wildlife rescue organisation. For more information, see wires.org.au (New South Wales), wildlife.vic.gov.au (Victoria) or wrq.org.au (Queensland).

Consider renting an electric vehicle Most of the big hire companies at least have hybrids available.

Grey water If you're travelling in a campervan or caravan, make your grey water more environmentally friendly by choosing natural, plant-based soaps and detergents, dry-wiping plates and cutlery with paper towels before washing up, and pouring vinegar and baking soda down drains to clean them. Also, empty your grey-water tanks regularly.

Choose reusable bags, cups and cutlery These make a handy ecofriendly travel kit.

BMPHOTOGRAPHER/SHUTTERSTOCK

GIVE BACK

Save koalas affected by fires, deforestation and disease by donating to the Australia Koala Foundation (savethekoala.com) or the World Wildlife Fund (wwf.org.au).

Plant a tree and help regenerate degraded land by donating to not-for-profit organisations like Carbon Positive Australia (carbonpositiveaustralia.org.au) and ReForest Now (reforestnow.org.au).

Volunteer a few hours of your time to an Australian Conservation Foundation (acf.org.au) or Conservation Volunteers Australia (conservationvolunteers.com.au) project, which range from planting and weeding to beach-litter cleanups.

Eat and shop at places that support and empower local communities and the disadvantaged, such as Streat (streat.com.au) and the Social Studio (thesocialstudio.org) in Melbourne, and Heart Cafe (heartcafe.com.au) and Song Kitchen (songkitchen.com.au) in Sydney.

DOS & DON'TS

Do experience an Indigenous perspective by seeking out First Nations–owned tours and cultural experiences.

Don't photograph Aboriginal ceremonies and sites of significance without permission.

Don't throw cigarette butts onto the street or in the landscape; it's illegal and can cause bushfires.

Don't cuddle a koala. It's stressful for the animals and has been banned in most states.

LEAVE A SMALL FOOTPRINT

Spend more time in fewer destinations. Not only will you shrink your footprint, you'll form deeper connections and memories in the place you're in.

Research neighbourhoods in large cities and base yourself in one with good public transport links and/or within walking distance of places that interest you.

Do not use plastic bottles Tap water is safe to drink along the East Coast; bring a reusable bottle.

Book tour operators known for their sustainability credentials. Many are listed at Eco Tourism Australia (ecotourism.org.au).

GLEN BERLIN/SHUTTERSTOCK

SUPPORT LOCAL

Support businesses that are small and independent over large chains, whether Australian or international.

Feast sustainably by visiting local farmers markets (farmersmarkets.org.au), organic and biodynamic wineries (organicwine.com.au), and eateries that champion local, seasonal produce and sustainably sourced coffee.

Buy souvenirs made by local artisans. When buying Aboriginal and Torres Strait Islander art, ensure that you are buying authentic items that support the artist and Indigenous communities (indigenousartcode.org).

CLIMATE CHANGE & TRAVEL

It's impossible to ignore the impact we have when travelling, and the importance of making changes where we can. Lonely Planet urges all travellers to engage with their travel carbon footprint. There are many carbon calculators online that allow travellers to estimate the carbon emissions generated by their journey; try resurgence.org/resources/carbon-calculator.html. Many airlines and booking sites offer travellers the option of offsetting the impact of greenhouse gas emissions by contributing to climate-friendly initiatives around the world. We continue to offset the carbon footprint of all Lonely Planet staff travel, while recognising this is a mitigation more than a solution.

RESOURCES

greentravelguide.org
discoveraboriginal experiences.com
socialtraders.com.au
worldanimalprotection.org.au
australiangeographic.com.au

ESSENTIAL NUTS & BOLTS

BYO
Bring your own (BYO) drinks to a barbecue, and ask whether you should bring a plate (a dish or salad) to share.

SHOUTING
Shouting (buying a round of drinks) is common when out drinking with friends. If someone shouts you, shout them back.

SMOKING
Smoking is banned in most indoor public spaces and some outdoor spaces. Ask before lighting up around others.

FAST FACTS

Time Zone GMT+10

Country Code +61

Electricity 230V/ 50Hz

GOOD TO KNOW

All visitors to Australia need a valid visa to enter the country (immi.homeaffairs.gov.au).

The legal drinking age in Australia is 18; public drinking laws vary between states.

Stand on the left on escalators and overtake on the right. Also, stay on the left when using stairs and footpaths.

If there's a queue, respect it and apologise if you accidentally cut in.

In case of emergency, dial 000 (police, fire and ambulance).

ACCESSIBLE TRAVEL

Key attractions, including some national parks, commonly provide access for those with restricted mobility. Numerous places also cater to visitors with restricted vision and hearing; see wheeleasy.org.

Hotels commonly have lifts, ramps and rooms with accessible bathrooms; see accessibleaccommodation.com.

Public transport in major cities and towns is usually wheelchair accessible, though some stations and stops are not.

Major taxi companies offer WAV (wheelchair-accessible vehicles); request ahead.

Tour operators with vehicles catering to mobility-restricted travellers operate from most capital cities.

Accessible dining can vary significantly. It's always best to call in advance.

Useful resources include deafaustralia.org.au, visionaustralia.org, ideas.org.au and scia.org.au.

PUNCTUALITY
If you're running more than 10 minutes late to an appointment, text or call ahead to apologise.

GARÇON!
Don't wave or shout to call your waiter. Wait to make eye contact and simply raise your hand.

CHRISTMAS CLOSURES
Many businesses close or reduce their trading hours from Christmas to the second week of January.

GOOD MANNERS

Australians are relatively casual and not especially big on formalities. Moderate swearing is common among friends and not always considered rude. Not saying 'please' and 'thank you' is considered rude. So too are intrusive questions about a person's age, weight or income.

FAMILY TRAVEL

Public transport is usually free for children aged under four or five. Older children usually pay half the adult fare.

Admission to some museums and galleries is free. Most paid attractions offer reduced-price tickets for kids.

Hotels can usually provide cots, with notice. Some boutique B&Bs and resorts do not welcome children.

Cafes, pizzerias and casual restaurants are child-friendly. Fine-dining restaurants usually discourage bringing babies or small kids.

Breastfeeding in public is widely accepted.

GREETINGS

Despite the stereotypes, most Australians do not speak like Mick Dundee or the Crocodile Hunter (especially in urban areas). The most common greeting among locals is 'Hi', 'Hello' or 'Hey'. A friendly 'G'day' is fine but less common than you may think.

FILEDIMAGE/GETTY IMAGES

LGBTIQ+ TRAVELLERS

Homosexuality is legal, and same-sex marriages are legally recognised in Australia.

Australians are generally open-minded, but you may experience some suspicion or hostility in more conservative neighbourhoods or regions. Inner Sydney and Melbourne have especially vibrant gay scenes.

Major events include the Sydney Gay and Lesbian Mardi Gras, and Melbourne's Midsumma Festival and Queer Film Festival.

Online resources include Visit Gay Australia (visitgay australia.com.au), which lists a number of LGBTIQ+ businesses across the country.

Index

000 Map pages

000 Map pages